ENCYCLOPAEDIA OF INDIAN GOVERNMENT: PROGRAMMES AND POLICIES

ENCYCLOPAEDIA
OF
INDIAN GOVERNMENT:
PROGRAMMES AND POLICIES

Vol. 26

Biotechnology

Edited by

Satish Tiwari

ANMOL PUBLICATIONS PVT. LTD.

NEW DELHI - 110 002 (INDIA)

ANMOL PUBLICATIONS PVT. LTD.
4374/4B, Ansari Road, Daryaganj
New Delhi - 110 002

Encyclopaedia of Indian Government: Programmes and Policies

First Edition, 2000
ISBN 81-261-0515-1 (Set)

PRINTED IN INDIA

Published by J.L. Kumar for Anmol Publications Pvt. Ltd., New Delhi - 110 002 and Printed at Mehra Offset Press, Delhi.

Contents

Preface

Encyclopaedia of Indian Government: Programmes and Policies contains authoritative information on about fifty departmental policies and their future developmental programmes.

Organised to be completed in 40 volumes, this gigantic work covers Agriculture, Atomic Energy; Chemicals and Fertilizers; Coal; Commerce; Communication; Culture; Defence; Education; Environment and Forests; External Affairs; Finance; Food & Consumer Affairs; Food Processing Industries; Health and Family Welfare; Home Affairs and Internal Security; Human Resources; Industry; Information and Broadcasting; Labour; Law, Justice and Company Affairs; Non-conventional Energy Sources; Ocean Development; Parliamentary Affairs; Personnel, Public Grievances and Pensions; Petroleum and Natural Gas; Planning and Programme Implementation; Planning and Statistics; Posts and Telegraphs; Power; Rural Development; Science and Technology; Social Justice and Empowerment; Space; States Affairs; Steel; Steel and Mines; Sugar and Edible Oils; Surface Transport; Textiles; Tourism; Urban Development; Water Resources; Women and Child development etc.

Based on the information derived from authoritative sources, this work contains authentic facts and figures. I am deeply beholden to all the scholars whose writings are cited or substantially made use of in the present work. I am also thankful to Anmol Publications Pvt. Ltd. for undertaking publication of this encyclopaedia. I am solely responsible for shortcomings in presentation of matter.

Encyclopaedic in nature, this will prove a dependable reference work for scholars and academics besides those appearing for different competitive examinations.

—Satish Tiwari

1

Introduction

India is well poised today for a bioindustrial development. The scientific expertise, infrastructural facilities and research leads obtained during the last 10 years are indicative of the rapid progress in the field of biotechnology. What is important is to further strengthen the relationship between research institutions, academia and industry in a symbiosis mode for conversion of research findings into products, processes and technologies. It is towards this endeavour that the Department of Biotechnology has made concerted efforts and has been able to transfer some innovations to industry for commercialization. As evident world over, biological resources would be the most important feed stock of bioindustrial revolution. Rules and regulations for the new patent regime especially in biotechnological innovations and the need for protecting our national biodiversity and intensification of research and development in all areas of modern biology would be the priorities. While supporting basic research, the department has kept in view the biotechnology based programmes for rural development, weaker sections and women in particular. A number of new initiatives have been launched in this direction.

The Department of Biotechnology through its multifaceted approach in furthering advanced research in modern biology has given a definite thrust to the sectors of agriculture, human health, livestock, environment and industrial development. A number of useful research leads have been generated. Validation and commercialisation of vaccines, diagnostic kits and bio-products have been the thrust areas for support. Genome research, molecular taxonomy, new vaccines and diagnostics, human resource development, expansion of bioinformatics network, repositories, biodiversity conservation and characterisation have progressed well.

New programmes have been evolved with the active support of various expert task forces and committees. Review of ongoing programmes and midcourse corrections wherever necessary have been essential features.

As part of the Golden Jubilee celebrations of the country's Independence, all the planned activities were completed. The Biotechnology Research and Promotion Committee (BRPC) and expert task forces have provided very high scientific content to various programmes of the department in giving approvals, monitoring, review and in their implementation. The department has made special efforts to interact with the scientific .community, industry and financial institutions. Revised guidelines for biosafety and for generating data for clinical trials of recombinant products have been brought out. For popularisation of biotechnology and better understanding of new areas of biotechnology and biosafety aspects, programmes, lectures, exhibitions land workshops were organised.

Programme wise salient features are briefly presented below:

Scientific advisory committees

The Scientific Advisory Committee of DBT (SAC-DBT) met on 21st April 1998. Issues pertaining to IPR, technology transfer and biosafety measures for testing recombinant products were discussed. It also identified certain areas for major multi-institutional projects. The Committee expressed overall appreciation of the activities of the department.

The ninth meeting of the Standing Advisory Committee - Overseas (SAC-O) held in the Department on January 8-9, 1999 discussed areas of basic and applied research including DNA Vaccines, protein profiles, protein structures, diagnostics for complex diseases, production of biomolecules, drug design and mechanism, transgenic plants and animals, genomics and genetics in agriculture and health, structural genomics and technologies, genes for resistance and virulence etc. Working scientists were invited for presentation. A greater role of the committee was envisaged through its association with some major programmes of the department.

The Biotechnology Research and Promotion Committee (BRPC) held two meetings. All together, 42 projects were considered and 17 recommended for support. The BRPC constituted expert monitoring committees for the recommended projects costing above Rs. 1.00 crore for regular monitoring including field visits. The expert task forces met; reviewed and recommended projects for financial support.

Research and development

As per its main mandate, the research projects generated through experts and received from individual scientists have been supported in carefully selected areas. Out of 517 projects received, 204 have been approved. Basic research, crop biotechnology and plants, medical and environment related areas received priority.

Research in modern biology

Some significant achievements in the area of basic research have been in structural biology. Elucidation of structural polymorphism in DNA encompassing with standard structures and pH induced transitions, using a 600 MHz FTNMR (TIFR, Mumbai); development of cross-linked efficient cellulose based absorbent beads for expanded bed operation of chromatography (UDCT, Mumbai); determination of three dimensional structure of an iron binding protein (AIIMS, New Delhi); isolation of a causative agent of Kala-azar and conclusion that UR6 has enough potential to be used specially for drug resistance (IICB, Calcutta) and elucidation of the structure - function relation of proteins at molecular level specially the difference in the substrate specificity of different plant proteases are noteworthy. Determination of the three dimensional structure of a novel 122 amino acid long protein of mosquito at University of Pune; utilisation of facilities for automated DNA sequencing by the scientists of the country for several projects, development of versatile phage and phagemid based display vectors for cohesive-end and blunt-end cloning and development of new phage display based system for epitope mapping using gene fragment libraries to identify immunodominant epitopes in HIV-1 gag using polyclonal IgG against p24 are some other research leads. The development of various protocols for the efficient use of display system in different applications (University of Delhi, South Campus and understanding the structural basis of promoter activity with X-ray Crystallographic study (University of Madras, Chennai) have progressed well.

Agricultural biotechnology

In a project on cotton, prolific somatic embryogenesis was achieved in coker. By using Cry ICE and np II as selection marker, transformation was achieved in both coker and agronomically important Indian cultivats. In a network project on wheat , two genes were tagged successfully for quality traits. Full length cDNAs of triticine were isolated and strong promoters for major wheat seeds storage proteins, gliadins and glutenin cloned using PCR approach.

For mustard, molecular methods using barnase and barstar genes for hybrid seed production and transformation of B. juncea cv Varuna with constructs have been developed. A number of transgenics developed with different barstar constructs and plants were selected in vitro on herbicide basta. Constructs have been designed in which influence of 35S promoter is limited and 250 transgenics with branase gene showing male sterile flowers were obtained. These plants are being field tested. On the molecular biology of fruit ripening, near full length clone of ACC synthase gene from banana have been cloned and partially sequenced. Further characterisation of ACC synthase transcription during ripening process of banana fruit was done. Cloning and sequencing of six genes were achieved. The implications are many i.e. seed storage for enhanced nutritional quality, PAL for plant pathogenesis and protein kinase for signal transduction. Transgenic potato, tobacco and rice plants containing AmA1 genes have been produced.

In order to develop insect resistant transgenic Brassica lines, synthetic Cry 1Abs gene was mobilised into Agrobacterium tumefaciens and transgenic cabbage plants obtained after selection on kanamycin. On development of transgenic Brassica for fungal resistance, cDNA constructs of basic chitinase of tobacco with 35S promoter and nos terminator in an agrobacterium vector was used successfully for transforming B. juncea. The department would be setting up a transgenic screening facility at NBPGR, New Delhi.

Biological control of plant pests, diseases and weeds

Four new biopesticide technologies are under feasibility studies for commercialisation. Events were also organized to disseminate knowledge on production and use of bioagents. About 26000 ha. were covered and about 5000 farmers benefited this year. Mass production technologies of some of the biocontrol agents like Trichograma (developed by IARI), Trichoderma (developed by RRL, Jammu) and Beaveria bassiana and Verticillium lecam (developed by AAU, Assam) are being patented. Successful field demonstrations of some of the biocontrol agents resulted in the recommendation for their use in various states.

Biofertilisers

In order to understand the basic mechanism of nitrogen fixation a number of projects on crop specific biofertilisers have been supported. High nitrogen fixing strains of rhizobium and blue green algae suitable for different agroclimatic regions were isolated and demonstrated in field conditions. Technology for the mass production of mycorrhiza is being transferred to industry.

A crucial step for host specific symbiosis is inducing nodulation genes of rhizobia by specific molecules like flavonoids. The studies have indicated that flavonoid synthesis/secretion is normal in non nodulating lines and may not be the reason for their non-nodulation and nodulation variants are probably blocked at the early stages of nodulation like initiation of root hair deformation or cortical cell division. Detailed characterization in shake culture and a 10L fermenter was carried out at GB Pant University of Agriculture & Technology. The studies indicated that strains GRP[3] and PRS9 were able to grow well in a wide temperature range of 10°C to 37°C.

A number of technologies have been developed by the department for large scale production of high quality biofertilisers specially rice, pulses, fodder, legumes and important forest trees. These technologies have been demonstrated and are under transfer to field. The mission mode programme on biofertilisers has resulted in increased awareness and capacity building in the country. The department has initiated a network programme i.e. Integrated Nutrient and Pest Management to develop a package of practices involving various biofertilisers for specific cropping systems and biopesticides.

Plant tissue culture

Protocol refinement continued for a number of species, along with field demonstration trials in association with the user agencies. A programme has been initiated on strengthening Tree Biology Research, for tackling specific problems of regeneration and improvement of important temperate species. Large scale production of elite neem varieties and its demonstration plantations at different locations is continuing. Mangrove propagation and its conservation is being done at the Genetic Resource Centre at Pichavaram, Tamil Nadu.

In the horticultural crops, the technology for complete plantlet regeneration of mango varieties is being refined under a coordinated programme. In Citrus, demonstrations continued for disease free planting material. A programme has been supported on developing a complete package of technology for regeneration and extension of banana in the field.

A project was supported for the scale up and refinement of the technology for Saffron and Kala Zira. A network programme on Coffee Biotechnology has been developed for coffee improvement using molecular biology tools.

The hardening facilities are scaling up protocols and production as per the requirement of the region. The testing of genetic variation in the tissue culture raised plants is continuing.

Bioprospecting and conservation

This multi-institutional collaborative programme on bioprospecting of biological wealth aims at characterization, inventorization and conservation of the biodiversity of different eco-geographical regions and prospecting of genes and biomolecules. The Department of Space has initiated the work of preparing biome maps for the region.

The Indian Institute of Science, Bangalore has been able to develop a biomonitoring system actively involving 13 colleges of 4 different States for montoring the biodiversity of the region. The plants of the cold desert region- Lahaul & Spiti are being monitored and those plants resistant to cold have been identified. Bioprospecting is now being done for the candidate genes and molecules in order to identify and characterise these genes for potential use in other groups of plants. Bioassay studies and chemotyping are being done to identify the active principles for use as a biocide, antifeedant and as industrial raw material. Studies are being conducted to identify those plant species which are present in both North-East and South-West region. DNA fingerprinting is being done to determine the variability existing between two groups of plants. In addition, plants of high economic importance are being collected and finger-printed for complete characterisation and cataloguing.

Efforts are being made to conserve these important plants through in-situ and ex-situ conservation. Regeneration protocols are being developed for rapid multiplication of elite material. A programme on molecular taxonomy has been initiated on identification, characterization and documentation of plant resources specially the crops of economic importance.

Medicinal and aromatic plants

The three gene banks set up by the DBT have nearly a

thousand accessions from different biogeographic regions of the country. They are conserving collected accessions of rare, threatened, endangered and economically important species in field gene banks, seed banks, in-vitro repository, DNA bank and through cryopeservation. An integrated programme on taxol, an anticancer compound obtained from the plant taxus has been launched covering conservation of germplasm, in vitro studies for micropropagation as well biotransformation of taxane derivatives such as 10-Deacetyl baccatin (DBA) for the production of taxol. A microbial process for biotransformation of taxena to 10-Deacetyl baccatin - III (10 DAB III) using Flavobacterium dehydrogenans has been developed. Active fractions (peptide) possessing hypoglycemic activity have been partially purified from seed extracts of Momoridica charantia. The hypoglycemic effect has been demonstrated in experimental diabetic rats. The butanol insoluble part of the crude extract of neem bark has been found to be highly potent in inhibiting gastric acid secretion and ulceration in animal models.

Seri-biotechnology

The work on constructing high density linkage map based on sequence tagged site (STS) markers in silkworm (Bombyx mori) continued at CDFD. A silkworm genome library from a non-diapausing strain of silkworm has been prepared with a view to cloning and characterizing many known and anonymous probes which could either be used directly or converted as STS probes. The fibroin protein from posterior silkgland of Antheraea mylitta (tasar silkworm) has been purified and characterized..

Expression of green fluorescence protein (GFP) has been successfully achieved in cell lines/ caterpillars of Bombyx mori after infecting with recombinant Bm NPV harbouring reporter gene (GPF). Studies have been initiated for expression of Hepatitis - E viral antigen using this system. Molecular characterization of different silkworm strains show that the diapause and non-diapause traits of silkworm are linked to some of the quantitative trait loci (QTL) associated with cocoon, cocoon shell weight and fecundity. The denodgram of 13 silkworm genotypes was constructed based on five microsatellite analysis. Protocols have been developed for production of gynogenic haploids and triploids in mulberry. Under a demonstration project for controlling uzifly in two tribal villages of Killi hills in Tamil Nadu, the increase in cocoon yield by integrating chemical and biological methods using Nesolynx thymus was recorded to be about 25 kg/100 DFLx over controls.

Biodiversity conservation and environment

An integrated biotechnological approach has been adopted for biodiversity conservation, germplasm characterisation, treatment of industrial effluent, waste treatment and conversion to useful products. A marine strain of Yarrowia lipolytica has been isolated which can degrade 58% of the oil present in treated palm oil mill effluent within 5 days. Efforts are on to demonstrate the technology at Karnataka Oswal Oil Mills. A complete process for treating azo dyes waste water has been developed on a pilot scale.

An efficient crude oil and oily sludge degrading bacterial consortium and pure bacterial strains viz. Acinetobacter calcoaceticus and Alcaligenes odorans have been selected. Contaminated land at the site of two oil refineries has been selected and carrier based material applied. 20 accessions of Artemissia representing 8 species were subjected to RAPID analysis to reveal the genetic diversity. Characterisation of 150 accessions of tea germplasm using RAPID markers is in progress Studies on genetic diversity using AFLP markers in 37 neem accessions from different regions of India and 4 exotic lines from Thailand are in progress.

Medical biotechnology and immunodiagnostics

Special efforts were made to generate projects in the area of major communicable and non-communicable diseases namely HIV, tuberculosis, Japanese Encephalitis, cholera, leishmaniasis, malaria, Helicobacter pylori and contraceptive vaccines. The funding of multi institutional projects has yielded good leads in terms of targets and objectives. Three assay systems for detection of HIV infection were transferred to industries. The Western blot test developed at CRI, Bombay would be marketed by the industry very soon. Three PCR based systems developed for early diagnosis of tuberculosis are in the advanced stage of validation. A number of test systems i.e. for cortisone, reproductive hormones, T3, TSH JEV, H. pylori are being validated through peripheral centres. Reagents for IgM Mac-ELISA test of dengue have been made available at NIV, Pune for supplying to various hospitals for early detection of dengue cases.

Phase I clinical trials of the first indigenously developed cholera vaccine, VA. 1.3 have been initiated at Post Graduate Institute of Medical Education and Research (PGIMER), Chandigarh; Sanjay Gandhi Post Graduate Institute of Medical Science (SGPGIMS), Lucknow and Society for Applied Studies (SAS), Calcutta with support from Institute of Microbial Technology (IMTECH), Chandigarh and National Institute of Cholera and Enteric Diseases (NICED), Calcutta. The vaccine strain has been found to be genetically stable. Efforts are being made to improve the immunogenicity and sustainability of hCG, a female contraceptive vaccine by using T-cell epitopes of infectious organisms. An Immunomodulator, based on killed Mw developed by NII and trade named as LEPROVAC is poised for manufacturing and marketing by M/S Cadila Pharmaceuticals.

A number of new vaccines are under development. A synthetic peptide vaccine has been designed for JEV. A

DNA vaccine using envelope and non-structural core protein for JEV has produced good antibody response in mice model and in generating Tlcell memory. Recombinant BCGs using 6 antigens from Mtb and surface antigen of Heptatitis B and E virus have been developed. Studies resulted in isolation from a culture of Indian strains of H.pylori and cryopreservation of the same. The molecular characterization for determining virulence factors are underway.

The use of human monoclonal antibodies for rabies virus has the potential for treatment of post exposure cases. Studies on envelope gene and genotype analysis indicate that subtype C of HIV is the most predominant in different geographical regions of the country. However, minor levels of subtype B, A and E have also been found, The absolute CD_4 cell count showed an inverse relationship with viral load. New programmes have been initiated on analysis of deletion of genes encoding for HIV-I co-receptors amongst healthy subjects and in high risk groups.

The initial phase of the National Brain Research Centre (NBRC) consists of a networking programme, coordination and funding of workshops, seminars, training etc. through NIMHANS, Bangalore. An interactive session on "Vision for Neurosciences in the Next Millennium" was organized by the department to prepare a plan of action for the coming decade.

Human genetics and genome analysis

In addition to molecular diagnosis for the common genetic disorders such as beta-thalassemia, Duchenne Muscular Dystrophy (DMD) and other haemoglobionpathies prevalent in the country, 14 genetic clinics have been established for genetic counselling of the affected families. Two major projects implemented pertain to: establishment of molecular genetic studies on schizophrenia and bipolar diseases at NIMHANS,

Bangalore and Molecular Genetics for the diagnosis of Haematological Disorders including bone marrow transplantation and Molecular Genetic Diagnosis for thalassemia, haemophilia, Glanzman's thrombasthenia at CMC, Vellore.

In a major programme on Functional Genomics implemented during 1997-98, a fast and efficient method has been standardised for isolation of DNA from 10 ml blood samples and PCR based analysis for SCA3, SCA1 and DRPLA disease detection standardised . A formal MOU has been signed on Functional Genomics with NIMHANS, Bangalore and AIIMS, New Delhi.

Vaccine research and development

Indo-US vaccine action programme

The focus is towards development of new and improved vaccines and immunodiagnostics. During the third phase, proposals have been generated in the areas of HIV/AIDS, tuberculosis, cholera, H.pylori etc. The 12th meeting of the Joint Working Group (JWG) held in Washington, D.C. reviewed the progress of the ongoing projects. Prior to this meeting, a Workshop on "Emerging and Re-emerging infectious diseases" was held at NIH, Bethesda. Two major diseases viz, HIV/AIDS and tuberculosis were discussed. The future areas of collaborative research have been identified. The meeting also discussed Group 'A' Streptococcus, DNA and therapeutic vaccines, development of experimental animal models and guidelines for generating pre-clinical and clinical data for r-DNA based vaccines, diagnostics and other biologicals. Significant progress under this programme includes initiation of phased clinical trials for rotaviral vaccines in USA; promising leads towards the development of diagnostics for hepatitis C; rapid, sensitive specific and non-invasive diagnostic test system for leishmaniasis and development of gene based PCR assay method for tuberculosis.

Bharat Immunologicals and Biologicals Corporation Limited (BIBCOL), Bulandshahr

For the first time, the company formulated 100 million doses of OPV, the target for reaching the full installed capacity. There was more than a 500% increase in sales turnover and OPV was supplied to the National Immunization Programme.

A WHO team inspected the BIBCOL facilities as a prelude to granting of WHO-GMP certificate by National Control authorities. The team felt that BIBCOL had created a production facility as per GMP specification and the facility is suitable for production of various vaccines and immunobiologicals. A formal visit was made by a team constituted by Drugs Controller General of India for grant of WHO-GMP accreditation. A diversification plan for production of BCG, Measles and Tetanus toxoid vaccines has been evolved.

Animal biotechnology

Transgenic mice using neomycin resistant gene, hepatitis B virus x gene and hepatitis B virus x gene with c-myc gene have been produced at Nil. Efforts on similar lines to produce transgenic animals are underway at Indian Institute of Science (IISc.), Jawaharlal Nehru University (JNU), Tamil Nadu University of Veterinary and Animal Sciences (TANUVAS) and National Bureau of Animal Genetic Resources (NBAGR). Embryo transfer (ET) techniques for camel were standardised and pregnancies established using the non-surgical method of ET. Biologicals for augmenting ET were produced at Delhi University.

Recombinant ovine growth hormone has been produced using a high cell density fermenter at N.I.I. A PCR method for identification of canine parvo virus and equine herpes virus has been standardised. Immunodiagnostic tests for trypanosomiasis including double immunodiffusion test, card agglutination test and enzyme linked immunosorbent assay have been standardised. Cell culture rabies vaccine produced for animals was taken up for studies on sterility, toxicity and potency . Recombinant protective antigen of anthrax was purified. This will be useful in developing a recombinant vaccine.

Aquaculture and marine biotechnology

Various projects were implemented on feed development, fish spawning agents, transgenic fish, bioactive compounds, development of bioreactors, diagnostics and vaccines. Indigenous prawn feed was developed for tiger shrimp and white shrimp semi-intensive / extensive farming. The technology has been taken up for transfer. Synthetic prostaglandin analogues developed for fish breeding showed encouraging results. Genomic libraries of catla, rohu and catfish were constructed. Efforts were made to produce transgenic fish using indigenous constructs. A national facility has been established for parasexual fusion and genetic modification of seaweeds. Studies were carried out on neuropeptides of cyanobacteria. Potent toxin producers like Oscillatoria, Synechocystis, Anabaena, Pseudoanabaena were isolated. New initiatives were taken on fish strain identification, pearl production in black lip marine oysters, immunostimulants, cell culture system for diagnostics, a pilot fresh water prawn hatchery in Panjab and a training programme in molecular biology for fisheries scientists.

Under the mission mode prawn aquaculture project, a hatchery facility has been established to produce prawn seed almost round the year at CIFA, Bhubaneswar. About 1.5 million seed have been produced and 0.1 million utilized for stocking in ponds. The remaining were supplied to the farmers for production of prawns. In a growout system, the prawns were fed with newly evolved improved growout pellet diet produced in the feed mill. About 670 kg. of prawns were harvested in 7 months from these 4 ponds (1.675t/ha.) The technologies have been transferred through training programmes to the interested farmers and entrepreneurs in different states.

Biotech product/process development and technology

Micropropagation technology parks

Large scale production and demonstration of tissue culture plants continued at NCL, Pune and TERI, New Delhi. 50 lakhs plants were in the field. Clonal trials were being conducted in multilocations. Complete technology packages are being transferred to the industry for commercialization. A technology for teak has already been transferred to international Plant Laboratory, UK. Technologies for 5 other species are being transferred. The parks are providing know-how to state Universities/ Institutes for setting up of laboratories at different locations on a turn key basis and also transferring the complete protocol package including training. In addition, protocols for different economically important species are being refined. A satellite park is being set up in the North East for popularization of the technology and for producing sufficient quantities of planting material for the region.

Tissue culture large cardamom — product plan

Evaluation has been taken up on the performance of tissue cultured plants of large cardamom (Amomum subulatum) in planters field over an area of 70 ha in Sikkim and Darjeeling district of West Bengal. During the 1998 planting season, an area of 12.25 ha in 49 units was field planted with tissue cultured plantlets. Three training programmes were organized and a total of 101 farmers participated.

Tissue culture vanilla— product plan

Performance of in vitro vanilla plants in farmers field over an area of 150 ha in the states of Kerala, Karnataka and Tamil Nadu is being demonstrated under this project. An area of 44 ha has been field planted during the 1998 season. Initial observations suggest that the number of nodes and leaves were more in tissue cultured plantlets than stem cuttings. Four training programmes on cultivation and processing of vanilla have been conducted and 216 beneficiaries/farmers participated.

Biotechnology based programme for SC/ST population

The programme lays emphasis on the application of biotechnological processes, tools and techniques for the welfare of SC/ST people. Cultivation and distillation of medicinal and aromatic plants, floriculture, mushroom culture, vermiculture, vermicomposting, spirulina production, fish farming, poultry farming, production and application of various biological control agents for plant pests, survey of genetic disorders and counselling have been the main activities. So far, a total of 33 projects have been pursued in 17 states and union territories. It is estimated that around 10,000 people would be benefited through training, demonstration and other activities under these projects. The programme has been found to be very useful for socio-economic upliftment of SC/ST population and has created awareness about the role of new technologies in improving their living standards.

Biotechnology based programme for women and rural development

The projects supported are in the areas of floriculture, cultivation of medicinal plants, agriculture and livestock based employment opportunities. Significant achievements were reported in food processing, wasteland development, waste management, floriculture, human health and environment protection. About 265 women and others in rural areas have benefited by extensive training programmes. The Biotechnology park for Women in Chennai is being developed as a model approach.

The model bio-village project which was started during last year at Mocha village near Porbandar was formally announced at the S&T exhibition on 3rd August 1998 at the National Stadium. This project is for improving the living conditions of the rural population through proven biotechnologies. Major efforts in training, demonstration and employment generating activities have been planned. The lead agency CSMCRI, Bhavnagar conducted farmers' training on use and production of biofertilizers and biopesticides at the village. Thirty farmers have been trained at the Gujarat Agricultural University Campus, Junagarh on 10th & 11th December 1998.

Biotech process engineering and industrial biotechnology

The projects approved during the year included development of rapid diagnostic kits based on PCR assay systems for detection of food borne pathogens, upscaling and application of alkaline proteases in tannery industries, development and designing bioreactors for treatment of industrial effluents, industrial products etc. The department also took the initiative to develop rapid detection protocols for argemone.

Food biotechnology

Four low cost nutrients as food supplements we re developed through biotech no logical approaches having more than 400 kilo calories in 80 gram formulations and costing less than Rs. 5/-. They were released by the Hon'ble Prime Minister Shri Atal Bihari Vajpayee on the Children's Day, the 14th November 1998. Measures have been taken to start their pilot level production and introduce them in mid-day meals in different states.

Microbial biotechnology

During the year, several leads were obtained for rapid diagnosis of breast cancer, food toxicants, pesticide residues in food, solvent free extraction of penicillin from fermentation broth, designing of bio-reactor models for enhancing hairy root cultures, development of low cholesterol egg through biotechnological approaches and clarification of fruit juices. Rejuvenation of manganese mine dumps with the application of mycorrhiza, bio-treatment of refectory gold ores and concentrates at Hutti gold mines progressed well. A collaborative project has been initiated on xylanases where a paper industry would participate by providing large-scale trials of this industrially important enzyme.

Biosafety, IPR and bioproducts

A roving seminar on biosafety was organised by the department at Delhi, Calcutta, Hyderabad, Pune and Bangalore. The workshops coordinated by BCIL were well attended at all the five places. Two meetings of the Review Committee of Genetic Manipulation (RCGM) were held and about 60 proposals cleared for rDNA research. The revised biosafety guidelines have been published and widely circulated. A monitoring cum evaluation committee has been constituted.

During 1998-99, the department filed seven Indian Patents as per the recommendations of the Patent Search Committee. Two US patents and three Indian patents were assigned to the department in association with the Universities. The negotiation for transfer of technology for one US patent is at advanced stage with a US based corporate, house.

Human development

Sustained efforts in generating trained human resource has given rich dividends in bringing excellence in this field and providing the skilled human resource for research and industry. Support has continued for running 31 Post Graduate, Post-Doctoral and Post MD/MS Certificate Courses at selected institutions in the country. Three new PG courses and a diploma course in Medical

Biotechnology of one year duration were approved. 26 scientists were selected for the Overseas Associateship and 14 scientists for the National Associateship for the year 1997-98. Around 20 scientists each are likely to be selected for the Overseas and National associateships for the year 1998-99. 18 Short-term training courses were sponsored for training mid-career scientists on emerging research techniques in biotechnology.

Financial assistance was provided for holding 80 national /international seminars/ symposia/conference/ works hops in various institutions. Popular lectures by experts, publications in biotechnology, participation in exhibitions, support to National Science Day celebration etc., were also continued. 15 best students in biology at CBSE 10+2 level were selected for scholarships to be awarded on the National Science Day. In order to encourage outstanding research in biosciences, 10 National Bioscience awards have been instituted. Major Universities have undertaken popularisation of biotechnology in the country. The department participated in the 86th session of Indian Science Congress Association whose focal theme was New Biosciences. It has been a highly successful session scientifically, as appreciated by a large number of distinguished Indian Scientists and many foreign scientists, including Nobel Laureates and Presidents of Academies. The participation of young scientists and students particularly in the exhibition, was a clear indication of the excitement of this field for the future generation.

Centres of excellence, facilities, repositories and service

Repositories

The seven repositories each on tissue cultured plants; blue green algae; marine cyanobacteria; industrial and allied microbes; cryopreservation of blood cell; filaria and reagents; medicinal and aromatic plants continued to get support. Augmentation of existing cultures, services and supplies continued. A brain storming session was held to identify new areas and evolve comprehensive guidelines for repositories. The repository on medicinal and aromatic plants at CIMAP, Lucknow, started in 1996-97 has more than 800 accessions of plant materials. Documentation of more than 1000 plant extracts and identification services were provided. In the repository on filaria and reagents at Sevagram, 55 samples of filaria isolates were preserved and 2 lakh units supplied. Sera were collected from patients and preserved. Attempts to construct cDNA libraries are on. The cryopreservation facility at IIH Bombay standardised methods for preservation of blood cells. In the BGA Facility at IARI, a Training programme was conducted for mass production. Participants from 18 states representing Industry, NGOs, Agricultural departments and Universities attended. The food pigment production technology utilising Cyanobacteria was transferred to Industry.

Programme support and centres of excellence

Under this scheme, the "Programme Support in high Priority areas of Modern Biology" funded at IISc, Bangalore was reviewed by the Apex Committee. In all the three Sub- Programmes : infectious diseases; drug and molecular design; genome diversity, the leads available are being pursued further involving 55 faculty members across various disciplines. Programmes during the period -encompassed human immune response to Japanese Encephalitis proteins, protective role of antiviral cytotoxic T-cells in mice against JEV, characterisation of candidate vaccine strains of rotavirus and the development of transgenic plants resistant to infection. In Mycobacterium tuberculosis, four genes and related promoters were cloned and characterised. The crystal structure of garlic and basic winged bean lectins as well as Physallis mottle virus were determined. Identification of signal transduction pathways of phytohormones using the cucumber system has been initiated.

Biotechnology facilities

The biotechnology facilities which continued to be supported include Animal Facilities at NIN, Hyderabad and CDRI, Lucknow; Centre for Genetic Engineering and Strain Manipulation at MKU Madurai; Biochemical Engineering and Process Research and Development, IMTECH, Chandigarh. The animal facilities supplied about 100,000 experimental animals to various institutions and laboratories. The facility at Hyderabad was reviewed by the Institute's Scientific Advisory Committee. Pilot scale experiments for production of daumycin, antibiotic from Streptomycin, important in import substitution was tested at pilot scale with cost reduction at MKU, Madurai. A new National Facility on mass spectrometry at IICT, Hyderabad was sanctioned jointly with DST.

Bioinformatics

The Biotechnology Information System (BTIS) is in the nature of a distributed database and a satellite based network system namely Biotechnology Information System Network (BTISNET) comprising 10 Distributed Information Centres and 38 sub-centres located at major R&D institutions and university departments in the country The BTIS today offers a single major information resource covering several inter-disciplinary areas. Bioinformatics has evolved to deal with the various issues related to biological data. It also covers the development of data analysis tools, modelling of biological macromolecules and their complexes, metabolic pathways, designing of new molecules such as drugs, peptide vaccines, proteins, etc. The Network has been expanded to cover 15 new centres.

R&D projects in Bioinformatics were initiated to build capacity in database management, software and development of tools for analysis of biological data. The

EMBnet node at CDFD, Hyderabad achieved the status of a National Node.

The International Conference and General Assembly meeting of CODATA was held in Delhi, for the first time in India in recognition of our strength in various inter-disciplinary aspects of Bioinformatics. A state of-the-art Local Area Network (LAN) was established by the Apex Centre in DBT to provide full Internet services to all scientific officers of the department.

International collaboration

There has been a steady increase in biotechnology collaboration with developed and developing countries. The ongoing programmes of collaboration with Germany, Poland, Sri Lanka, Switzerland, Sweden, UK, USA progressed well. New programmes are being developed with Cuba, France, Japan, Israel, Italy, Russia and Tunisia. Interactions were organised with Australia, Brazil, Egypt, Hungary, Norway, Romania, Slovenia and other countries for possible collaborations. Agreements were signed with the National Centre for Scientific Research (CNRS), France and Biotechnology and Biology Research Councils, United Kingdom. Draft agreements were exchanged for collaboration with GBF (Germany), S&T Ministries of Egypt and Sri Lanka. A new phase of bilateral collaboration in the area of agriculture and environment has been agreed to with Switzerland. Under Indo-Polish collaboration, a new project on immunomodulators has been implemented at NII, New Delhi.

Multilateral collaboration amongst SAARC countries, in biotechnology is under consideration. Projects are being developed in the areas of vaccines and diagnostics, medicinal and aromatic plants and plant transformation. Three r projects with ASEAN countries in the area of plant biotechnology are ,being taken up for implementation.

Gene banks for medicinal and aromatic plants

National gene banks at CIMAP, Lucknow, TBGRI, Thiruvananthapuram, and NBPGR, New Delhi under the aegis of G-15 group of countries were further strengthened. The gene banks have made significant progress in terms of collection and conservation of species. The department participated in the G-15 exhibition held during the eighth G-15 sumit at Cairo during May, 1998 and in the ninth G-15 summit at Jamaica in February, 1999. Exhibits on various aspects of medicinal and aromatic plants including products were displayed.

Farmer Centred Agriculture Resource Management (FARM)

The UNDP/FAO supported FARM project activities continued. Case studies of successful demonstration of all member countries were documented. A Regional workshop on the Application of Biotechnologies to Rainfed Farming Communities was organized. The biovillage concept has been demonstrated in all member countries. A Participatory Assessment and Planning training was also organized for the Site Working Group members from the three National Sites. This exercise was done mainly to bring the farmer to the centre of decision making and to formulate an action plan for watershed sheds with a bottom-up approach.

Jute biotechnology

The UNDP supported project aims at developing an improved enzymatic retting protocol and developing transgenic jute genotypes with desirable genes. Studies initiated have shown good leads and a laboratory level protocol has been developed. Desirable genes have been identified, and a transformation protocol is being standardized.

International Centre for Genetic Engineering and Biotechnology (ICGEB)

Research projects in frontline areas are being pursued at ICGEB by six groups for Malaria, Virology, Immunology, recombinant gene products under Mammalian Biology Programme; Plant Molecular Biology and Plant Transformation, Insect resistance under the Plant Biology Programme. Significant leads have emerged in these areas. The centre has transferred technologies to industry for HIV-I and II diagnostics, HEV diagnostics, HBV vaccine and Gamma interferon. Nine Post-Doctoral fellows from member countries are undergoing advanced training and over 20 students are doing Ph.D. The centre also organised two practical training courses during the year.

Autonomous institutions

National institute of immunology

This institute has emerged as a Centre of excellence in basic immunology, infectious diseases, molecular design, reproduction etc. Immunological products from plants were investigated for both immunopotentiating as well as immunosuppressive properties. NII-60, an isoquinoline isolated from Berberis aristata was shown to possess T cell inhibitory property and its efficacy in endotoxin induced septic shock. A flavanoid from Azadirachta indica was seen to inhibit phospholipase A2, a player in inflammatory reaction and establishment of infection by certain parasites.

Japanese encephalitis virus was studied to determine the genetics of virulence. The NS1 nonstructural gene was cloned under the SV40/CMV promoter and is being optimized as a putative DNA vaccine. Ribozymal intervention to arrest HIV-1 replication resulted in the development of a hammer-head ribozyme that could cleave the truncated 178 bp long HIV-1 envelope gene in vitro. Studies on the CCR5 coreceptor suspected to aid viral entry and progression of the disease were carried out. An individual was identified with a heterozygous mutant allele for the CCR5 coreceptor. The Mycobacterium w-based leprosy vaccine progressed through immunprophylactic trials at Kanpur dehat. The 1mmunotheraupeutic product has been given to industry for commercialization. Multidrug resistance in tuberculosis was explored with genetic probes. PCR primers specific to RNA polymerase b-subunit were designed to reveal mutations that lead to resistance against rifampicin.

The birth control vaccine for women hCG is being optimized for the remaining stages of clinical trials. In order to achieve greater effective coverage, the immunogenicity of the vaccine formulation is being enhanced by the inclusion of T helper epitopes from seven infectious organisms. The problem of carrier-mediated suppression encountered with the vaccine is also being investigated. The zona pellucida of oocyte has been investigated as a potential antifertility vaccine candidate. Synthetic immunogens to B cell epitopes of zona pellucida (ZP) were made and their immunogenicity evaluated. Human zona was also characterized using polyclonal antibodies generated against recombinant bonnet ZP1, ZP2 and ZP3.

A research programme for developing transgenic animals has been initiated using two reporter transgenes namely, green fluorescent protein (GFP) and neomycin (Neo). A transgenic mouse model for hepatitis B is also underway. The doctoral programme of the Institute continued to receive the best talent from across the country.

The Institute continued as a WHO Collaborating Centre for Research & Training in Immunology, on FAO's Asian Network on Biotechnology as Applied to Animal Reproduction & Health, UNESCO's Centre for Molecular & Cellular Biology, as a Centre of Excellence of the Third World Academy of Sciences and also as a node of the Hybridoma Databank.

National centre for cell science, Pune

The. Centre is now focusing in areas of basic research and has attracted very good talent from India and abroad. The activities of the cell repository, human resource development through teaching and training programmes, workshops were-continued. Concerted R&D efforts have culminated in the development and transfer of two technologies related to large scale expansion of human skin In culture for treatment of burns, vitiligo and non-healing ulcers and cryopreservation of cord blood and haematopoetic stem cells. Training has been provided to end users, medical centres/hospitals. Research continued on regulation of melanin skin pigmentation, signal transduction pathways involved in the stem cell amplification, fetal liver infusion (FLI) therapy, basic studies in cell biology, immunobiology, neurobiology and parasitology. The results obtained from FLI studies indicate that fetal liver cells bring about stimulation of haematopoiesis by secretion of TGF beta 1. A novel growth factor from pancreatic islets beta has been' isolated and partly characterised. This seems to be a new protein molecule.

New Institutions

National Brain Research Centre (NBRC)

A National Brain Research Centre is being established with the main objective of consolidating the efforts in the area of neurosciences and basic brain research. An interactive session on, "Vision for Neurosciences in the Next Millennium" was held during the year in which neuroscientists from all over the country participated. An Action Plan for the next decade has been drawn.

National centre for plant genome research, New Delhi

Realising the potential of the human genome project, the task of analysing the genomes of other organisms and plants with the aim of cataloging genes, obtaining genetic and physical maps of genomes and sequences is under way.

The research work has started from the existing Centre of Plant Molecular Biology (CPMB) and Genetic Engineering unit (GEU) facilities supported by DBT. Within a short period, a number of transgenics of important crop plants have been produced.

Centre for DNA Fingerprinting & Diagnostics (CDFD)

The total number of forensic cases received at CDFD during the year was 197. These included paternity dispute cases and crime, including rape, murder and swapping of infants. Several cases of genetic disorders also were handled and results provided to the hospitals. The scientists have developed three single locus probes named as Bpf 3.8, B2 and T5 which are being used along with their multilocus probe to reduce the chances of error. Training courses were organised to expose more people to DNA Finger Printing Techniques. These courses were attended by participants from national and international institutes.

Administration

Efforts were made to implement the Official Language Policy for the progressive use of Hindi. The officers and the staff were encouraged to do more work in Hindi. A Hindi Fortnight was celebrated from September 1-14, 1998. Competitions in Hindi essay writing, debate, etc. were organised and cash awards given to the winners. Various vacant positions have been filled. Modernization of office, less paper approach and expeditious clearance system are being adopted for efficient functioning. All parliamentary matters have been attended to on time.

A presentation was made to the Department related Standing Parliamentary Committee. Follow up action has been taken. The subject of the meeting of Consultative

Committee of the Parliament for Science departments was Biotechnology. Detailed scientific presentation was made before the Committee.

The progress of expenditure has been good. The SFC and EFC memos have been processed and approved. The effort is continuing to expedite the financial approvals and ensure timely release of grants to research institutions.

In the field of biotechnology there is a seamless flow of basic research becoming directly applicable to humankind. Considering the enormous biodiversity and biological wealth in this country, basic research and modern biology, product oriented research for new generation of vaccines, diagnostics, recombinant products and other bioproducts specially the eco-friendly technologies would be the priority agenda for the next millennium. The preparedness and the desire of biologists to harness the research results for the socio-economic progress of the country is evident from their demand for undertaking a large number of research programmes of excellence and relevance. It is also clear that the quality of publications has increased substantially. The human resource being generated through the biotechnology teaching programmes at various universities is considered high quality and is competing very well in the national UGC and GATE examinations. The importance of transgenic research for increasing food productivity and nutritional security as also for diversification of our bread basket has been fully recognised in the country as elsewhere in the world. The department has made concerted efforts to prepare biosafety guidelines in consultation with the scientists for instituting appropriate monitoring and reviewing mechanisms. Application of biotechnology to improve the living conditions of the poor people, the SC/ST population, women in rural areas has gathered momentum. Integrated projects like Biotechnology Park and Biovillage have been taken up with a view to ensuring the impact of biotechnology on the target group. These programmes would be expanded further. Biotechnology is using the tools of information technology in expanding its bioinformatics network in the form of new database and information systems. This is probably the unique network being used by a large number of scientists in the country. Biotechnology programmes have been initiated in different states. The department has made sustained efforts to establish close linkages with the user ministries and departments, state level organisations, industries and NGOs. Special attention has been paid to strengthen the university infrastructure for basic research and expand the human resource development programme. There are great expectations from this field and focussed efforts particularly in the areas of plant biotechnology, documentation of biological resources, vaccines and diagnostics, bioremediation, genomics etc. offer great promise for generation and application of biotechnology products, processes and technologies. The efforts of the department in close association with the scientific community, academia and industry in this cumulative endeavour are yielding significant dividends. This trend will continue as we enter into the next millennium..

2

Advisory Committees

The department since its inception has functioned with the advice of the SAC-DBT and SAC-O, expert task forces and individual scientists. This has continued over the years successfully.

Scientific Advisory Committee of DBT (SAC-DBT)

The chairman of various task forces highlighted the specific issues pertaining to that task force. Some of the areas suggested were:

— Transgenic research

— DNA chip development

— Molecular taxonomy

— Drug development specially for tuberculosis

— Value addition and post-harvest technologies etc.

The specific suggestions given by the Committee were:

— Developing large inter-disciplinary, inter-institutional projects

— Mission Mode programme to be taken up and

— Special programme for rural development.

Detailed area wise suggestions were made by SAC, which have been implemented during the year.

Standing Advisory Committee Overseas (SAC-O)

The Ninth meeting of the SAC(O) was held in the Department on January 8-10, 1999. In basic research, discussion focussed on agriculture biotechnology including plant molecular biology; medical biotechnology; molecular biology and structural biology. Under applied sciences towards products and technology, discussion focussed on agriculture biotechnology including plant molecular biology; medical biotechnology, product development, technology transfer and patenting, environment and biodiversity conservation. The Committee was informed of the setting up of the National Brain Research Centre at Gurgaon and the National Centre for Plant Genome Research at JNU, New Delhi. Presentations were made by five young scientists in different areas of research. The SAC(O) members were appreciative of the high standards of research carried out at different centres in the country and made specific suggestions with regard to improvement in the protocols and research studies.

Specific suggestions made at the meeting included support to collaborative projects, commercial exploitation of areas where leads are already available. Research areas suggested included DNA vaccines; protein profiles; protein structures; diagnostics for complex diseases; use of natural products in treatment; transgenic animals; production of biomolecules and therapeutics; drug designing; drug mechanism methodology development; transgenic plants; genomics and genetics in agriculture and health; structural genomics and technologies; microbial prospecting with study on antimicrobial peptides; genes for virulence; identification of genes for resistance; chromosomal studies; protein nutrition enhancement; studies of biological molecules using mass spectroscopy and crystallography etc. The committee also discussed effective ways of associating the SAC(O) members in the monitoring of major programmes of the department.

Biotechnology Research and Promotion Committee, (BRPC)

The Biotechnology Research and Promotion Committee (BRPC) was constituted in April 1997, to consider and recommend all projects costing above Rs. 45 lakhs. During the year, two meetings were held, 42 projects were considered, and 17 recommended for support. During the fourth meeting, the terms of reference of the BRPC were revised. The new procedure for consideration of proposals is as follows:

- BRPC would consider only proposals costing above Rs. 1.00 crore.
- Individual proposals costing Rs. 1 crore and above after peer review would be placed before the task force. Only proposals recommended by the task force would be considered by BRPC.
- Proposals of Programme support, Mission projects, Integrated multi institutional projects and generated projects costing above Rs. 1.00 crore would be placed directly before BRPC, for consideration after obtaining the comments of the respective expert committees.

The BRPC also constituted Monitoring Committees for the recommended projects costing above Rs. 1.00 Crore. Each committee comprising 3-4 experts in the related subject area will monitor the projects once a year and report to BRPC.

3

Research and Development

Under the overall guidance of BRPC and expert task forces, 204 projects were approved for financial support.

Basic research in modern biology

This Task Force was formed with the realisation that progress in hi-tech areas such as biotechnology is intimately linked with the progress in basic research. The Task Force is not restrictive in terms of priority areas and invites proposals with innovative ideas pertaining to biotechnology A continuous interaction with other task forces is maintained to avoid overlapping areas. During the year, 25 new research proposals were approved for financial support. Highlights of some of the ongoing projects are as follows:

Molecular biology

Role of Innate Immunity in Visceral Leishmaniasis; IICB, Calcutta: It was demonstrated that in leishmanial parasite, UR6 is an avirulent variety. The ability of the leishmanial parasite to act as an immunoprophylactic and immunotherapeutic agent against experimental visceral leishmaniasis in a hamster model was tested. The parasite lacked lipophosphoglycan but possessed abundant message for kinetoplastids membrane protein-II and failed to induce visceral infection when given through the interactive route, unlike the virulent

Leishmania donovani, AG83, the causative agent of kala-azar. It has been concluded that UR6 has enough potential to be used specially for drug unresponsive kala-azar cases. The investigators have isolated Leishmania donovani from a drug unresponsive kala-azar patient.

Expression of Wild type and Mutant Human Eukaryotic Initiation factor2 (aeIF2) Sub-unit in Spodoptera frugiperda insect cells to characterize the importance of aeIF2 phosphorylation in the regulation of protein synthesis; Univ. of Hyderabad, Hyderabad: Impressive expression (15-20% of the total protein) of wild type and a mutant form of human initiation factor aeIF2 was achieved in insect cells using the baculovirus expression system. The recombinant viruses are recognised by southern hybridisation and the proteins by monoclonal human eIF2a antibody and are found to migrate at 38kDa position on SDS-PAGE. The expressed sub-units of human eIF2 alpha are phosphorylated to the same extent in-vitro by purified reticulocyte heme-regulated eIF2a kinase.

Pathogenicity of Candida albicans and N-acetylglucosarn-ine inducible catabolic pathway; JNU, New Delhi: A cDNA clone of NAG1 gene was obtained by immunoscreening a GlcNAc induced cDNA library in Igt 11 with an affinity purified anti-GlcN-6-phosphate deaminase antibody. The cDNA was then subcloned in pTZ18U at EcoR 1. This cDNA EcoR 1 fragment was then labelled and used as a probe to screen a genomic library of C-albicans in I-EMBL3.

Recombinant DNA technology

High level inducible expression of cloned recombinant Streptokinase (rSK) in the culture filtrate of E.coli; IMTECH, Chandigarh: Significant progress has been made in developing a highly efficient and cost effective process for the preparation of large quantity (300-400 mg) of pure native-like recombinant streptokinase extracellularly from E.coli. The technology for overexpression of recombinant streptokinase is being perfected

Protein engineering

Development of phage display based protein engineering systems for diagnostics, prophylactics and therapeutics; University of Delhi (South Campus.): Versatile phage and phagemid based display vectors have been developed which can be used for cohesive-end and blunt-end cloning, and direct cloning of PCR amplified inserts by T/A cloning, ligation-independent cloning and by a new PCR-Script cloning procedure (A1). A new phage display based system for epitope mapping using gene fragment libraries has been developed. This system was efficiently used to find out immunodominant epitopes in HIV-1 gag using polyclonal IgG against p24 and for mapping epitope in Glutathione S Transferase (GST) recognised by a monoclonal antibody, D431 (A2). Both linear and constrained phage display random peptide libraries were constructed using a method which does not involve the use of restriction enzymes. These libraries contained several million independent clones. These libraries were evaluated by screening for Streptavidin binding phages and a new binding peptide (CLYPWHNFWTC) was identified which works as a constrained peptide. These libraries were also used to identify the epitope recognised by Mab E311, which showed strong reactivity to the envelope glycoproteins, both HIV-1 [gp41] and HIV-2 [gp36] (A3). Various protocols have been optimised which are required for the efficient use of phage display system in different applications.

Macromolecular crystallography and molecular modelling

The structural basis of promoter activity. X-ray

crystallographic study; University of Madras, Chennai: Several dodecanucleotides which have the central six bases corresponding to the consensus region were designed. The studies are likely to reveal important information regarding the structure of the promoter sites especially since these decamers may be compared with the dodecamar structures to eliminate the effects due to packing.

Purification, Biochemical characterization, X-ray structure determination, structure function relationship of native Apo and Iron Metal saturated Lactotransferrin from Buffalo Colostrum; AIIMS, New Delhi: Three dimensional structure of buffalo lactoferrin has been solved. Lactoferrin, a protein controls the iron levels in higher organisms through their very tight but reversible binding of iron.

Structural basis of differences in Catalytic mechanism of different cysteine proteases by X-ray crystallography and molecular modelling; Bose Institute, Calcutta: Studies are underway for elucidation of the structure-function relationship of this protein at molecular level specially the difference in the substrata specificity of different plant proteases. The investigators successfully crystallised a batch of diffracting crystals and complexes are being formed with a set of inhibitors-BAPA, Chloromethyl ketone, E-64, Leupeptine and cystain.

Biochemical engineering and enzymology

Expanded bed chromatography for protein purifications; UDCT, Mumbai & IIT, Delhi: It was found that in expanded beds the axial mixing, unlike assumed universally, is not a function of system physical property alone. A new cellulose based super-macroporous beaded adsorbent matrix for expanded bed operation was also developed.

Enzymology and molecular biological investigations of

b-gluclosidase from thermophilic yeast Pitchia etchellsii; IIT, Delhi: Detailed structural and functional characterisation of the cloned gene pitchia in E.coli including cloning and expression of truncated gene and its products, sequence analysis have been carried out. Kinetic analysis of the original yeast enzyme as well as recombinant E.coli expressed enzymes has also been done. The partially purified enzymes were used for biosynthesis of methyl - b-D - glucosides and oligosaccharides.

Enzymatic Synthesis of Chiral b -Adrenoreceptor Agonist Salmeterol; RRL, Jorhat: The manufacture of single isomer products has become an important growth area for pharmaceutical industries. The main aim of this project is to study stereoselective synthesis of the active R enantiomer of salmeterol through chimoenzymatic pathway The prochiral carbonyl precursor for synthesis of the target molecule R-salmeterol has been prepared by first chloromethylation of p-hydroxy acetophenone with paraformaldehyde in presence of concentrated hydrochloric acid under catalytic influence of a little amount of zinc chloride -whereby 3 -chloromethyl 4-hydroxy acetophenone was obtained in quantitative yield. 39 microorganism were isolated from soil collected from near a local brewery, municipal dumping ground and compost heaps. Four isolates responded in the microbial reduction. The enzymes isolated from Rhodotorula rubra was purified and immobilized on silica. The reduction of phenacyl bromide was studied in various conditions.

Biochemical studies on Basidiospore formation in oyster mushroom (Pleurotus spp.); IICB, Calcutta: One of the major problems encountered in oyster mushroom cultivation is that the people involved in cultivation activities at times complain of general fatigue, pain in limbs, headache, cough and fever. It has been established that this illness is an occupational allergy caused due to the inhalation of spores. Studies were carried out to find out the levels of key enzymes of carbohydrate metabolism and laccase during developmental stages of P.florida and isozyme pattern of laccase at different stages of fruit body formation. The oxygen consumption of semi-purified low molecular weight substance of sporulating fruit body extract in presence of laccase and the Km of displayed fruit body laccase in presence and absence of heat killed semi-purified compound of mature fruit body of P.florida have been determined.

Agriculture biotechnology

Plant genetic engineering methods have the potential to provide novel means of accelerating the introduction of traditionally desired agronomic traits such as enchanced pest resistance within or even beyond traditional breeding barriers to capture the benefits of biologically based pest control. They also provide the means to create novel species and unique traits for agronomic practices. The impressive variety of old and new applications of plants has attracted a great deal of commercial and academic interest. There are presently three types of ongoing activities: R&D projects in priority crops, two multi-institutional projects on development of transgenic cotton and quality trait studies in wheat. The department also supported plant biotechnology programmes at JNU, New Delhi; MKU, Madurai; TNAU, Coimbatore; Osmania University, Hyderabad; Bose Institute, Calcutta; NBRI, Lucknow and Delhi University. The mandate of these programmes relate to problems of local crops, basic research in the area of plant molecular biology and generation of transgenics. The salient achievements made are highlighted below:

Rice (oryza sativa)

A project on development of insect resistant transgenic plants by introduction of a modified delta endotoxin gene of BT is being implemented at ICAR Research complex for NEH region, Barapani. Agrobacterium tumefaciens strain EHA 105 harbouring a binary vector containing synthetic cry 1A (c), hygromycin phosphotransferase (hph) and gus-gfp fusion was used. A number of hygromycin resistant gus and gfp positive seedlings of RCPLI-3c and IR 36 were recovered and amplification of Cry 1 A(c) through PCR indicated the presence of Cry 1 (c). In another project at HPKVV, Palampur RAPID analysis was performed to characterise genetic variability in more than 85 Pyricularia grisea isolates collected from different epidemiological regions of H.P. A number of isolates of P.grisea were grouped into 13 pathotypes on the basis of differential reaction on isogenic lines containing resistant genes. The resistant genes were found effective against more than 90% isolates.

Three institutions are working on the molecular characterisation of Indian isolates of rice tungro viruses and development of molecular diagnostic probes. The project aims to establish symtomatic variants, to survey the extent of disease and also to develop models for forecasting. The component at BCKV, Kalyani is engaged in on-farm studies on the disease and the monitoring of insect vectors for this disease. IARI, New Delhi is engaged in collection, maintenance and symtomatology of tungro virus isolates from various locations. The University of Delhi is carrying out molecular analysis of the viruses and development of diagnostic probes. Viral isolates are being cloned to bring out similarities and differences between them at genomic level. The information generated has been used to develop a set of probes to detect one of the viruses.

Rapeseed and mustard (brassica campestris and b.juncea)

In a study on development of transgenic Brassica for funga resistance, the cDNA construct of basic chitinase of tobacco with 35S promoter was used for transforming

B.juncea. Putative transgenic plants rooting in kanamycin medium were obtained. Also transgenic tobacco plants having truncated chitinase have been shown to express chitinase enzyme in extracellular spaces. Another project on transfer of male sterility from different sources to vegetable Brassicas through protoplast fusion and incorporation of endotoxin gene into combiner lines for insect resistant hybrid production was implemented at IARI, New Delhi. Donor-recipient protoplast fusion was carried out to recover cybrids of vegetable Brassicas. Trachystoma balli and Moricandia arvensis were used as cytoplasm donors. A total of 38 independent and cybrid plants of three vegetable Brassica having different cytoplasm have been produced. In order to develop insect resistant transgenic vegetable Brassica lines, synthetic cry1 Abs gene was mobilised into Agrobacterium tumefaciens. Transgenic cabbage plants were obtained after selection on kanamycin.

On development of molecular methods using barnase and barstar genes for hybrid seed production in mustard at University of Delhi, it was reported previously that different constructs with both wild type and modified barstar gene under the control of tapetum -specific promoter A9 or TA29 and bar gene driven by CaMV35S double enhancer promoter as selectable marker were developed. The transformation of B.juncea cv Varuna with the above constructs was initiated. A substantial number of transgenics were developed with different barstar constructs and selected in vitro on herbicide Basta. The T_0 transgenics were grown under controlled conditions and analysed for the integration pattern.

Further, constructs have been designed in which influence of 35S promoter is limited and transgenics with barnase gene showing male sterile flowers were obtained. Approximately 250 transgenics with different barnase constructs and 150 with barstar constructs have been transplanted under contained conditions.

Chickpea, pigeonpea and mungbean (cicer arietinum, cajanus cajan and vigna radiata)

In a project on development of transgenic plants of chickpea at HAU, Hisar, multiple shoots via organogenesis was reported earlier. Transformation experiments using three agrobacterium strains were carried out and putative transformants were histochemically analysed for the presence of GUS marker gene. Also protocol for biolistic transformation o: two day old pre-cultured embroyos and calli were standardized. The development of genetic transformation studies in pigeonpea are being carried out in UDSC, New Delhi. Regeneration of shoots via somatic embroygenesis was achieved from cotyledonary explants.

At IARI, on genetic transformation of pigeonpea to express insecticidal proteins of BT, 10 lepidopteran-specific Bt delta-endotoxin were tested for their efficacy towards larvae of H.armigera and cry 1AC was found most effective. Further, a synthetic gene encoding Cry 1AC which was optimised for plant expression was cloned in a binary vector (PCAMBIA 1304). This vector has genes coding for hygromycin phosphotransferase (HPT), green house flouresent protein (GFP) and GUS. The transformants were in the rooting medium.

Genetic transformation studies of Vigna radiata are being carried out at M.D University, Rohtak. Embroygenic axes with 100% exposed apical meristematic region were bombarded with naked particles prior to incubation with agrobacterium strain EHA 105 carrying binary vector. The regenerated shoots were visualised for gfp expression and found positive. These shoots were excised and rooted in MS medium containing IBA.

Wheat (triticum aestivum)

AFLP and RAPD linkage map has been constructed for the A genome of cross T.boeoticumX T.monococcum in a project at PAU, Ludhiana. The mapping population possesses large variation for morphological and agronomical traits as well as resistance to leaf rust, stripe rust and cereal cyst nematode. This population therefore, is being used to tag the genes of economic importance. Testing of parents and F3 progenies of the mapping population with single spore isolates of leaf rust has shown that T.monococcum possesses two genes for resistance to widely prevalent pathotype of leaf rust. Also F3 progenies with stripe rust, Karnal bunt and nematode resistance were identified in various interspecific crosses. These progenies were used to tag genes for resistance as well as for transfer of resistance.

Other crops

In a project on the use of antisence RNA to delay fruit ripening, implemented at Bose Institute, Calcutta, ACC synthase enzyme activity assay was standardised from tomato fruit extract. RT-PCR was also done using ACS-2 specific primers and RNA from ripened tomato. Also tissue culture conditions to get regeneration was standardised. RFLP and RAPD analysis of powdery mildew resistance in pea at IARI, New Delhi, a SCAR (sequence characterised amplified region) generated primer has been identified which could detect polymorphism between two near isogenic lines. Marker aided selection using this primer is in progress. Also NILs are being developed for er gene in different genetic background to facilitate molecular tagging of er gene directly. A project has been supported on molecular mechanism of Alternaria helianthi resistance in sunflower at UAS, Bangalore. A.helianthi secretes a toxin into the culture media during vegetative phase. Further, purification of the toxin and screening of some of the germplasm for resistance was carried out. The focus is on toxin binding proteins and their isolation and analysis of transcripts.

A project was implemented on the induction of genetic variability and rapid clonal propagation of tikka disease resistant variety of Arachis hypogea at Visva-Bharati, Santiniketan. Attempts were made to induce healthy callus using different explants in the presence of various auxins. A project on molecular probes for the detection and diagnosis of TLCV was taken up at IISc, Bangalore. After overcoming initial problems in establishing virus and vector culture for producing required quantities of tissue, whitefly inoculated technique has been standardised.

Project support

Specific programmes are being supported at six institutions/universities namely, NBRI, Lucknow; TNAU, Coimbatore; Osmania University, Hyderabad; Bose Institute, Calcutta; MKU, Madurai and Delhi University, South Campus. The salient achievements are:

National Botanical Research Institute, Lucknow: The group has cloned and partially sequenced the near full length clone of ACC synthase gene from banana. RT-PCR was carried out using promega RT-PCR access system. The 1.8 kbp cDNA amplicon was obtained and cloned subsequently in pMos blue vector. Further characterisation of ACC synthase transcription during ripening process is in progress.

On nuclear organelle genome interaction studies, more than 80% of total populus chloroplast genome has been sequenced. Studies on expression of chloroplast genes from populus suggest that various factors govern expression of these genes. Preliminary data based on Northern analysis suggest that light plays an important role in splicing petD intron. The data further suggest that psbN transcript is of 380 nt and is regulated by light. On molecular organisation of plant viral genome and raising of transgenic lines with built in virus resistance, chimeric constructs and mobility of coat protein gene of TLCV were studied earlier. Screening of resistance to TLCV was studied. Transgenic plants were analysed for replication of virus by PCR amplification using specific primers to amplify replicas gene of TLCV. However, ELISA test for checking the CP expression could not be done. On development of chickpea/pigeonpea and tomato plants expressing BT endotoxin gene for insect resistance, two chimeric plant expression vectors pRAT 103 and 201 harbouring BT Cry 1A(C) were employed. The results showed single copy insertion of transgene and the leaves of these plants showed differential toxicity against neonatal larvae of Spodoptera.

Tamil Nadu Agricultural University, Coimbatore: DNA fingerprinting studies of rice varieties released by TNAU has been carried out. Among the 40 varieties released, 19 were amplified using 10 operon primers. A total of 1588 loci were amplified using these primers. Out of 116 common loci amplified with all the varieties, 76 were found polymorphic and 40 were monomorphic, recording 65.5 % of polymorphism. On identification of QTLs for yellow stem borer resistance in rice, W1263 was identified as a moderately resistant cultivar. F1 was fixed by crossing Co43 as succeptible parent with W1263. A number of individual F2 plans were phenotyped by challenging with YSB larvae. The nature of resistance was found to be polygenic.

The third project is on tagging gene(s) for leaf folder resistance in rice. In earlier studies three RAPD markers linked to the major genes of leaf folder were identified. From the seeds obtained by crossing IR36 and TNAULFR 831311, F 1 plants were raised -in the field and out of 65 plants, 2 were fixed based on their morphological parameters. On tagging genes for BPH resistance, RILs (178) were developed by crossing IR 50 and IR 54745. Both RAPD and STS markers were used to screen the polymorphism. Among 300 operon primers, 19 showed polymorphism and bulk segregant analysis with 109 RILs confirmed that 4 primers were linked to BPH (Biotype 4) resistance gene. Of the 20 microsatellite used, RM 18 and RM 168 were found polymorphic and further confirmed that they were 1.3 cM and 1.9 cM away from the resistance locus.

Osmania University, Hyderabad: A cDNA library was constructed from 171 mM NaCl stressed roots of Porteresia coarctata in gt 10 vector. The library was screened with a heterologus probe (pA 9) from Medicago sativa. The insert analysis of the putative positive clones revealed that the size of the insert is 0.8 kb. Northern analysis revealed that the gene is under the control of NaCl inducible system and expression is confirmed in root and rhizome. P.coarctata root specific library was constructed in gt 10 vector. The isolated mRNA was used for cDNA synthesis and ligated onto gt 10 vector arms. This cDNA was packaged in phase lysate, The library was screened using the cDNA heterologous probe pA 9. A total of 3,37,943 sequences were searched and homology profile determined. The sequence was used to determine putative open reading frames in all the six frames.

Agrobacterium plasmid constructs were made and used for transformation studies using indica rice varieties. Twelve indica rice varieties were tested for tissue culture response and transformation efficiency based on transient gus A and gfp gene expression. The embryogenesis calli after co-cultivation with 5 Agrobacterium strains were selected on medium containing hygromycin. The putative transformed rice plants were regenerated and further molecular studies taken up.

Bose institute Calcutta: A decline in photosynthetic

activity noticed in salt-sensitive cultivars was found to be correlated with inhibition of both cytosolic and chloroplastic Fructose-1, 6 biophosphate activity. Such inhibition was negligible in salt-tolerant cultivars. The decline in enzyme activity was not associated with decrease in specific transcript or the immuno-detectable protein during the stress period. In contrast, the enzyme either from salt-tolerant cultivars of rice or from Porteresia coactata show no such in vitro inhibition by NaCl.

In another project on cloning of molecular markers associated with salt-tolerance, to generate cDNA for already known probable marker, Rab 16 A, for salt tolerance and the bacterial genes for samdecarboxylase, spermidine synthesis were amplified by PCR. Characterization and subcloning in plant expression vector was taken up. In order to identify the cDNA for upregulated mRNAs, differential display experiments were initiated. In respect of the project on genetic approaches for improvement of aromatic rice, approximately 2000 individuals identified in a promising F2 population have been characterized and 537 individuals, representing the spectra of variation in agromorphological traits were selected and F3 families planted. The study showed ample genetic variation amongst them for direct improvement. GLC analysis confirmed 2-acetyl-pyroline as the major principle conferring aroma in rice.

Madurai Kamaraj University: On development of Vigna mungo plants with YMV resistance, one of the DNA B clones (pKA22) of VMYMV was studied. The DNA A and DNA B clones were confirmed as infectious by agro infection studies using partial tandom repeats of DNA A and DNA B in Agrobacterium binary vectors. Also, embryonic axes from mature V.mungo seeds subjected to transformation by microprojectile bombardment showed about 60% of the explants to be GUS+ in transient assays.

A broad host-range plasmid PBAL3 was constructed by cloning the pTiB0542 Vir and Vir C genes. In another project on development of constructs for plastid transformation of sunflower/groundnut, isolation and purification of chloroplast DNA (cp DNA) of sunflower was standardized.

In the third project on development of indica rice with drought and salinity tolerance; cultivars of indica rice namely, ADT-36 and IR-50 were assessed for the accumulation of proline and induction of P5CS gene under salinity and heavy metal (cadmium) stresses. IR-50 was found to bernore sensitive to both the stresses. Embryogenic calli derived from mature seed embryos of IR-50 were co-bombarded with pUBP5CS and PHX4 (hph gene). Transformed calli were selected with hygromycin (50 mg/1). Promising leads were obtained in the development of transgenic, virus-resistant cardamom by expressing the coat protein gene of Indian cardamom mosaic virus (ICdMV). The RT-PCR product (752BP) obtained by using degenerate primers in the coat protein and nuclear inclusion protein genes of Potyvirus has been cloned in pBSILKS and both strands sequenced.

University of Delhi, South Campus: With a view to isolating novel genes and regulatory elements, sequencing of another photosynthesis- related gene psb Q has been completed. Three stage-specific cDNA library of rice, were evaluated for their quality and insert size. By differential screening and Northern hybridization, several cDNAs specific to root, pre-pollination or post-fertilization stages were isolated. To understand the molecular mechanism of photomorphogenesis, the unusual potential of Arabidopsis is being exploited. The HLS 1 gene has been PCR amplified both from the wild-type and pho 1 mutant, with the aim of sequencing and defining the molecular lesion in pho 1 which elicits constitutive photomorpho-genesis.

Work on wheat resulted in the development of

regeneration protocols for mature and immature embryos of wheat varieties HD2329, CPAN1676 and PBW343. The protocols developed for induction of somatic embryogenesis are being utilised for transformation of wheat employing co-cultivation with Agrobacterium and biolistics. Various parameters influencing gene delivery and expression of the introduced gene have been investigated and others are being optimised. Transgenic rice (variety Pusa Basmati 1) obtained via co-cultivation with Agrobacterium have been analysed for inheritance of gene by measuring the activity of resistance and reporter gene as well as by genomic hybridization. Transgenics were found to have one to six copies of the gene inserted.

Genomic analysis of abiotic stresses such as submergence, drought, salinity and low/ high temperature have been done. The protein profile alteration induced by flooding has been examined in two contrasting rice cultivars namely, FR13 A and IR 54 by two-dimensional gel electrophoresis. Some of the prominent proteins showing altered expression in response to flooding stress were excised and subjected to microsequence analysis. The results indicated that imposition of these stresses elicit increased rate of glycolysis, alcohol fermentation as well as channelling of carbon towards pentose phosphate pathway shunt.

Development of transgenic cotton varieties: for resistance to cotton bollworm

The synthetic cry 1CE gene was placed in front of 35S CaMV native promoter to study the toxicity level against bollworm. Transgenic plants of tobacco were developed as a model system to examine the performance of synthetic gene. The TO plants were grown to maturity and tested for expression. On feeding Spodoptera litura larvae, 100% killing of larvae upto 5th instar was observed. Prolific somatic embryogenesis was achieved in

Coker cotton. Using uidA (GUS enzyme) as a reporter gene or synthetic cryICE as the desired gene and nptll (kanamycin resistance) as the selection marker, transformation was achieved in both Coker and agronomically important Indian cultivars. However, the transgenic callus obtained after Agrobacterium mediated transformation of cultivars selected for agronomic performance could not be regenerated into plants. An alternative method of biolistic mediated transformation gave chimeric transgenic plants.

Characterisation and using quality traits in wheat aided by molecular markers

Thousands of wheat grain samples were analysed for HMW glutenin subunits. The results confirmed that the parents HI 977 and CPAN 3004 chosen for good bread quality and HD 2329 for poor bread making properties were correct. The crosses were attempted for bread quality for the development of RILs between various varieties. These have been taken to F5 and F6 generations. To find molecular markers for three quality traits viz. protein content, pre-harvest sprouting tolerance and seed size in bread wheat, three different populations were developed. A study of polymorphism between the parents of these populations has identified 89 polymorphic RAPD loci between low protein and high protein; small and bold seeds.

PCR based approaches (STMS, STS) detected adequate polymorphism. One QTL for grain protein content has been tagged using STMS marker. Also, full length cDNAs of triticin have been isolated and strong promoters for major wheat storage proteins gliadins and glutenin have been cloned using PCR approach. For studying durum wheat quality, a partial genomic library of MACS9 has been constructed. Studies on genetic variability in 64 Indian durum wheats were carried out. An efficient regeneration protocol has been developed from mature embryo explants after experimenting with media composition and genotype response. Transient expression of GUS and anthocyanin reporter genes was achieved in immature/mature embryos after biolistic transformation.

Biological control of plant pests, disease and weeds through biotechnology

Crop pests are considered to be the vital factors affecting crop yield. The concept of Integrated Pest Management (IPM) for sustainable development has emerged with the increasing realisation of the importance of sustainable agriculture. The farmers who were using chemical pesticide in the 60's and 70's are now looking for biorational methods of IPM. IPM implies combining better and more effective agricultural practices with judicious use of pesticides for better yield. Biological control fits in very well in the IPM concept of plant protection. Their efficacy has been successfully demonstrated in substantial areas (60,000 ha) throughout the country covering important crops like cotton, rice, chickpea, tobacco, sugarcane, groundnut, sunflower, safflower, blackgram, greengram, pigeonpea and other pulses, sesamum, cauliflower, tomato, chilli and other vegetables.

Research and technology development

Microbial Pesticides and Other Natural Enemies: Under the project on "Scaling up of biopesticides production and widespread use under IPM for 'Green Cotton Production' (TNAU), surveillance for cotton pests and natural enemies was carried out in 15 holdings. Sorghum maize, sunflower, cowpea, castor, redgram and bhindi were included in the cropping system approach to pest management by way of trapping the pests, enhancing natural enemy population, providing pollen to adult entomophages and as barrier crops for sucking pests.

Among the biocontrol agents, the fungal, antagonist Trichoderma viride was used as seed treatment to prevent root pathogens. B.t, NPVs of Helicoverpa armigera and Spodoptera litura and fungal pathogens, Beauveria bassiana and Noruraea rileyi were used against sucking pests and bollworms. Trichogramma chilonis, egg parasitoid of bollworms was produced in large quantity and used successfully. Conservation and natural augmentation of green lacewing fly predator, Chrysoperla carnea could be done in the winter cotton season by providing pollen yielding plants and avoiding pesticides. Neem products Vitex negundo, Pongamia glabra, Madhuca latifolia, Ipomea carnea, Jatropha glandulifera, Prosopis juliflora, etc. were used extensively in the project area.

In a project on "Mass production formulation and application of an entomopathogenic fungus Beauveria bassiana for coffee berry borer control", at University of Mysore. Intensive surveys, conducted in the pest infected areas revealed the existence of six species of fungal pathogens affecting coffee berry borer. Of these Beauveria bassiana was the most common, which caused upto 50% insect mortality under favourable conditions. This fungus was isolated from 10 coffee growing areas and only one of the isolates showed the required virulence against the borer, first in the laboratory and later in the field. Beauveria bassiana was mass multiplied on selective liquid media and conidia harvested from 1-day old culture and the conidia III were Iyophilized. After six days of incubation a maximum of 80% insect mortality was observed. The fungus completely colonized the insect and killed it.

In a project on "Electrophysiological approaches 'of Insect Plant Volatiles in Biocommunication" at Loyola College, Chennai, behavioural, neuroanatomical and electrophysiological studies were underway on the role of plant volatiles in relation to feeding behaviour of Spodoptera litura and Rhapidopalpa foevicollis and its effects on the parasites of S.litura. Undamaged leaves (e.g. castor, mulberry and cotton) produce low levels of green leaf volatiles as compared to plants damaged by S.litura larvae or mechanically damaged plants which emit high levels of green leaf volatiles. Behavioural studies involving the role of known chemoreceptors in the adults of Rhapidopalpa foeicollis in the discrimination between hosts and non hosts were observed.

At TNAU - In a study on "Biological control of nematode pests of potato grapevine and citrus" two field experiments cum demonstration trials established that application of Pseudomonas fluorescens considerably declined the infestation by the citrus root nematode Tylenchulus semipenetrans, 45 days after application, by significantly reducing the nematode population in soil and root. Results of two field trials for the management of potato cyst nematodes, Globodera spp showed that application of Pseudomonas fluorescens formulated in talc, at 10 kg/ha significantly reduced the parasites on the root and increased the yield by 30%. The cost benefit ratio was of the order of 1:3.

At IARI, New Delhi, an outstanding strain of Aspergillus niger (AN27) has been used to manage six soil borne pathogens (Fusarium oxysporum, F.solani, Macrophomina phaseolina, Pythium spp. Rhizoctonia solani and Sclerotinia, sclerotiorum) belonging to different classes of fungi by a single application under different agroclimates in diverse groups of crop plants. A rare antifungal compound and two growth promoting compounds and siderophores have been identified. The formulations have been tried in cultivators' fields in muskmelon, watermelon bottle gourd, cucumber, rice, rabi sorghum, safflower, aonla, onion, crucifers and solanaceous vegetables, ornamentals and sunhemp in Delhi, Haryana, UP, Andhra, and Maharashtra.

At Lucknow University, a yeast bioformulation prepared from Debaromyces hensenii has been found very effective against post harvest disease management of mango and citrus. Aqueous suspension of yeast bioformulation was found suitable as fruit coating as well as a spray agent. The bioformulations can be stored in granular powered form.

At Allahabad Agricultural Institute, Steinernema carpocapsae in combination with Xenorhabdus luminisens have proved a potent biocontrol agent in the management of important pests of economically important vegetable crops like -okhara, brinjal, tomato, potato etc. A bioformulation encapsulating the nemotode and bacteria was packeted in sodium alginate in the form of beads or pearl was developed for field use against several pests of vegetables.

At IARI, New Delhi, under "Nemic germplasm collections for fundamental and applied research services" biocontrol of Lepidopteran insects with nematodes was established. New hosts of the entomophagus nematode, Steinernema glaseri were recorded in brinjal and bhindi fruit borers, Leucinodes arbonalis and Earias vitella, respectively. Corcyra sp. was the most preferred host among the three insects as increased harvest of nematodes was recorded from the same number of larvae of these insects. Interestingly, even a better insect host was found for this nematode in adult cockroach, Periplenata americanum in which approximately one hundred thousand nematodes could be harvested from a single insect. This harvest from a single insect gave the required impetus to boost the availability of the nematode population needed in field application for the biocontrol of insect-pests of various economically important crops.

For the bio-control of aphids and mites infesting crops, mass culturing of a potent fungal pathogen, Fusarium pallidoroseum was done at KAU, Kerala using low cost substratas. Among the different substratas tried, rice bran was found to be the best substrata for growing the fungus. Mass multiplication of the fungus in polypropylene bag was found to be ideal for sterilizing the media.

In a TNAU-NCL Collaborative project on "Development of Microencapsulation formulation of Nuclear Polyhedrosis Virus of Helicoverpa armigera and Spodoptera litura" - NPV of H. armigera and S.litura with greater virulence have been isolated and characterized by restriction endonuclease, analysis of DNA. An efficient method of mass production of the viruses has been developed which has almost doubled the yield of polyhedra from a single larva in in vivo production system. Adopting these improved techniques, the NPVs; were mass produced.

At TNAU, mass culturing of P.xylostella has also been standardized. An ovipositonal cage suitable for P.xylostella has been fabricated. Three strains of granulosis virus (GV) have been isolated from P.xylostella and DNA characterisation was done using the restriction enzymes Pst1, Hind3, BamH1 and EcoR1. There were no genetic variations among the isolates. Mass production techniques were standardized. Studies on storage stability of the formulation is in progress. Biobit was more effective than Delfin against P.xylostella. Susceptibility of P.xylostella larvae was tested against Beauveria, B.brongniartii, Metarhizium anisopliae, Verticillium lecanii, V.chlamydosporium and Paeilomyces fumosoroseus. Out of these only B.bassiana, M.anisopliae and P.tumosoroseus were found to be infective.

At NCL Pune: Myrothecium verrucaria organism itself and its chitinase preparation were effectively used to control Sclerotium rolfsii infection of ground nut. Disease incidence was reduced to 25% after daily irrigation of plants with enzyme. Viability of conidia in commercial carriers and organic materials like marine chitin waste was promising (95% after 1 month at room temperature).

At PDBC, Bangalore: For biological control of Argotis spp. intensive surveys were undertaken for isolation of entomophilic nematodes in different states viz., Andhra Pradesh, Tamil Nadu, Kerala, Goa, Karnataka, Assam, Gujarat, Bihar, Sikkim and West Bengal for collection of soil samples from potato growing areas and other host crops of Agrotis spp. Three Steinernema spp. and two Heterorhabditis spp. have been isolated. Activity of EPN in sand and soil columns against Agrotis spp. was also evaluated. Compatibility of Steinernema sp. PDBC EN 3.2 and Heterorhabditis sp. PDBC EN 13.3 with pesticides commonly used in potato ecosystem viz., Endosulfan, Malathion, Mancozeb and Carbofuran were evaluated in aqueous solution. Nematodes were found to be compatible with the pesticides evaluated. Hetrorhabditis sp. was more resistant to pesticide than Steinernema sp.

At the "National Repository of Natural Enemies of Crop Pests and Weeds" natural enemies belonging to various groups of (i) Trichogrammatids, (ii) Coccinellid predators, (iii) Weed insects, (iv) Braconids, (v) Chrysopids, (vi) Eulophids and Scelionids, (vii) Anthocorids, (viii) Parasitoids of coconut leaf caterpillar. (ix) Ichneumonids, (x) Encyrtids, aphelinicls and predatory mites, (xi) Fungi against weeds, nematodes and insects were isolated by regular field surveys in and around Bangalore. Various biochemical parameters were undertaken for the purpose of host preferences.

Transgenic bt./molecular aspects

At CTRI, Rajahmundry, flue cured virginia tobacco cultivars, Hema and Jayasri were transformed with insecticidal crystal protein genes (Cry 1A (b) and Cry 1

(c) from Bacillus thuringiensis (Bt) employing Agrobacterium mediated transformation. ELISA studies with resistant plants of R_3 and R_4 generations indicated that they had enough quantity of sendotoxins (Bt protein) to kill the larvae of S.litura and H.armigera. The toxic protein is tissue specific and harmless to birds and mammals. The material has become stable and eligible for open field evaluation. The Review Committee on Genetic Manipulation (RCGM) has approved open field evaluation of these Bt plants.

At SBI, Coimbatore, studies on "Genome characterisation of Sacchrum using RFLP and its utilisation in breeding varieties resistant to red rot disease have been undertaken. 644 progenies of Sacchrum from 13 crosses involving commercial varieties differing in red rot reaction were screened for red rot resistance. For characterisation of red rot pathogen - genome DNA extracted from four isolates of red rot pathogen (CoC 671, Co 7717, Col 148 and Co 85061 isolates) was studied using PCR technique. Five random primers were used for the PCR amplification, of which three produced polymorphism.

Insect cell lines

At VMSRF, Chennai, in a study on "Primary Neuronal cell cultures as screening systems for potential Neurotoxic Biomolecules" the structural details of the histological sections of brain tissue of Heliothis armigera were elucidated. Standardisation of MTT assay to study the effects of selected limonoids isolated from neem on the growth of primary neuronal cell cultures was also done. A simple assay has been developed to assess the toxic effects of Azadirachtin on the primary cell cultures developed from Heliothis armigera & Spodoptera litura.

At NII, New Delhi, in an attempt to develop large scale insect cell culture in bioreactor for the production of bioinsecticides and recombinant protein, baculovirus growth kinetics of insect cells were studied in suspension culture. Cell densities of 4-5X10[6] 6 cell/ml were achieved in 4-5 days of culture, which was 5-10 times higher than that achieved in simple T flask culture. Insect cells were found to utilize glucose and reduce sugar from the medium for growth.

Pheromones/other semiochemicals,

At SPIC Science Foundation, Chennai, efforts were made to synthesise pheromones of a few target pests (Cnaphalocrosis medinalis, Scirpophaga incertuals, Helicoverpa armigera, Earias vitella, Spodoptera litura and Chiloacchariphagus indicus) and evaluate them in the field. All the pheromone components were synthesised through divergent synthetic strategy from 10-undecenoic acid, a readily available material from castor oil. Large scale synthesis of pheromones of Chilosacchariphagus indicus has also been achieved. A simple slow release dispenser has been developed for attracting the male insects of Chilosacchariphagus indicus. Field evaluation of the synthetic product led to the development of a successful mating disruption technique by trail following method. The technology has been demonstrated in about 25 acres. A significant increase in cane yield was observed in all the trial plots.

At NCL, Pune, The pheromones of the insects of H.armigera, Chilo pertellus, Plutella xylostella, Ducus doraslis, Agrotis ipsilon and Trichoplusia ni have been synthesised. These pheromones are useful for IPM in a number of crops e.g., gram, potato, sorghum, maize, red gram, cotton, tomato cabbage, mango and other fruits. Wind tunnels of different sizes were designed and fabricated for assessing insect response to pheromones. Electro-aritennogram assembly was set-up. Bioassay techniques were developed for evaluating synthetic pheromones of Helicoverpa armigera, Chilo partellus, Plutella xylostella and Daccus dorsalis. Some of the pheromones were formulated and supplied to Mahatama Phule Krishi Vidyapeeth Agricultural University for testing in fields. Synthetic pheromones of H.armigera and P xylostella were tested in eight different fields in Maharashtra. Crops used were mainly tomato, chickpea and cabbage. Pheromones showed very good activity in terms of insect catches in all the field tests. New analogues of pheromones of oriental fruit fly were examined and found to be effective at low population level of the pest in the field studies.

At DRR, Hyderabad, in a study on the management of rice, yellow stem borer, Scirpophaga incertulas through pheromone mediated mass trapping and mating disruption mass trapping technique was developed for direct control of rice yellow stem borer Scripophaga incertulas, a key pest of rice in India causing crop losses ranging from 5-95%. This technique involved installing 20 pheromone sleeve traps per hectare baited with 5mg of pheromone, 1015 days after transplanting. This removed maximum male population in the field and checked consequent pest build-up.

This technology was demonstrated at the farmers' fields at Medchal village in AP. Entire rice cropping area of 300 acres consisting of about 50 small holding farmers of Medchal was taken as treatment site and a neighbouring village, Athivelli, at a distance of 3 km was selected as Farmers practice site where farmers observed conventional control practices. Results indicated a significant decline of YSB infestation by about 25-50% at both vegetative and reproductive stages in pheromone treated area resulting in yield increase of 40-60%.

Botanical pesticides

Under the development of biodegradable and ecofriendly botanical pesticides, several projects were implemented and they showed promising results. The plants under active investigation for their insecticidal properties at various centres include: Annona squamosa, Derris tephrosia, Acorus calamus, Melia azedarach, Walsuria trifoliata, Dysoxylum ficiforme, D.malabaricum, Azadirachta indica, Vitex negundo etc.

Studies were carried out on Development of Insect Growth regulators from Natural Products of Medicinal and Aromatic Plants at CIMAP, Lucknow. Bioassay studies done in thirteen different extracts and fraction of Catharanthus roseus L.G. Don variety L-31 and variety Nirmal, tested against various economic insect pests species namely tobacco caterpillar (S. litura Fb.) gram pod borer (H.armigera Hb.) and green peach aphid (Myzus persicae Sulzer) showed that CR-7 (leaf extract of L-31) had maximum insecticidal insect growth regulator activity against (S.litura) and (H.armigera) as compared to a promising synthetic insecticide dichlorovos and a neem based botanical insecticide -NEEMACTIN.

Popularization of biopesticide technology through extension activities and training programmes

Popularization of biopesticide technology is an important component of the programme and as such several workshop-cum-farmers' Melas/field days and other extension activities were organised in Tamilnadu, Karnataka, Gujarat, U.P, Maharashtra, Andhra Pradesh, J&K and Assam. During Krishi Melas, exhibition-cum-information cell and consultancy/ biocontrol stalls were arranged to popularise the importance of bioagents as eco-friendly measures to manage target pests and diseases at various centres. These extension activities were very useful to disseminate the knowledge on production and use of bioagents in IPM for end users. At MKU, farmers, farm labourers and extension functionaries were trained in the proper use of biological control agents and botanical pesticides in IPM. Farmers' Field School (FFS) on cotton IPM was organised alongwith State Department of Agriculture. In the current 199899 winter cotton season, cotton IPM modeling experiments were conducted in 30 panchayat unions in 15 cotton growing districts in about 300 acres of farmers' holdings. These Krishi Melas and extension activities were attended by subject matter specialists, students, farmers, field functionaries, scientists from Govt. organizations and representatives from industries and NGOs.

Wide publicity of the biocontrol agents under IPM was also given through farmers' field school, and through mass media which included newspaper, magazines/popular articles/radio talks, video films etc. Besides, press meets were also organised and the significance of biocontrol under IPM was highlighted.

Training programmes on production, application and management strategies of biocontrol agents were also conducted at various centres. Training was imparted to scientists from State Agril. Universities, State Agril. Dept., Sugar factories, progressive farmers, private entrepreneurs. Over 1000 farmers, representatives from state government and state agricultural university participated. Besides, several on farm demonstrations were made for the farming community. Publications on mass production and mode of application strategies of various biocontrol agents under IPM were also prepared in various regional languages and distributed among the farmers.

Demonstration of biocontrol technology

Development, Production and Demonstration of Biocontrol Agents under Integrated Pest Management was an important aspect taken up.

At RRL, Jammu - Fermentation studies: An Indian

patent application entitled "A novel composition of a Fermentation Medium useful for Economic Mass Production of viable Spores of Trichoderma viride used for Crop Protection" based on the development of a novel medium composition involving inexpensive industrial by-products for the mass production of spores of Trichoderma viride has been filed. The technology has been packaged and transfer to a suitable enterprise is being negotiated through BCIL and DBT, New Delhi. Several fermentation batch runs at 100 1 fermentor scale using the patented media composition were made for the mass production of the biocontrol agent. The biocontrol agent was supplied to SKUAST, Agriculture departments of Jammu & Kashmir and to many private agencies for validation of efficacy for wilt and root-rot based diseases in different crops.

Field Studies: Biological control agent, Trichoderma viride and Gliocladium virens were also tested on chilly crops infected with wilt complex during kharif 1998 in Jammu, Udhampur and Kathua dists. of J&K. With biocontrol treatment, 16-18% average increase in germination and overall productivity was recorded in comparison to untreated control.

At CTRI, Rajahmundry - An area of 1273 ha. of different crops viz., tobacco (204 ha.), cotton (234 ha.), groundnut (600 ha.), chillies (228 ha.) and pigeonpea (7 ha.) belonging to farmers of East Godavari, West Godavari and Krishna districts of Coastal Andhra Pradesh was covered under demonstration of IPM of S.litura (1032 ha) and H.armigera (241 ha). In the demonstration of IPM of S.litura in tobacco nurseries at Morampudi in East Godavari, it was seen that IPM practice nursery growers obtained 33,50,000 seedlings with a net profit of Rs. 70,333/ha in comparison to chemical control nursery growers with 30,20,200 seedlings/ha and net profit of Rs. 46,346/ha. The C.B. ratio for IPM was 1:1.45 whereas in chemical control it was 1: 1.29.

At PDKV, Akola the demonstration of bio-agents in an area of over 850 hectares was undertaken in the farmers field covering 188 farm families. The field experiments have indicated fairly good incremental cost benefit ratio in the adoption of IPM programme over the conventional practice of pesticide application. At IISR, Calicut- an economic substrata was developed for Trichoderma. Apart from sorghum meal and decomposed coffee husk, tea waste and coconut water also supported good growth and sporulation of T.harzianum. Shelf life of T.harzianum in tea waste was good even after 3 months ($277X10^5$) in neem cake. An efficient Trichoderma harzianum isolate was used for all the field evaluation against Phytophthora root rot of black pepper covering an area of 6300 ha which included nursery management in black pepper and cardamom. The percentage of field establishment of pepper biocontrol treated cuttings was as high as 85-90% compared 5055% in untreated controls. Field evaluation trials conducted in Kerala and Karnataka against foot rot of black pepper showed slow but steady protection.

At IIPR Kanpur, field demonstrations of HaNPV against Helicoverpa armigera in chickpea crop were carried out in 200 ha area in the districts of Hamirpur, Jalaun and Kanpur. Endosulfan (0.07%) treated and untreated crops were compared with HaNPV (250 LE/ha). Results showed that mass larval population ranged from 2 to 6, 1 to 4.5 and 19 to 35 in NPV, endosulfan and untreated plots, respectively. Reduction in percent pod damage varied between 14.2-31.2 in NPV and 22.2-47.7 in endosulfan treated plots over control plots. The cost-benefit ratio varied from 1:5 to 1:9 in case of HaNPV whereas it ranged from 1: 11 to 1: 19 in case of endosulfan.

At OUAT, Bhubaneswar, field demonstrations on the performance of HaNPV on chickpea, pigeonpea and tomato in 125.5, 74.0 and 262.0 ha and that of S1NPV of, groundnut in 396 ha. area were conducted ir the fields of 2726 farmers farmers of 51 villages in eight districts viz., Cuttak, Puri, Khurda, Nayagarh, Ganjam, Jajpur, Keonjhar and Mayurbhanja of Orissa state. On the use and performance of HaNPV and S1NPV on different crops, 120 farmers' training programmes were conducted and 2726 farmers participated.

At Assam Agricultural University, Jorhat, Biopesticides for Integrated management of tea pests in North - East India were developed, Shelf-life of the product was prolonged to 9-12 months for the first time. The technique is under patent. An area of approximately 10 ha. of tea crop was covered with biocontrol agents like Verticillium lecanii, Beauveria bassiana Chrysoperla carnea, Trichogramma chilonis, an, NPV against different pests of tea. The technique of mass culturing of biocontrol agents and method of their application were also exhibited to farmers.

A major R&D programme on the role of Biological Resources for integrated nutrient and pest management for increasing agriculture productivity for existing cropping system is being launched. This programme has a major component on Biological Control under, integrated pest management. This particular component of the programme has been developed based an the success achieved in the biocontrol R&D network programme and subsequently in the mission mode programme of the department. In this programme 14 centres are involved from various states viz U.P., Kerala, Tamil Nadu, J&K, Assam, Gujarat, Karnataka, Andhra Pradesh, Maharashtra, Orrisa, Andaman & Nicobar islands. The main objective of this programme is to integrate the use of biopesticides, natural enemies alongwith other components of IPM and INM for developing a package of practices in different crop systems.

Biofertiliser

A number of projects were supported on crop specific

biofertilisers in order to understand the basic mechanism of nitrogen fixation which will help technology development. High nitrogen fixing strains of rhizobiurn and blue green algae, suitable for different agroclimatic regions have been isolated and demonstrated in field conditions. Technology for the mass production of mycorrhiza has been transferred for commercialisation. A network programme on Integrated use of Biofertilisers in Nutrient Management for specific cropping systems prevalent in the various zones of the country as been started.

Rhizobium

The chickpea nodulation variants ICC4918M and ICC4993M developed by pure line selection from their normal nodulating patents ICC4918 and ICC48993 lacked nodulation but formed normal root hairs. Studies indicated that flavonoid synthesis/secretion is normal in NN lines and may not be the reason for their non-nodulation and nodulation variants are probably blocked at the early stages of nodulation like initiation of root hair deformation or cortical cell division.

Studies conducted at Centre for Biotechnology, New Delhi demonstrated sugar specific binding of peanut root lectin (PRA II) to peanut specific bradyrhizobial lipopolysaccharides (LPS), by gel retardation assay and lectin based ELISA. Sephadex G-50 gel purified high molecular weight polysaccharides from NC 92 LPS bind PRA II most efficiently Binding of NC 92 LPS only to PRA II and not to PNA, SBA and PSL by Western blot analysis suggests that this lectin-LPS interaction is tissue as well as species specific. Human and rabbit erythrocyte agglutinating activities were specifically inhibited by lactose/cellobiose (SLII) and methyl a-mannoside (SLI) respectively. Actively growing tissues like newly emerging young leaves and elongating stem contained more SLII activity in comparison to mature tissues. Immunological tests indicated that all the vegetative tissue lectins are serologically related.

In order to develop a suitable technology for large scale cultivation of the two proven growth promotory strains, PRS9 and GRP3 of Plant Growth Promotory Rhizobacteria Fluorescent Pseudomonads, detailed characterization in shake culture and a 10L fermenter was carried out at GB Pant University of Agriculture & Technology. The studies indicated that strains GRP^3 and PRS9 are able to grow well in a wide temperature range of 10°C to 37°C. While both exhibit optima of 29°C, strain GRP3 is a rapid multiplier than PRS9. Farm yard manure was better than storage of nutrient enriched carriers at room temperature (15-20°C).

Experiments confirmed the lysogenic behaviour of a Bradyrhizobium strain (A025) isolated from pigeonpea nodule at BHU, Varanasi. Strain A025 induced phage (RT2) in culture during growth phase. Phage RT2 formed distinct turbid plaques on another Bradyrhizobium isolate A039. Both lysogenic and phage-indicator strains produced effective nodules on five different legumes (pigeonpea, mungbean, urdbean, cowpea and siratro) under axenic environment. Symbiotic interaction of the isolated antibiotic resistant and auxotrophic mutants of both Bradyrhizobium strains were studied on two legumes (pigeonpea and siratro). The results indicated that all selected mutants of both lysogenic and indicator Bradyrhizobium strains successfully nodulated siratro plants and increased significantly the plant dry weight. Three mutants of the strain A025 (L3, L5 and L8) and one mutant of the strain A039 (M4) were unable to produce nodules on pigeon pea plant. This suggests that the host infectivity of some mutant strains were changed. Symbiotic effectiveness of the mutant Bradyrhizobium strains was studied on three pigeonpea cultivars namely ICPL83072, Bahar and T-21 under controlled conditions showed a significant difference for all the symbiotic traits at 1 % probability level. The nodule number varied from 5 to 26, maximum being on ICPL 83072 and minimum on Bahar cultivar.

Blue green algae

A study was undertaken by Utkal University, Bhubaneswar to determine the distributional pattern of blue-green algae in the rice soil at 45 locations covering 9 agroclimatic zones of Orissa. In all, 120 species of heterocystous blue-green algae belonging to Nostoc, Cyclindrospermum, Calothrix, Rivularia, Aulosira, Tolypothrix, Scytonema, Westiellopsis and Hapalosipon and 23 non-heterocystous forms of the genera Oscillatoria, Lyngbya and Aphanothece were recorded. Wide variation in the growth rate and nitrogen fixing capacity among the isolates of each genus and between different genera was observed.

Although many Anabaena, Nostoc and Cylindrospermum species possessed higher growth rate, their nitrogen fixing capacity was much less in comparison to the species belonging to Calothrix Rivularia, Tolypothrix, Aulosira and Westiellopsis which were generally found to be slow growing forms. Field trials to assess the performance d isolated blue-green algae during Kharif revealed that yield was increased by 25-32 percent than control.

In a survey conducted at Rajendra Agricultural University, Pusa, Bihar, 42 species of cyanobacteria belonging to the genera Microcystis, Chroococcus, Gloeocapsa, Aphanotheceae, Oscillatoria, Phormidium, Lyngbya, Microcoleus, Cylindro-spermum, Wollea Nostoc, Anabaena, Aulosira, Scytonema, Calothrix, Gloeotrichia and Westiellopsis were identified. Out of these, 26 species were non-heterocystous and 16 species heterocystous forms. Wide variation was recorded in cyanobacterial growth and nitrogenase activity in incubated soil samples collected from different soil types. The soils rich in 'organic matter showed maximum algal biomass but nitrogenase activity was minimum at these sites.

Field trials revealed that application of different cyanobacterial inoculants alone or in combination with fertilizer nitrogen brought about significant increase in grain and straw yield over the respective controls in both the years.

Rice fields of forty localities in ten districts viz., Allahabad, Pratapgarh, Raibareli, Fatehpur, Jaunpur, Hardoi, Bareilly, Varanasi, Basti and Moradabad were surveyed by Allahabad University for the growth of Blue green Algae.

Ten localities of Allahabad district were kept under close observation for gradual change in floristic pattern during the paddy season and also for their recurrence in subsequent years and strains were isolated. At present non-heterocystous and filamentous forms (Oscillatoriales) 58 strains, and Nostoc Anabaena complex (Nostocales) 80 strains, are being maintained. These strains were characterized on the basis of morphological and physiological parameters. C.S. Azad University of Agriculture and Technology, Kanpur also conducted similar studies and a number of promising strains of BGA were isolated and characterized.

Mycorrhiza

At Madras University, Chennai, mycelium isolates of the ectomycorrhizal fungus, Pisolithus tinctorius were collected from Eucalyptus plantations of the coastal regions of Madras. Two types of inocula were produced using the ectomycorrhizal fungus. Inoculum of

G.mosseae and Bradyrhizobium sp. significantly improved the plant growth and mycorrhizal development when compared to the uninoculated control.

JNU and Hamdard University, New Delhi successfully raised Bacopa monnieri and Artemisia annua plantlets on a defined and simplified media and also achieved success in the interaction of arbuscular mycorrhizal fungi with that of tissue culture raised plantlets. The rate of survival was as high as 93.1% as compared to control. The rate of growth of mycorrhiza inoculated plantlets was much better than those without mycorrhiza.

Regular survey of various crop-fields of minor millets of Santhal Pargana and Bhagalpur divisions was conducted by T.M. Bhagalpur University. Three crops namely Sorghum bicolor, Zea mays and Panicum miliaceum grown in the experimental plots, showed dense association of VAM fungi. Minor millet crops i.e. P.miliaceum, E.coracana, P.scrobiculatum, Echinocloa frumentacea, Setaria italica were grown in experimental plots which were devoid of cultivation for a long duration.

Role of biofertilisers in integrated nutrient management

The department initiated a network programme to develop a package of practices involving various biofertilisers for specific cropping systems. The objectives of the programme are as -follows:

Basic Issues for study:

(i) Extent of phenotypic and genotypic heterogeneity in microbial population in rhizosphere and bulk soil under existing cropping pattern/practices and changing crop component.

(ii) Relative contribution of microbial biomass in C and N pools in the presence of organic and inorganic fertilizers.

Table: Varietal performance of TC derived black pepper plants as compared with conventional propagules.

	P1	P2	P4		Karimunda			
Characters	TC	Cutting	TC	Cutting	TC	Cutting	TC	Cutting
Plant height (m)	2.6	3.2	22.4	3	3	3.5	2.6	3.7
Internodal length (cm)								
Lateral	6	7.4	5	6	5.1	6	6.6	8.5
Main shoot	8	7.5	7.5	8	5.6	7.5	8	8.5
Leaf area (cm^2)								
Lateral	91.73	114.80	91.95	83.07	84.5	86.7	55.66	44.9
Main shoot	83.07	79.52	97.26	71	99.4	70.29	52.68	42.6
No. of lateral	63	38	78	50	93	30	87	30
No. of spikes/ lateral	1.5	1.4	1.75	1.5	2	1.5	2	1.25
Length of spike (cm)	11.3	11.3	8.3	8.3	7.5	8.2	8.9	5.5
% set	85.71	94.28	83.75	95.71	68.18	88.46	93.16	64.28

(iii) Influence of turnover rates of organics on in situ microbial activity and soil health.

(iv) Efficacy of mixed microbial consortia as against monoculture in nutrient dynamics and budgeting.

(v) Development and use of molecular tools for quantitation and characterization of phenotypic and genotypic heterogeneity under in-situ conditions, particularly for legal protection of strains.

(vi) Understanding the critical role played by microbial consortia in uptake mechanisms, partitioning and relocation of nutrient resource using microcosms and mesocosms.

Applied Issues for study:

(i) Evaluation of appropriate biofertilisers with organic and mineral fertilisers within given cropping systems and crop management packages under changed emphasis on organics for sustainability of a system.

(ii) Monitoring the trend of individual crop yields, productivity and soil quality parameters of the system through intensive experimental trials.

(iii) Integration and study of known and new microbial inoculants in the existing practices for improvement of input-output ratio and soil health decreased dependence on chemical inputs.

(iv) On farm validation of technology] packages developed.

Technology development and transfer

A number of technologies were developed and demonstrated for large scale production of high quality biofertilisers specially for rice, pulses, fodder legumes and important forest trees. These are under transfer to industry.

Tree and woody species, application of tissue culture

Plant tissue culture

The projects focused on protocol development and demonstration for important species of forest trees, horticultural and plantation crops. Regional hardening facilities catered to the requirements of specific ecological regions.

(i) Forest trees

In the Arid zone region, the regional hardening facility at Jodhpur produced nearly 10.000 plants which were field planted in association with the State Forest Departments. Nearly 16000 plants of Wrighitia arborea were produced and hardened. The growth performance is being evaluated.

Studies on Dalbergia species focussed on inter specific protoplast fusion. Plant regenerations from cell suspension protoplasts of Dalbergia latifolia and D.sissoo were achieved and plants were transferred to soil. Mass propagation of high yielding azadirachtin clones were continued and approx. 1.5 lakh plantlets; were field planted at multilocations. Variability studies in neem were also conducted and samples collected from different provinces. RAPD studies indicated that in neem the extent of variability was low and possibility of a narrow genetic base. Plant regeneration from mature explants of Maggar bamboo has been standardized. High frequency somatic embroyogenesis has been achieved and synthetic seeds were obtained. In vitro cultures have been established for Pinus wallichiana, P.geradiana, Cedrus deodara, Quercus leucotricophora, Q.semacarpifolia and Q.glauca. Somatic embryos of Q.semecarpifolia germinated to form well-developed plantlets, which were hardened and transferred to pots. Studies were taken up on some endangered and rare tree species of Western Ghats.

Good progress was achieved in the tissue culture regeneration of canes and rattans. Plantlet regeneration through somatic embroyogeneis was achieved and plantlets transferred to soil. Studies continued on Mangrove species. Protocol for six species were perfected and nearly 60,000 plants were transferred to the field at the Genetic Conservation Centre. A large number of species were mass multiplied. In order to study the genetic variability of the TC raised plants vis-a-vis the control, studies are on using DNA fingerprinting and RAPD techniques. Protocol for DNA isolation and RAPD probes for a number of species (eucalyptus, teak, desert sps, coffee, pepper) have been standardised.

The DNA fingerprinting of plant genome of Populus species was taken up. Three different clones were characterized. These are useful for phylogenetic analysis and for screening of inter-specific hybrids. PCR based markers were developed for analysing genetic variation. RAPD assay was done to study genetic diversity in P.ciliata and P.deltoides. The clustering of genotypes in both species was found to be in accordance with the geographical distribution. Different factors affecting micropropagation of Gmelina arborea were studied. Seasonal recalcitrance shown by nodal explants was overcome by application of hormone and antioxidants and a successful microporpagation method was established. The hardening facility at Calcutta became operational. Protocols of economically important species are being refined by 5 different groups and plantlets being hardened at the facility. The field demonstration have been initiated in association with State Departments and NGO's.

(ii) Horticultural crops

Under a coordinated project on mango, studies continued on a number of commercially important varieties namely Dasheri, Chausa, Langra, Alphonso, Amrapali, Totapari,

Neelam etc. Tissue culture regeneration protocol is being worked out using different explants - zygotic embryo, nucellar embryo, axcillary buds et promising leads were obtained. Somatic embryogenesis was induced and further, proliferation of embryos achieved. Nucellar erbryogenesis has been augmented in root stock varieties. Nucellar embryo proliferation was sustained in a long-term culture. Synchronize development of nucellar embryo was obtained and plantlets regenerated.

In Citrus species, shoot meristems less than 1 mm were regenerated into complete plants. Micrografting was successfully done and in vitro raised plantlets transferred to soil. A production system for disease free (Tristeza, greening of Darjeeling orange) plants micropropagation has been established and plants are now being field demonstrated. The double grafted plants were more vigorous with greater canopy diameter and more flowering. 600 plants micrografted on tissue culture raised rootstock of Rangpur lime and rough lime were produced. A protocol to produce nucellar cultures of Darjeeling orange has been developed.

Banana plants resistant to Bunchy Top virus infection were produced through mutagenesis. One tissue culture raised clone of dwarf Cavendish, showed tolerance to the virus even after repeated inoculation. The BB 7 tolerant clone was multiplied to 80-multi-cultures and tested. More than a thousand cultures were screened 3000 tissue culture raised plants were screened. A programme for developing transgenic eggplant resistant to abotic stress was supported.

Agrobacterium mediated transformation was standardized. This now being used for transferring polyamine biosynthetic genes. Microprogation protocols were standardized for a number of commercially important species of orchids using different explants. In a few species like Aerides rosea, Vanda stangeana, Vanda parishii, Aerides odoratum Vanda stangeana and Renodes, protocols for hardening were being standardized.

Mutations were being induced for improvement of a few varieties. In an attempt to produce commercially important hybrids, studies were initiated on breeding interspecific and inter-generic hybrids of Orchids. Mother plants of 52 varieties of sympodial and 67 varieties of monopodial orchids including wild varieties were being maintained. Hybridization and inter specific crossing experiments were initiated.

Studies were continued for regenerating chrysanthemum and rose from gamma ray treated explants of capitulum, pedicle, floret and petal in an attempt to manage the chimera. Plant regeneration was achieved from floret. The regenerated plants survived well and flowered true to floret colour types.

(iii) Plantation crops

Viable protocols were developed for a number of economically important crops. Commercially viable protocols were developed for Coffee - Cavery/Catimor, Sln9, CxR and BR varieties. Nearly 2000 plants were produced and field transplanted in 7 Coffee growers estates for comparison with seedling raised plants. The TC raised plants showed good vegetative growth. Nearly four thousand Black Pepper varieties - Panniyur 1,2,3,4 and KS-27 were produced through tissue culture and planted in the farmers field in 3 districts of Kerala - Thrissur, Idukki and Waynad.

The field performance has been evaluated in comparison to seedling plants. 90% survival was recorded and the performance of TC raised plants observed to be better than the control in a number of parameters such as number of laterals, flowering branches, yield/vine, % fruit set etc. No abnormalities were observed in spike or berry characters.

The genetic stability and clonal fidelity of TC raised plants were being tested at field levels, using molecular markers.

Studies are continuing for protocol development of regeneration of clove, nutmeg and cinnamon from various explants. Protocol standardization was taken up for cashew from shoot tip explants. A protocol for somatic embryogenesis of ginger from leaf and vegetative bud has been established. A high rate of conversion of these somatic embryos into plantlets has been achieved. Three elite tea clones UPASI-3, 26 and 27 were mass multiplied and their performance studied vis-a-vis vegetatively propagated (VP) plants. Approx. 95-100% survival was reported in TC plants as against 91 % in the case of vegetatively propagated plants, the number of laterals in the case of TC plants was more.

Studies were underway for establishment of an anther/pollen culture protocol in tea. 100 androgenic calli lines were maintained and artificial seed production attempted. Somatic embryogenesis was achieved and attempts were made to enhance the conversion rate.

Table : Biomass removed at the time of tipping and centering.

Clone	Biomass removed Centering	g fr. Wt/plant Tipping
VP plants	4.34	15.6
TC plants		
UPASI - 3	12.40	9.6
UPASI - 26	11.50	3.4
UPASI - 27	14.50	16.0
CID P 0.05	6.08	8.1

Bioprospecting

This multi-institutional collaborative programme on bioprospecting of biological wealth aims at characterization, inventorization and conservation of the bio-diversity of different -eco-geographical regions and prospecting of genes and bio-molecules.

Survey of biodiversity

The Dept. of Space initiated the work of preparing biome maps for the region. Initial studies concentrate on the NorthEastern region. Field work for ground data collection is being done and digital analysis of data is under progress. The vegetation and land use maps generated by remote sensing data have been integrated with other thematic layers. These images are being use for assessing biological richness. The Indian Institute of Science Bangalore developed a biomonitoring system actively involving 13 colleges -4 different States for monitoring the biodiversity of the region.

Bioprospecting of molecules/genes

The plants of cold desert region - Lahul & Spiti were monitored and those plants resistant to the cold region were identified. Bioprospecting is now being done for the candidate genes and molecules in order to identify and characterise these particular genes for potential use in other groups of plants. Bioassay studies and chemotyping are being done to identify the active principle of utility as a biocide, antifeedant and as an individual raw material.

DNA Fingerprinting/genetic variability

Studies were initiated to identify those plant species present in both North-East and South-West regions. DNA fingerprinting is being done to determine the variability existing between two groups of plants. In addition, plants of high economic and medicinal importance are being collected and finger-printed for complete characterisation and cataloguing. In the first phase of activities, approximately 10 species were selected for the North-East region, South-Western Ghats and Western Himalayas.

Tissue culture and conservation

Efforts, were on to conserve these important plants through both in-situ and ex-situ conservation methods. Regeneration protocols are being developed for rapid multiplication of the elite material.

Molecular taxonomy

In view of the urgent need of evolving suitable research strategies for proper inventorization and cataloguing of the biological resource, a programme on molecular taxonomy has been initiated. The programme concentrates on identification, characterization and documentation of the plant resource specifically the crops of economic importance, region and species wise.

Medicinal and aromatic plants

Various projects have been launched on conservation, micropropagation, production of secondary metabolites, biotransformation of intermediates into pharmaceutically important products and genetic improvement of medicinal and aromatic plants.

National gene banks for medicinal and aromatic plants:

National bureau of plant genetic resources, New Delhi

Seven explorations were undertaken and a total of 432 germplasm accessions collected. Chemical evaluation was undertaken on germplasm collections of Acorus, Mucuna and Psoralea and evaluation of at least 30 accessions of Mucuna for L-DOPA content carried out. The L-DOPA content ranged from 2.34-3.79%. Ten accessions of Psoralea were evaluated for psoralin content which was found to range from 0.97-1.39%. In in vitro repository, shoot cultures of Gentiana could be conserved for over two years. In Crocus, low temperature was found to induce dormancy as sprouting of bulbs was delayed for eight months. Experiments continued to improve the medium term conservation protocol.

Central institute of medicinal and aromatic plants, Lucknow

The germplasm collection of 25 accessions of all prioritized plant species has been further strengthened by adding more threatened plant species and accessions including the plants used in folklore medicine. In field gene banks, 196 species of medicinal and aromatic plants are being maintained. A total of 41 species in Seed Gene Bank and 23 species in DNA Bank are being conserved. In addition to these, 35 plant species are also being maintained in the form of callus, multiple shoots microplantlets and hairyroot cultures in this gene bank.

A library of 251 cell lines covering 22 plant species is being maintained as hairy root gene bank. Two new anthroquinone derivatives Rheum emodi were identified. Four hype, alkaloid producing Catharanthus roseus genotypes were identified out of 23 accession Out of 84 genotypes of palmarosa collected from different parts of the country, ten best genotypes have been selected for a bench scale trial. Variability in yield and quality of sweet basil accessions was estimated to define core group Characterization of 170 accessions of Citronella led to identification of 34 core accessions for their essential oil quality and quantity In vitro evaluation of Cantharanthus roseus accession was carried out for tolerance towards 5-methyl tryptophan selection.

One stable genotype tolerating 100-120 mg/I 5-methyl tryptophan was identified. A detailed screening of taxol and 10-deacetyl baccatin - III contents in the stem, bark and needles of Taxus baccata individual trees has revealed that these antineoplastic compounds were present in higher concentrations (0.02%) in the germplasm collected from Himachal Pradesh than the accessions collected from Kashmir, Uttar Pradesh and Arunachal Pradesh.

Tropical biotanical garden research institute, Thiruvananthapuram

Conducted ten plant collection trips to collect germplasm from different parts of Kerala, Tamil Nadu and bordering areas of Karnataka and Andhra Pradesh. Four hundred and twelve accessions were introduced into the nursery the field gene bank. These include three target species - Berberis nilgherrensis, Piper pykarensis and Piper schmidtii.

Seeds of 20 species were studied in detail with regard to their viability, storage and germination aspects. Twenty six species with 29 accessions are maintained in the in vitro repository.

Three accessions one each of Crataeva magna, Geophila reniformis and Janakia arayalpatra were added during the period under report. The in vitro protocol for mass multiplication of Mahonia leschenaulti (rare) has been successfully developed. Shoot tips derived from shoot cultures of Holostemma annulare, a vulnerable medicinal plant was successfully cryopreserved in liquid nitrogen through an encapsulation-dehydration protocol.

RRL- Jammu

This project has been recently initiated to understand the present status of availability of resources in three regions of J&K state, identification of endangered and threatened plant species of the region, and to collect enlisted plant species from Ladakh, Kashmir and Jammu region and their conservation by establishing field gene banks and by in Vitro methods.

Micropropagation

At IISc, Bangalore a high frequency embryogenic system with considerable synchrony has been developed for sandalwood. The efficiency of the protocol was tested on several trees of sandalwood and the protocol was found to be applicable to the cultures of all trees sampled. The protocol of embryogenesis ensured proper morphological maturation of embryos and conversion of these embryos into plants.

Eight populations of Rheum and Acontium species have been identified with considerable variations in seed protein profile and active ingredients (glycosides in case of Rheum and aconotine in case of Aconitum in rhizomes at Garhwal University, Srinagar, Garhwal. All superior types identified for higher active ingredients have been transplanted in temperate and alpine nurseries. The modified protocols for Rheum species have been developed for tissue culture. Culture conditions for Aconitum atrox and A.heterophyllum were established. Economically viable and simple technology has been developed to obtain 10-12 fold increase in the tuber yield in two Himalayan Aconite species. It also helps in a five-fold increase in number of tubers per plant in A.atrox.

Studies have been initiated for micropropagation of Swerta chirata - an endangered medicinal plant. Natural population will be screened to identify genetically superior and elite clones and germplasm conservation of identified clones genotypes carried out using in vitro culture strategies. In vitro studies have been initiated on Cartaeva nurvala at Birla Institute of Scientific Research, Jaipur. Plant material has been collected from different areas for screening of higher lupeol (antiurolithiatic agent) content. Various media combinations were used to test the morphogenetic potential of various explants.

Nodal segments were proliferated into multiple shoots. The shoot tips and leaves of these plants have produced profusely proliferating callus cultures. Attempts are being made to induce regeneration in these cultures.

The work on developing micropropagation protocol for two medicinally useful Asclepiadaceous members -Decalepis hamiltonii and Hemidesmus indicus has been initiated at Sri Krishnadevaraya University, Anantapur. Studies on in vitro induction of salinity tolerance in the aromatic grasses (Cymbopogon martinii and C.flexuosus) have been initiated at RRL, Bhubaneshwar. At Kerala Agricultural University, Trissur, in vitro propagation protocol for Gymnema sylvestre has been developed. Tissue culture derived plants were transferred to field and the growth rate observed. The calli derived from leaf and internodal segments of G.sylvestre were analysed at different intervals for presence of secondary metabolities.

Production of secondary metabolites biotransformation of intermediates

Studies on production of therapeutic agents in tissue culture of Withania somnifera and Azadirachta indica were continued at Kakatiya University, Warangal. The procedures for extraction and HPLC method for the estimation of Azadirachtin and Withaferin- A were standardized and established. Cell suspension cultures were maintained by sub-culturing at regular intervals. The studies on influence of precursors, polymeric adsorbents and stress inducers on the bioproduction of secondary metabolities have been initiated. At Kakatiya University, Warangal, procedures have been standardized for establishment and maintenance of static and suspension cultures derived from explants of Taxus wallichiana and T.baccata. The callus cultures could be effectively maintained for four passages of five weeks each and later on browning of the cultures and necrosis of callus was observed. The analytical profile could be established using HPLC method and extraction method for taxane from biomass was developed.

An active fraction has been partially purified at JNU, New Delhi from Momordica charantia (Karela) to bring down the blood glucose levels in diabetic rats and improve glucose tolerance significantly. Purified fraction elicits hypoglycemia to almost an equal extent observed with insulin. The fraction also possessed lipogenic activity for increasing blood glucose utilization. At NCL, Pune, the callus cultures from cotyledonary explants of Mappia foetida have been raised towards developing a methodology for production of desired anticancer compounds such as Camptothecin in some combinations. Organogenetic responses was obtained from hypocotyl, immature and mature embryos, immature cotyledons and induction of embryogensis from callus is in progress.

Molecular biological studies on cardio-protective properties of Terminalia arjuna continued at AIIMS, New Delhi. In order to investigate any antioxidant effect of chronic feeding of T.arjuna on cardiac ischemic-reperfusion injury, dried and pulversised bark of the plant (500 and 750 mg/kg) in 2% carboxymethyl cellulose was administered orally to Wistar albino rats (200 - 250 mg) at 6 days/ week for 90 days. Hearts were then subjected to in vitro ischemic reperfusion injury in a Langendorff's apparatus to observe the effect on oxidant stress in cardiac 1 -R injury.

The results suggest the involvement of oxygen free radical in I-R injury in isolated rat heart. The crude neem bark extract has been found to have potent antisecretory and antinuclear activity in animal models at IICB, Calcutta. It inhibits both drug (mercaptomethylimidazole) and pylorus - ligation induced gastric acid secretion nearly 90% at a dose of 10 mg / kg.

The extract is highly potent to -block stress-induced gastric ulcer almost completely at a dose of 20 mg/kg. The bioactive material which is more potent than pure ranitidine and omeprazol in inhibiting acid secretion and gastric ulceration has been purified. Future studies would be directed to investigate the mechanism of action.

AT IIT, New Delhi, callus cultures of Podophyllum hexandrum are being raised from the seeds collected from Tunmarg, Srinagar (J&K) and I.H.B.T., Palampur. Efforts are also being made to initiate suspension culture from the callus culture of P hexandrum.

At PAU, Ludhiana, the studies have been initiated for production of capsaicin by immobilized bell cultures of Chilli pepper, Capsicum annuum and C.frutescens. Composition of culture medium has been standardized for the initiation and proliferation of callus from pericarp and placenta of nine varieties of C.annuum. Callus proliferation was found to be slow in high capsaicin varieties than low capsaicin variety. Work is in progress for determining capsaicin content in the callus and establishing cell suspension cultures.

Genetic improvement

Studies have been undertaken at CIMAP, Lucknow to develop high bacoside (memory enhancer) yielding genotypes of Bacopa monnieri and for genetic fingerprinting of the selected plant material toward the domestication of this species. Different accessions of B.monnieri were subjected to RAPD analysis to determine genetic variation and to define them into distinct clusters. The band similarity index for individual primers was calculated, and a similarity matrix was prepared by taking the average of band similarity indices of all 20 primers. Based on the similarity matrix, a phylogenetic tree (dendrogram) was constructed.

In an attempt to generate variability within the existing germplasm of Pelargonium graveolens, calliclones were raised in the widely adopted Algerian variety. Eighty five randomly selected calliclones were subjected to field trials alongwith their controls in randomized block design. Out of these 85 calliclones, 31 exhibited serrated leaf phenotypes resembling the parental type, whereas 54 can be grouped as less serrated leaf phenotypes. The total content of the stem distilled essential oil mostly varied between 0.15% to 0.23% in the serrated leaf calliclones and 0.11 to 0.21% in the less-serrated leaf calliclones, Whereas the control plants showed a range of variation from 0.15 - 0.16%. About 16% of the serrated leaf phenotypes and 9% of the less - serrated phenotypes produced 0.21 % of oil which are normally found in higher oil yielding Bourbon variety. Under natural infection in the field conditions, 48% of serrated leaf calliclones and 13% of less-serrated were found to be resistant to leaf blight (Alternaria alternata). A few calliclones having desirable oil profile, yield and resistant to leaf blight have been selected for further studies.

In vitro cell lines of Artemisia annua were identified which contain high artemisinin (antimalarial drug) and artemisinic acid, at CIMAP, Lucknow. High artemisinin yield can be obtained under subtropical agro-climatic conditions of North-Indian plains by cultivating A.annua at a very density as 2.22 x 10 plants / ha. A.annua at this population density yielded 7.4 kg of artemisinin and 91 kg of essential oil. A.annua population has been characterized at molecular level using DNA fingerprinting. Using unique RAPD profiles developed, it is possible to identify each chemotype distinctly from others. An improved single step process was developed for the conversion of artemisinic acid into artemisinin.

Studies have been continued at Zandu Foundation for Health Care, Ambach, Gujarat to develop novel germplasm of Mucuna pruriens with high L-Dopa content, improved yield characters and lacking of itching trichomes on pods. Seeds of 23 lines collected from different regions of India were used as parents in the breeding programmes. New lines of 48 F-1 hybrids, 16 BC - 1 and 10 BC-2 have been developed and evaluated for the seed associated characters. Of these 48 F-1 hybrids, 36 lines have-shown non-itching trichomes on pods, white in colour with medium size of seed while 12 lines had non-itching trichomes on pods, striped with-medium to bold seed size. Fourteen BC-1 lines were found to be with non-itching trichomes and two BC-1 lines showed itching trichomes on their pods. Six crosses of BC-2 lines were found to possess non-itching trichomes on pods, white in colour and medium-to-bold seed size ranging between 97 and 138 gm/100 seeds. Four crosses of BC-2 showed itching trichomes on pods, small-medium size (31-64 gm/100 seeds). Analysis of L-dopa content in the seeds, back crossing and selection of desired lines are in progress.

At IHBT, Palampur, studies have been initiated on protoplast culture and somatic hybridization of rose species (R.damascena and R.bourboniana). Callus cultures from nodal, stem and leaf segment from freshly sprouted to one-year-old field-grown plants were raised. Fast growing cell suspension cultures were produced from the friable callus subcultured into liquid medium. Protoplasts were isolated form actively growing freshly harvested suspension cells at varying intervals after subculture and cultures at different densities ranging from $4x10^5$ to $0.25x10^5$ in liquid medium. Thin alginate layer (TAL) technique was employed and callus was formed within three weeks. Work on introduction / improvement and demonstration of better agrotechnologies of some of the selected medicinal (Withania somnifera, Catharanthus roseus, Cassia senna,

Amomum subulatum) and aromatic plants (Mentha arvenis, Cymbopogons winterianis and C.flexuosus) has been recently initiated at CIMAP Lucknow.

Integrated programme on taxol

At NCL, Pune, the callus of Taxus has been raised from the needles and stem bits collected from Shimla and Himachal Pradesh. The callus growth rates in various media and growth regulator combinations are being compared. Various anti-bacterial and anti-fungal agents were tried out to reduce contamination and promising leads obtained. Several dormancy breaking treatments such as gibberolic acid application, embryo excision and vernalization were employed for precocious germination of seeds of Taxus. Some of these treated cultures exhibited precious germination. Microorganisms from repositories have been used for testing biotransformation of taxol congeners present in Taxus wallichiana at RRL, Jammu. Microorganism No. RRL-189 was found capable of enhancing the 10-DAB-III content present. Various unidentified baccatins present in the biomass have also been enhanced by the enzymes present in the microbe.

At CIMAP, Lucknow, several accessions of Taxus wallichiana collected from Arunachal Pradesh and Darjeeling were chemically screened to identify the trees with maximum content of taxol or its analogues. The presence of taxol, 10-deacetyl baccatin III (DAB) and seven taxoids were detected through TLC in all the samples of Arunachal Pradesh but the Darjeeling samples revealed the absence of taxol and presence of DAB alongwith six taxiods only.

The HPLC analysis of the Arunachal Pradesh samples showed the presence of taxol ranged from 0.00027 to 0.0427 % and DAB in the range of 0.0103 - 0.17%. Callus cultures were from different explants of T.wallichiana collected from the Jammu and Kashmir. The ethylacetate fraction of the callus extract yielded a major phenolic compound which is found to possess anticancer properties. A procedure was developed to detect the presence of taxol during the initial phase of callusing using cell division inhibition technique.

A large number of bark needles from marked trees of Taxus sp. in four locations were collected for chemical analysis and propagation studies at I.H.B.T., Palampur. Taxol, bacctin III, 10-DAB-III and cephalomanine were estimated by HPLC. Taxane content in all the samples showed marked variation.

The technique for vegetative propagation of Taxus through stem cuttings has been standardized. Four hundred and fifty rooted stem cuttings were field transferred under its natural habitat at Barangi Tirthan Valley (2000 m) in the Great Himalayan National Park, Kullu. About 1300 rooted stem cuttings were also planted in the institute experimental farm.

At RRL, Jorhat, population of Taxus species growing in Meghalya and Arunanchal Pradesh were surveyed and collected with an objective of mapping the Taxus growing areas in the region, their variability studies, characterization and conservation strategies. Based on the habits and habitats of the plant population growing in the region, four variants of the species were evaluated for their macro and micromorphological characters from a taxonomic point of view.

Two samples of needles one each for both male and female population collected from Meghalaya region were chemically evaluated. Presence of both taxol and 10-DAB contents in the extracts of samples has been ascertained.

Seribiotechnology

A number of projects have been launched on different aspects of application of biotechnology for improving the productivity and quality of -silk alongwith improvement of host-plants in both mulberry and non-mulberry sericulture.

Development of better races of silkworm for increased productivity

At MKU, Madurai, transient expression of the CAT activity in the progenies of silkworm (Bombyx mori) has been successfully achieved. The transcription of CAT gene in the testis of infected batches has been demonstrated. Studies have indicated that a sperm membrane-bound protein may facilitate the internalization of DNA into the sperm. This protein was not detected in the female h reproductive tissues or haemolymph or fat body. Ten multivoltine silkworm (B.mori) races were screened for the presence of mariner elements using insect specific mariner primers at MKU Madurai. Silkworm-specific primers were designed. Studies have shown the presence of mariner copy in the screened races. The presence of three diverged mariner elements in B.mori genome reflects the invasion of this genome by horizontal transfer of mariner elements from other organisms.

The investigations on genetic and molecular basis of pattern formation during development in silkworm (Bombyx mori.) were continued at IISc, Bangalore. A method has been developed for studying silkworm embryonic development using DIC microscopy. The expression of Proliferating Cell Nuclear Antigen (PCNA) has been examined in the dechorionated embryos using antibodies raised against Drosophila PCNA.

The expression of PCNA has been visualised using the anti-body (conjugated to FITC) technique, under confocal microscope. This technique is now being used to study limb development during silkworm development using the heterologous antibodies (raised against distal-less). Oligonucleotide primers have been designed to clone the wingless gene from B.mori in order to investigate its role in development.

At Seribiotech Research Laboratory (SRL), Bangalore, work on RFLP analysis in silkworm (B.mori) for resistance to nuclear polyhedrosis virus (NPV) was continued. The LD 50 assay has provided adequate information on divergent response of silkworm races to the NPV. The analysis of data suggest that the resistance to NPV in silkworm is polygenic. Twenty five single / low copy probes from Pst I subgenomic library were selected based upon scorable bands, simple restriction profiles and their inheritance pattern in F1 hybrids of Nistari and NB1 races.

These clones are being used as probes for southern hybridization to find out any close linkage with virus resistance / susceptible character using bulk populations developed in the laboratory. The studies on identifying DNA markers in the silkworm breeds having low and high cocoon shell ratio have been continued at CSR&TI, Mysore. Six hundred recombinant clones and about 350 low copy probes have been developed for RFLP studies.

The work on molecular characterization of silkworm varieties using micro and minisatellite DNA has been concluded at SRL, Bangalore. The studies have demonstrated that the silkworm genome is abundant with di-and trinucleotide repeats and microsatellite repeats are conserved in the diversed saturniid moths. The results of genetic analysis of recombinant inbred lines show that the diapause and non-diapause traits of silkworm are linked to some of the quantitative trait loci (QTL) associated with cocoon, cocoon shell weight and fecundity. The diapausing trait seems to be invariably associated with higher metric traits while the opposite seems to be the case in non-diapausing silkworm strains.

The results provided important clues for selection of silkworm strains in silkworm improvement programme.

Studies on characterization of High Mobility Group (HMG) of proteins isolated from silkworm, B.mori were continued at University of Calcutta, Calcutta. HMG proteins from B.mori have similar antigenic property as that of Drosophila and mammals. These proteins were found to be present in all the developmental stages of silkworm larvae and pupae in a consistent manner.

At IIT, Kharagpur, amino acid composition analysis showed that Antheraea mylitta fibroin is rich in glycine. N-terminal and internal peptide amino acid sequences of the purified protein have been determined. Comparison of amino acid sequence data with that of A.pernyi in the nucleic acid sequence database revealed its high homology (95%) confirming the purified protein as fibroin. A cDNA library was constructed from the isolated m RNA of posterior silk gland in - ZAP II vector and screened with the raised polyclonal antibody and I Protein A. Seven positive phage clones were obtained after first round of screening.

The work on morphological and molecular characterization of a virus infecting A.mylitta has been continued at IIT, Kharagpur. Scanning electron microscopy revealed the presence of various shapes (icosahedral, cubical, pyramidal) and sizes (2-4 m) of polyhedra from a single infected host. Transmission electron microscopy of these purified virions showed that each virion particle is icosahedral in shape and 65-70 nm in size with spikes projecting from each vertices.

The total nucleic acid was isolated from the purified virion and analysed by agarose and polyacrylamide gel electrophoresis. Ten bands from 3.7 kb to 1.15 kb were observed in ethidium bromide-stained gel having characteristics of type IV Cytoplasmic Polyhedrosis Virus of Reoviridae family. These results suggest that viruses infecting A.mylitta and A.proylei (oak tasar silkworm) represent Cytoplasmic Polyhedrosis Virus containing 10 segmented double stranded RNA genome.

At the Institute of Advanced Study in S&T, Guwahati, seven eri silkworm (Philosomia ricini) stocks collected from different locations in North-East region were evaluated for their rearing performance on castor leaves during different seasons. Borduar race was found to be the best with respect to fecundity, larval weight, ERR, cocoon weight and shell weight.

Significant variation in the bovine serum albumin protein was noted among the stocks, however, variation among the strains of Titabor and Borduar were found to be insignificant. Protein profiles of different stocks of eri silkworm are being compared.

At NII, New Delhi silk proteins from eri silkworm have been purified to homogeneity. Significant differences were noted between the mulberry and non-mulberry silkworms in respect of fibroin as well as sericin protein. Antibodies have been raised against the silk proteins (fibroin and sericin). The cDNA expression library using m RNA isolated from the posterior silk gland of eri silkworm has been constructed. Isolation of the genes encoding fibroin (heavy and light chain) from the library is underway.

The fibroin proteins (both heavy and light chain) were isolated from the cocoons as well as the silk glands from different developmental stages of eri silkworm. The silk proteins were expressed in a development-specific fashion. The fibroin protein was also detected by Western blot to be expressed in a tissue specific manner.

Development of control measures for major diseases/pests of silkworm

Field trials of immunoassays for the detection of infectious flacherie diseases (Bm IFV) of silkworm (Bombyx mori) were conducted by CSR&TI, Mysore. PALLAS test was found to detect Bm NPV (up to 75 ng/ ml) in a sample, Tests have been standardized to detect the infectious flacherie in field samples. At CTR&TI, Ranchi, three monoclonal antibodies (Ig G type) were stabilized against Nosema sp. infecting tasar silkworm (Antheraea mylitta) in collaboration with NII, New Delhi.

These monoclonal antibodies (MA - 575, MA - 576 and MA - 577) are specific to Nosema sp. A sandwich ELISA was standardized. The results with MA-575 were found to be encouraging and may be useful to develop an assay. One step gluteraldehyde conjugation assay with monoclone MA-576 was developed and tested. Further standardization of immunoassays is in progress.

Field trials of integrated management of uzifly (Exorista bombycis) - a serious pest of silkworm have been completed at Semmedu village of Kolli hills in Eastern Ghats of Tamil Nadu by TNAU, Coimbatore. By integrating mechanical (uzinet), chemical (uzicide and uzi tablet) and biological method (through release of hyperparasite - Nesolynx thymus), the uzifly incidence was reduced to 8.25% from 19.75% in controls. Integrated Pest Management (IPM) treatment in cross breed (Pure Mysore x NB4 D2) registered a cocoon yield of 58 kg/100 DFLs as against 35 kg / 100 DFLs in controls. IPM trials have been recently initiated in Tharampuri and Pallapalayam villages to study the sequential release of different hyperparasities in conjuction with other methods of controls. Five training courses were organised on management of uzifly and 150 tribal farmers of Erode district participated.

Haemolymph samples obtained from bivoltine and multivoltine races of silkworm (Bombyx mori) reared under natural and in disease free conditions were analysed by SDS - PAGE at KSSR&DI, Bangalore. Several polypeptide bands of molecular weight ranging from 200 to 12 k Da were observed. These polypeptides were classified into five major groups. Haemocyte studies revealed that the total haemocyte count was high in bivoltine races as compared to multivoltines. However, the proportion percentage of plasmatocytes and granulocytes to the total haemocyte count was higher in multivoltine than bivoltine races.

Silkworm genome programme

The work on constructing high density linkage map based on sequence tagged sites (STS) markers in silkworm (Bombyx mori) has been continued by a core group established at CDFD, Hyderabad. A silkworm genome library from a non-diapausing strain of silkworm has been prepared with a view to cloning and characterizing many known and anonymous probes which, either could be used directly or converted as STS probes. The homologous sequence from the silkworm library has been picked up by using Bkm 2 (8) as a probe which would serve a probe for future DNA profiling research in silkworm. A cDNA library has been prepared from the ovary of silkworm to use array of cDNAs as expressed sequence tags for genomic research.

Silkworm as a bioreactor

At IISc, Bangalore, the hepatitis E coding sequences ORF 2 and ORF 3 have been procured for conducting studies on expression of recombinant viral antigens through Bombyx mori·Nuclear Polyhedrosis Virus (Bm NPV). The ORF 2 and ORF 3 regions have been subcloned in to p AC 1393 vectors for optimized expression. Recombination in to Bm NPV have been generated for ORF 3 and protein expression is being achieved. Using the plaque purified recombinant virus harbouring Hepatitis E-ORF3 (v Bm ORF3), B.mori larvae have been infected.

The expression of the recombinant protein in the haemolymph and fat bodies of the recombinant virus infected larvae has been demonstrated. The overall yields were not very high. Recombinant v Bm NPV harbouring the reporter gene Green Fluorescent Protein (GFP) has been generated by a similar technique. High levels of GFP are synthesized in recombinant virus infected cell lines.

On infection of cell lines, significant Green Fluorescence is emitted by the recombinant infected cells which provide a convenient means for the study of apoptotic cell death following virus infection. Olignonucleotide primers for PCR based cloning of the late expression factor gene (lef 2) have been synthesized. A functional role of Bm lef 2 in late gene transcription of Bm NPV (both polyhedrin and p 10) has been established.

Processing of silk

At IIT, New Delhi, a process was developed for pretreatment of spun silk with protease and cellulase enzymes. Spun silk fabric was subjected to bleaching and protease enzyme treatment in tandem. This improved the wettability and whiteness of the fabric without effecting its strength. A protease, degummase was used for biopolishing of silk. In continuation of this work, two proteases were used for biopolishing of different varieties of tasar silk. The enzyme treatment was most effective in case of bleached tasar silk. Bactosol SI was used for this purpose and the process conditions were being standardized.

The technology developed for degumming of silk with fungal protease was patented during this period. Efforts in the direction of conducting industrial trials and transferring the technology to industries are continuing. Studies have been recently initiated at Manipur University, Manipur for developing a better technology for processing of oak tasar silk using pineapple extract containing proteolytic enzyme (bromelain)

Improvement of host-plants

At University of Delhi South Campus (UDSC), New Delhi, seeds of Morus indica var K-2 were germinated on MS medium and in vitro differentiation capabilities of 7-10 days old explants (cotyledon, hypocotyl, root, leaf and petiole) were investigated. Previously developed protocol for the isolation of leaf mesophyll protoplasts was modified for in vitro grown explants. High density of healthy protoplasts was obtained in a combination of cellulase, macerozyme and pectolyase in CPW salts.

A protocol has been developed to establish continuously growing callus from immature endosperm of Morus alba at University of Delhi, Delhi. The initial association of embryo promoted endosperm callussing. When subcultured on a medium containing BAP (5 M) and NAA (1 M), 75% of the calli regenerated, with an average number of 11 shoots per culture. The regenerated shoots were multiplied and rooted in vitro. The potential triploid plants have been established in the field. Cytological analysis of these plants confirmed their triploid (3n = 42) nature.

At the University of Jammu, Jammu, a procedure for callus formation in Morus alba var. Chinese White and Ichinose has been standardized. Optimum callus initiation was achieved from leaf explants on MS medium supplemented with 2,4-D and BAP. Of the three explants tested, leaves proved to be the most suitable explant for callus initiation whereas petioles produce a small amount of callus.

At JNV University, Jodhpur, the evaluation of defoliation tolerance of four varieties of castor viz. Aruna, GCH-4, RCH-1 and NES-6 revealed that increase in rate and / or the frequency of defoliation resulted in higher foliage yield. Maximum foliage yield was recorded in GCH-4 among the four varieties tested. Difference in growth parameters and yield due to frequency of defoliation was non-critical at lower rates of defoliation. However, it was highly critical at higher rates. Castor varieties did not cause any significant variations in leaf bioassay using eri silkworm (Philosamia ricini) larvae. The parameters used for this were consumption index, approximate digestibility, efficiency of conversion of digested food and conversion efficiency of ingested food.

Different explants (cotyledons, hypocotyls and leaves) of Terminalia tomentosaa host tree of tasar silkworm were cultured on MS medium containing different concentrations of auxins and cytokinins individually at Kakatiya University, Warangal. Callus initiation was observed at the cut ends of the explants after 7 to 10 days. Somatic embryos were developed on MS medium fortified with 2,4-D and 2, 4, 5-T individually. Efforts continued for regeneration of plants directly from explants; and through callus mediation.

Studies were initiated at Kakatiya University, Warangal for improvement of mulberry through somatic hybridization. Cuttings of different mulberry varieties (K-2, S-13, S-36) were obtained from CSR&TI, Mysore and established in the field. Axenic shoot cultures of Morus indica cvs. K-2 and S-36 were initiated via axillary bud cultures and shoot apex cultures by obtaining explant material from the field. Multiple shoot formation was induced from axillary bud explants on MS medium supplemented with BAR These shoots were rooted on MS medium supplemented with IBA. Experiments have been initiated to isolate protoplasts from mesophyll tissues of field grown material.

Work has been recently initiated at the University of Calcutta on DNA fingerprinting of different castor accessions and development of DNA markers to tag desirable characters in castor for eri silkworm rearing.

Insect host-plant interaction

The work on studying protein quality in tasar food plants in relation to the yield and quality of tasar silk was continued at University of Delhi, Delhi. In order to assess the nutritional quality of the leaves, crude protein extracts, purified proteins and tannins were assayed in vitro for inhibition of bovine trypsin protease activity using toluene Sulphonyl Arginine Methyl Ester (TAME). In young leaves, crude exracts showed 90% inhibition as compared to the controls, purified protein showed 68% inhibition whereas tannins showed 32% inhibition. In semi-mature leaves, maximum inhabitation upto 76% was observed in crude extract, the purified protein showed 53% whereas tannins showed 37% inhibition. In mature leaves, the maximum inhibition was shown by tannins as compared to proteins.

Studies on rearing performance of eri silkworm on different castor genotypes, effect of different botanicals and iodine compounds were continued at UAS, Dharwad. Twenty four castor genotypes collected from FIRS, Raichur were evaluated for rearing performance. Late maturing triple bloom castor genotype RG-323 was found to be the best with respect to larval growth and development, cocoon traits and fecundity as compared to other genotypes. Further, 40 genotypes collected from

DOR, Rajendranagar, Hyderabad were also evaluated. The results indicated that the early maturing, double bloom castor genotype RG-902 showed significantly better performance than others.

Supplementation of an aqueous extract of Amaranthus spinosus (10%) during V instar significantly improved the larval growth and cocoon traits. The gain in larval weight, cocoon weight and shell ratio was 6.3, 7.8 and 14 per cent respectively over controls. The extract of Tridax procumbens (20%) resulted in increase in fecundity by 13%. Exogenous dust application of Cassia sericea (20%) once on 48 h old v instar eri silkworm larvae significantly increased the larval weight (6.1 %), cocoon weight (8.8%), shell ratio (15%) and fecundity (15%) over controls.

Biodiversity conservation & environment

The Task Force on application of Biotechnology for Biodiversity Conservation and Environment held two meetings and reviewed the progress of ongoing projects as well as research leads are as follows:

Biodiversity conservation

In a project at Karnataka University, Dharwad, extensive survey of Western Ghat regions of Karnataka and Maharastra was undertaken. Platanthera susannae L. and Habenaria crinifera L. have become rare plants in this region and only few populations of Platanthera susannae L. were located in the Amboli Ghat area, near Sawanthawadi of Maharastra. Similarly, Habenaria crinifera L. plants were collected from Anasi Ghat area of North Canara of Karnataka. Asymbiotic seed germination and induction of protocorms into seedlings have been achieved. Investigators at St. Anthony College, Shillong conducted 3 exploration tours and more than 3000 orchid plant's belonging to about 200 species were collected.

These plants are under cultivation. Tissue culture work included (1) age of the capsule in relation to percentage germination (2) seed culture of Vanda coerulea, Dendrodium aphyllum, Dendrobium nobile and Nepenthes khasiyana. Protocols have been determined. Mericloning had been done for Vanda coerulea and Nepenthes khasiyana.

Scientists at Vikram University, Ujjain were engaged in vegetative propagation of many ferns and angiosperm and seeds of many forest species, which are important for conservation, have been collected and germinated in controlled growth chamber and transplanted at Pachmarhi. In vitro studies were initiated in 4 plant species.

In a project at IHBT, Palampur, DNA fingerprinting programme on Artemisia was initiated by collecting 20 Artemisia accessions representing 6 species from different locations of western Himalayas by RAPD analysis. Out of 27, random 10 mer primers employed to characterise the germplasm, 5 gave no amplification products while the rest gave reproducible bands. Out of 22 responding primers, 4 primers gave considerable polymorphic bands and were selected for initial analysis of the results. Inter and intra species variability was observed. Studies have been initiated characterisation of available tea germplasm using RAPD markers. Initially 25 important Indian tea cultivars representing 3 types (13 Assam, 10 China, 2 Cambod) and 2 ornamental species i.e. C.sasanqua and C.japonica were characterized by RAPD markers. Results indicate high genetic variability of 95.2%.

At TERI, New Delhi, genetic diversity was estimated through AFLP markers in 37 neem accessions from different eco-geographic regions of India and 4 exotic lines from Thailand. Seven AFLP selective primer combinations generated a total of 422 amplification products. Scientists at Manonmanian University have reported a new species of Mahseer, Tor moyarensis in Moyar river, Nilgiri Biosphere Reserve (NBR). A new species of Horalabiosa has been described from Santhamparai stream in Periyar river basin. A new species of Salmostoma from Moyar river in Nilgiri Biosphere Reserve (NBR) has been found.

Investigators at Punjab University, Chandigarh have successfully cultured immature embryos in Dendrobium chrysotoxum and Paphiopedilum spicerianum and regeneration competence of shoot apical meristem (Vanda coerulea), stem explants (Cymbidium hookerianum, Dendrobium chrysotoxum) pseudobulb segments (Dendrobium chrysotoxum), leaf segments (Cymbidium hookerianum, Dendorbium chrysotoxum, Paphiopedilum spicerianum, Renanthera imschootiana), and inflorescence segments (Renanthera imschootiana, Vanda coerulea) was successfully tested.

In vitro florigenesis was induced in leaf segment derived PLBs of Vanda Coerulea. Scientists at Himachal Pradesh Krishi Vishwavidyalaya, Palampur have collected mature plants of P.hexandrum from Jalori Pass and Kothi (District Kullu) and Khajjiar (District Chamba) from an altitude of about 8000 ft. Analysis of podophyllotoxin content in roots by HPLC showed comparatively higher content (1.88 - 7.8 % on dry weight basis) from Jalori pass than in root samples collected from Khajjiar (1.0 - 4.21%). Investigators at Marine Biology Research Institute, Sagar Island collected surface and sub-surface soil samples from near the root systems of salt marsh grass (Porterasia coarctata), immature and mature mangrove plants (Avicennia marina). Benthic algal samples were collected from brackish water impoundments as well as paddy fields of Sagar Island and the tidal creeks of mangrove forests.

Samples are being treated for analysis & estimation of the microbial population associated with certain nutrient mobilization activities. Horseshoe crab is an important component of this gene pool. The blood of this organism has been found to be a potential source of a diagnostic reagent which is highly sensitive and useful for the rapid and accurate assay of gram-ve bacteria even if they are present in a very minute quantity upto the level of 10^{-10} to 10^{-12}gm.

Industrial effluent treatment

Scientists at NEERI, Nagpur have obtained soil samples from various oil contaminated environmental niches including refineries and industrial sites which were used as inoculum for enrichment of strains. The enrichment cultures streaked on nutrient or minimal medium led to isolation of 40 bacterial isolates based on enrichment source and colony morphology An isolate R3 that could transform dibenzothiophene relatively more rapidly than others was selected for further studies. Genomic DNA and plasmid DNA were prepared. The availability of the DNA sequences matching genes encoding desulphurization in isolated organism was determined by a dual target PCR.

In a collaborative project between IIT, Delhi, IIT Bombay and IISc, Bangalore, design of plausible molecular receptors for toxic metal ions and organic compounds has been carried out. It has been observed that the synthesized bisazobiphenyl calixarenes (BICALs 4-7) are present in the 1,3-alternate conformation of the calix(n)arene moiety. Novel heterocyclyl calix(n)arenes have also been synthesized for binding metal ions. Efforts were made to probe the interaction of metal ions though PANI-calix(n)arene matrix.

The conformational structures of the heterocyclyl

calix(n)arene systems synthesized by the IIT, Delhi team have been examined by IIT, Bombay. IISc, Bangalore group has synthesized several cholic acid based molecular receptors by utilizing a pyrene carboxylic acid as the fluorescence sensing unit in the cholic acid framework. Scientists at ITRC, Lucknow collected tannery effluent sample from tanneries located at Unnao and Kanpur (U.P.).

The samples were analysed for isolation of chromate resistant bacteria on plate count agar amended with chromate using pour plate method. Around 167 bacterial strains tolerant to different concentrations of chromate were isolated, of which 41 strains resistant to chromate level > 50-ug/ml were selected for detailed study. Scientists at RRL, Trivandrum are aiming a developing an economically viable bioreactor system using immobilised microbial cells and enzymes to degrade textile dyes especially sulphonated azo dyes which constitutes 80% of the dye used in India. In a project at NEERI, Nagpur, a soil perfusion apparatus has been fabricated for isolation of microorganisms through enrichment technique for the removal of odorants.

The apparatus is being used for enrichment of culture from soil using the existing odorants viz. ethylamine and pyridine. At Jaipur University, trials for the optimisation of dye waste water treatment were conducted, and optimal conditions for dye degradation in the system were identified. The treated waste water had no adverse effect on the growth of most susceptible aquatic plant species as Azolla, Hydrilla, and Spirodela including cultivated ones as Cymopsis.

In a project at TERI, New Delhi, very efficient crude oil and oily sludge degrading bacterial consortium and pure bacterial strains viz. Acinetobacter calcoaceticus and Alcaligenes odorans have been selected. Eight different carrier materials have been tested for immobilization of selected crude oil and oily sludge degrading bacterial strains. Contaminated land at the site of two oil refineries has been selected and carrier based materials are applied at contaminated sites. The in situ bioremediation rates and survivability of strains at contaminated sites was monitored. Scientists at RRL, Trivandrum are engaged in isolation and screening of potent organisms from soil and marine environment for the degradation of common commercial dyes. About 11 organisms were selected for the dye degradation studies and the comparison with the known lignin/dye degrading microorganisms is in progress. The known lignin degraders were studied for their dye degrading capacity.

Bioremediation

Experiments carried out at Delhi University, Delhi showed that S.paucimobilis could degrade gamma HCH and other isomers of HCH efficiently. The genomic DNA of Sphingomonas was transformed into competent E.coli cells and the recombinants were obtained. Out of almost 4500 colonies screened, two clones gave positive signals with the fin A probe. In a project at RRL, Trivandrum, batch, fed-batch and continuous studies were conducted in shake flasks, 1.0 and 1.5 litre glass reactors, 13.0 litre fluidised bed reactor and 13.0 litre biological activated carbon reactor to study biodegradability of chlorinated aromatic compounds. Biodegradation of chlorinated phenols was possible in both aerobic and anaerobic systems.

Scientists at NEERI, Nagpur have selected contaminated site sampling regimes and have worked out protocols for isolation. GC-MS Finger printing of polycyclic aromatic hydrocarbons contamination in soils has been initiated. Investigators at IARI, New Delhi have isolated a strain of Penicillium from sewage sludge which degraded about 30% atrazine in broth when amended upto 400 ug ml-1 level. Out of various soil fungi examined Aspergillus niger possessed highest degradative ability. A bacteria isolated from sewage water possesses ability to degrade 80% metolachlor in broth when amended upto 50 ppm level. Investigators at Goa University are engaged in studies in the fields of bioremediation of oil spills and tarballs using the bacterial consortia. Horizontal gene transfer constituted studies to determine the extent of gene transfer between the bacterial species in microcosm.

Waste treatment and conversion to useful products

Scientists at CTCRI, Trivandrum have isolated potential microorganisms from the starch factory effluents namely Aspergillus sps. Bacillus sps. and Saccharomyces sps. which have been screened for the production of cellulase, amylase, linamarase, rhodonese and polyphenol oxidase activity.

Investigators at NEERI,. Nagpur are aiming at developing economically viable solution to the problem of obnoxious industrial emissions based on a biotechnological approach with recourse to molecular sieves and microorganisms, as the existing physicochemical processes for odour control are cost and energy intensive.

Nitrogenous odorous compounds, viz. aniline, triethylamine, pyridine, and sulphurous odorous compounds, viz. carbon disulphide, diethyl sulphide were initially used for standardization of a monitoring technique using gas chromatography coupled with a mass-spectrophotometer (GC/MS) fitted with DB624 column. The standardized technique has been subsequently developed for characterization of the odorants generated from the viscose rayon and pharmaceutical industries.

Medical biotechnology

The Department made special efforts to generate projects in areas of important communicable and non-communicable diseases. This approach of inviting projects in specific areas has paid rich dividend in terms of meeting set targets and objectives.

Two meetings of the Task Force were conducted. Thirty new projects were considered and sixty ongoing projects were evaluated for their progress. Projects were implemented in the areas of: HIV - I & II virus bank; characterisation; collection of serum/plasma from sero positive individuals from different regions of India; genotyping of HIV - I, mutations in co-receptor $CXCR_4$ CCR_3 and CCR_5 amongst healthy subjects and in high risk groups, long term progressers and HIV cases to assess resistance to the outcome of infection, mucosal antigen delivery system using peptide sequences of envelope and core proteins of HIV-I; susceptibility of Indian strains of Herpes simplex virus and cytomegalovirus against antiviral agents; physical mapping of S.dysenteriae type I and investigation on the interplay between plasmid and chromosomal borne delta endotoxin gene(s) of B.sphericus and B.thuringiensis and evaluation of the heme biosynthetic pathway in the malaria parasite as a potential drug target.

HIV/AIDS

Several multicentric and interactive projects on different dimensions of HIV/AIDS have been implemented.

Nested PCR for envelope gene and Hetroduplex Mobility Assay for genotype analysis of HIV-I in circulation in different geographical regions of the country revealed it to be predominantly belonging to C subtype of HIV-I. However, recent sero-converters have equal distribution of C2 and C3 quasi species of HIV-I, C subtype while those with history of sero conversion of more than one year, a majority had CS quasi species. In addition to C subtypes, the country has a minor level of the subtype 6, A and E also. The north eastern region, where transmission is mainly through intravenous drug abuse, also has subtype C.Recombinant A/C has also been identified with "env" and "nef" of subtype A and core of subtype C. Studies on immunological and virological parameters in HIV infection were carried out at PGIMER, Chandigarh and AIIMS, New Delhi. The procedure for quantification of HIV RNA was standardized for HIV-I. The absolute CD4+ cell count showed an inverse relationship with viral load. The level of soluble TNF alpha receptor II in plasma showed positive co-relation with viral load and a negative co-relation with absolute CD4 count. Levels of circulating nucleosomes were estimated in the sera of patients by ELISA.

The difference between the AIDS and sero positive groups was significant. Using FACS analysis and staining with annexure V, six out of five patients studied so far gave a strong staining with annexure V with more than 40% cells undergoing apoptosis. Studies were carried out on antisense/ribozyme against HIV-I at NII, New Delhi. A hammerhead ribozyme against the (p24) gag gene which is conserved among all known isolates of HIV-I was constructed. Primers were synthesized that amplified the gag gene.

The amplified fragment (~740 bp) was cloned under the T7 promoter. Preliminary evidence suggested that the di-ribozyme was able to clear the gag specific RNA. A DNA-enzyme with 10-23 catalytic motif against the conserved region of HIV-I envelope was reported for the first time. New programmes on analysis of deletion of genes encoding for HIV-I co-receptors like $CXCR_4$, CCR_2,

CCR_3 and CCR_5 amongst healthy subjects and in high risk subjects like sex workers, thalassaemics, long term progressors, HIV sero positive without AIDS and those with AIDS have been initiated at NII, New Delhi and NIV, Pune respectively. A study on mucosal delivery of genes/antigen for HIV has also been initiated. In addition, an HIV viral repository has been established.

Tuberculosis

Studies on development of species and strain specific gene amplification technique for ribosomal gene region-restriction analysis (ARDRA) for clinically important pathogenic mycobacteria have been carried out at JALMA, Agra. Several primer combinations targetting 16S rRNA, 23 rRNA, 5S rRNA and spacer sequencing of pathogenic mycobacteria were designed and synthesized oligonucleotides were employed. A primer combination targeting 16S rRNA gene amplifying only the known pathogens has been identified. Results of testing of various strains show only limited variations within the region so amplified. This region shows specificity at the species level and could be more useful for detection and identification of pathogenic species. Another PCR assay amplifying part of 16S and 23S genes and entire spacer region has been found to elicit variations among the strains of M.tuberculosis and M.leprae. Further efforts are being made to develop this as a DNA fingerprinting system for molecular epidemiology.

In a study carried out at IISc., Bangalore, three monoclonal antibodies have been generated for gyrase A and epitope mapping with monoclonal antibodies have been made. The monoclonal antibodies have been employed to identify DNA gyrase inhibitor. Studies on the T-cell subtypes, T-cell receptor (TCR) and MHC haplotypes in tuberculosis susceptibility in South India were carried out at MKU, Madurai. A high risk caste group for pulmonary tuberculosis (PTB) has been identified. HLA DRB1 1501 was found to be predisposed for PTB and to drug resistance and DQB1 0601 is a high risk allele for PTB. HLA DPB1 04 is preventive and epistatic and DRB1 1501 and DQB1 0601 responsible for predisposition to PTB.

The distribution of high risk and preventive alleles was strikingly different between the patients and controls belonging to the high risk identified caste. Cytokine expression studies revealed that Th1 phenotypes were predominant in BCG scar positive endemic controls but not in BCG scar negative controls. However, the cytokine expression and lymphoproliferative response were not found to correlate with either the presence of high risk allele DRB1 1501 or the extensiveness of lesions.

Multi-centric, multi-investigator projects on tuberculosis resulted in a collection of about 700 isolates of M.tuberculosis (M.tb). These strains have been well characterised genotypically. A large number of sensitive and drug resistant strains of M.tuberculosis either to one drug or multidrug (MDR) deposited at Mycobacterial Repository Centre at JALMA from different parts of country have been characterized for their sensitivity profiles and included in the molecular studies at JALMA, Agra and Nil, New Delhi. Studies are being conducted on riboprobe analysis, DNA fingerprinting using IS6110, rpoB resistance, PCR amplification and sequencing of rspL, rspG , gyr A & B , Inh A and kat G at JALMA, Nil & AIIMS simultaneously.

Three DNA based PCR system for early detection of Mtb were evaluated and are being improved for desired specificity and sensitivity. The investigations carried out at South Campus, Delhi University, have resulted in development of a recombinant BCG. Genes for 6 antigens of M.tuberculosis and surface antigens of Hepatitis B and

E viruses have been cloned and expressed in M.bovis BCG under different promoters. Immunological as well as efficacy studies in experimental animals have been planned.

The studies at CDRI, Lucknow utilising M.habana as an alternative vaccine to BCG have indicated protection against M.tb in vaccinated mice. Comparative studies on M.habana vis-a-vis M.bovis BCG are being carried out.

Typhoid

At AIIMS, New Delhi, diagnostic potential of the PCR assay system was evaluated by screening of 200 blood samples from suspected enteric fever cases. Eleven cases were detected positive by PCR of which only 2 could grow positive in culture after 48-72 hrs. In another experiment, the PCR assay was modified in order to amplify the whole Salmonella specific flagellin gene (1530 bp). The test system was used to screen over 40 stool samples to detect Salmonella spp. By gene specific RK1 & RK2 primers, following nested amplification (486 bp), five additional cases were detected. Non-radioactive probes for identification and detection of these amplified products have been developed. A 486 bp amplicon (nested) has been generated as probe by incorporation of Digoxigenin labelled dUTPs during PCR using previously amplified flagellin gene as template. The probe is useful in detecting flagellin gene (1530 bp) from both S.typhi and S.paratyphi are common agents for enteric fever.

A Salmonella specific insertion sequence based on 692 bp probe internal to the IS 200 element has been found to be useful for epidemiological investigations, particularly tracing the origin of strains with MDR. This probe was used to investigate an out break of enteric fever due to S.paratyphi A in a residential colony near AIIMS during September-October, 1996.

Twenty strains of S.typhi, representing both drug resistant and drug sensitive groups were characterised using molecular probe IS 200. The drug resistant group showed profiles that were unique and distinctly different. Efforts are on to characterise the isolates belonging to both drug resistant and sensitive groups. Further diagnostic potential of this assay will be carried out.

Leishmaniasis

In an effort to develop nucleic acid probes for diagnosis, detection and epidemiology of kala-azar at RMRC, Patna, samples were collected from patients, cultured and cryopreserved. Out of twenty one isolates, 15 were obtained from visceral leishmaniasis (VL) and 6 from post kala azar dermal leishmaniasis (PKDL) cases. DNA and rDNA were isolated. The digestion pattern of DNA extracted from the isolates of responsive and unresponsive cases to SAG revealed five restriction sites amongst DNA of VL isolates digested with HaeIII while DNA of isolates from PKDL cases digested with HaeIII had two restriction sites. The base pair analysis with Eco RI indicated that responsive isolates are in the range of 2.77 - 39.15 kb and resistant ones are in the range of 5.6 - 28.3 kb.

At AIIMS, New Delhi, 10 isolates of L.donovani were successfully maintained in M199 medium supplemented with 10% decomplemented Fetal Calf Syrum (FCS). One isolate was found to be a rapid grower. Subsequently, M199 medium was supplemented with 10% human urine which also supported the parasite growth in a continuous culture. No changes in any of the characteristics including antigenic and genotyping characteristics were found. This seems to be a promising cost effective growth supplement.

Studies on L.donovani at IICB, Calcutta revealed that a maximum of 29 chromosomes of several Indian strains of L.donovani could be resolved under different conditions of pulsed field gel electrophoresis (PFGE). Hybridization of PFGE-resolved chromosomal blots with different gene probes showed conserved chromosomal locations among different strains, although a few differences were apparent. The genes for DNA topoisomerase II, adenosine kinase and Gp63 have been localized on the chromosomes of L.donovani Ag83 and L.donovani D1700 by PFGE and Southern hybridization. Experiments are underway to map these genes in the respective chromosomes.

DNA topoisomerase II from Leishmania has been purified substantially. While studying DNA topoisomerases from Leishmania, a novel endonuclease was identified and purified to homogeneity. The endonuclease termed EndoM is a single polypeptide of molecular weight 52 kDa. DNA topoisomerases I and II have been studied as targets for various agents derived from indigenous plants. A plant derived bisnaphthoquinonoid compound "Diospyrin" has been identified. This compound has been found to be a novel inhibitor of type I DNA topoisomerases of leishmania. Two more plants have been selected. The plant extracts have been fractionated and are being studied for their antileishmanial activities as well as inhibitory activity towards DNA topoisomerases.

In an in vivo study, by utilising mannosylfucosyl receptor on macrophages, attempts were made to target antileishmanial agent capsulated in mannosylated or fucosylated liposomes for the treatment of experimental leishmaniasis in hamster model. Mannosylated liposomes were found to be more potent in delivering antileishmanial agent to phagocytic cells. The liposomes loaded with an indigenous drug Andrographolide, a diterpenoid isolated from Indian medicinal plant

Andrographis paniculata, were tested against experimental leishmaniasis in hamster model. Mannosylated liposomes loaded with the drug were found to be more potent in reducing the parasitic burden in the spleen.

No side reactions were noticed. Studies suggested that Leishmania has specific receptor for laminin, a major extracellular matrix protein of liver and spleen. The receptor has a molecular weight of 67 kDa, is glycoprotein in nature and N-linked oligosaccharides play a part in the interaction of laminin to the binding protein.

The leishmania strain repository at IICB, Calcutta already has 40 isolates of Leishmania which comprises of 22 isolates of Ldonovani, five isolates each of L.infantum, two isolates of L.major, L.tropica, L.amazonensis each, one isolate each of L.mexicana, L.chagasi and L.braziliensis. In addition, 13 stibanate sensitive and 21 stibanate resistant clones have also been isolated. These strains and clones have been characterised through isoenzyme analysis.

Filariasis

Studies on molecular tools for the detection and quantification of larvae of lymphatic parasites, W.bancrofti and B.malayi in vector and humans at VCRC, Pondicherry have been carried out. cDNA libraries of mf and L3 stages of W.bancrofti and B.malayi have been constructed. These libraries are being used to locate precise molecular probe of these parasites. Monoclonal antibodies to excretory and secretary of L4 stages of W.bancrofti have been produced.

One of the monoclonals has been noticed to be specific to L4 excretory/ secretary antigens. This monoclonal will be utilised in clinical subjects to identify L4 antigen for a diagnosis.

Malaria

Towards the development of PCR primers for predicting drug susceptibility in P.falciparum malaria at Delhi University, Delhi, a couple of P.falciparum isolates were established in continuous In vitro culture. Their susceptibility to pyrimethamine and fansidar was determined. Clones were obtained by the limiting dilution technique and their susceptibility was determined. Resistance could be induced in vitro either by exposing parasites to single heavy dose or by repeated subcurative doses. In the former case 760 fold increase in inhibitory concentration (IC) 50 value of pyrimethamine resistant line to sulfadoxine were obtained, but in pyrimethamine sensitive line only 34 fold increase in IC 50 value to sulfadoxine was noticed. Genomic DNA from these selected lines has been isolated for genetic basis of drug resistance. It was apparent that pyrimethamine resistant lines are predisposed for faster selection of resistance to sulfadoxine.

Amoebiasis

Studies were carried out at PGIMER, Chandigarh on identification of distinctive genes coding for copro-antigens of pathogenic and non-pathogenic E.histolytica strains with cDNA clones in order to differentiate symptomatic and asymptomatic amoebiasis. A cDNA library with HMI (E.histolytica) strain was constructed and screened with coproantigenic monoclonal antibody. Results showed a positive signal. Further characterisation is in progress.

Helicobacter pylori

In a collaborative activity on diagnostics; molecular and immunological characterization of H.pylori strains, collection of clinical samples, cultivation (more than 150 cultures) and cryopreservation of H.pylori strains have been accomplished. All the strains have been found to be sensitive to tetracycline, ciprofloxacine, norfloxacin, while all tested isolates were resistant to metronidzole. The AIIMS and Taramani Centre at Chennai have modified and improved a recently developed broth culture medium for optimization of cellular growth to yield sufficient material for isolation of purified genomic DNA for further characterization. Preservation media have been developed by AIIMS and Taramani Centres. In-house ELISA has been developed and standardized. This will be validated by other investigators. Immune response to CagA, VacA and other gene products (35,30, 26.5 and 19.5 kd) were analysed.

The CagA antibody which is a major indicator of infection with invasive H.pylori in the developed countries may not be helpful in differentiating duodenal ulcer cases from non-ulcer dyspepsia in India. PCR assay using published primers of ureaseA, CagA and VacA genes has been standardized. The CagA PCR with 297 bp products showed a high diversity of the Indian strain in the region while CagA PCR with 1400 bp products showed less diversity.

The data suggest a need to examine the molecular nature of Indian strains carefully. Similarly, adherence assay as an initial test for virulence of the organism has been standardized. Immunoblot analysis studies have suggested the necessity of using more than one antigen for diagnostics.

Japanese encephalitis

The collaborative projects on Japanese Encephalitis Virus (JEV) has led to a collection of about 300 CSF samples at NIMHANS, Bangalore and KGMC, Lucknow. These are being stored at NIMHANS, Bangalore and NII, New Delhi. The JEV isolates are being sent to NIV, Pune for a JE virus bank. IgM MAC ELISA test developed by KGMC using monoclonal developed by NIMHANS is being validated using CSF samples.

In an attempt to develop a vaccine for Japanese Encephalitis using chimeric B cell-T helper cell synthetic peptides by NIV, Pune & Binformatics Centre, Pune, two different continuous peptide epitopes from envelope glycoprotein (Egp) of JEV, capable of inducing virus neutralising antibodies have been delineated. Molecular modelling studies have resulted in delineating conformation epitopes and confirming the conformation of peptides in free form and in the protein. Immunological studies in mice with these peptides provide a protective efficacy in about 66% of animals.

In the project to develop tissue culture derived vaccines against JEV, an Indian strain has been adapted to grow in vero cells at titres higher than 10^7 pfu/ml. A micro-carrier technology yielding requisite number of virion for vaccine production has been developed. Development of DNA based vaccines has resulted in construction of mammalian expression cassettes producing envelope and non-structural (NS1) proteins. These have been characterised. Immunogenicity studies have shown seroconversion in mice inoculated with plasmid containing cytomegalo virus promoter. Mice innoculated intra-dermally using envelop or NS1 proteins made antibodies against relevant viral proteins and had T-cell memory generated against the virus.

Cholera

Phase I clinical trials of oral recombinant vaccine based on VA 1.3 strain of Vibrio cholerae were initiated after the approval by the Drugs Controller General of India. The trials are being carried out at SGPGIMS, Lucknow; Society for Applied Sciences, Calcutta & PGIMER, Chandigarh. Three other centres i.e. NICED, Calcutta;

IICB, Calcutta; & IMTECH, Chandigarh are associated with these centres.

Chikungunya

Studies on genetic and molecular basis of susceptibility of Aedes aegypti to chikungunya (CHIK) at NIV, Pune, demonstrated the presence of putative virus specific receptor of 38 and 60 kDa on brush border membrane fraction of midgut of larva and adult Aedes aegypti. Dot blot experiments showed recèptor difference in chikungunya virus specific genotype as compared to refractory genotype of mosquitoes. This tends to indicate susceptibility of mosquito due to quantitative trait loci. Scanning electron microscopy of the midgut showed two types of cells. Studies are being carried out to determine if the virus specific receptors are located on a particular cell type. A new rapid method of identifying the red eye and rosy eye colour mutants of A.aegypti mosquito within 30 minutes has been developed which will new help researchers to determine the mutations.

Rabies

Studies on the use of recombinant variable fragments of human antibody molecules in the prevention and therapy of rabies was performed at AIIMS, New Delhi. The rabies virus (strain PV 11) was grown in bulk in the vero cell line and the glycoprotein antigen of rabies virus (GPRV) molecule has been purified. Human CD3-e (hcD-E) cDNA has been cloned.

The human IL-2 molecule has been cloned and purified. Using a phage display library, recombinant generating human monoclonal antibodies has been identified. Such a lead may help to replace anti rabies hyper immune serum raised in horses which has side effects. The use of human monoclonal antibodies to rabies virus has the potential for treatment of post exposure cases of rabies.

Development of contraceptive vaccines

Based on the leads obtained in the development of three candidate vaccines namely, PhCG, oFSH, anti-RCP for contraception, efforts are being made at Nil, New Delhi to improve the immunogenicity and sustainibility of PhCG by using T-helper peptides from circumsporozoite protein, the 38 kDa antigen from Mtb, 1 A from RSIP, measles virus F protein, influenza virus haemagglutinin and from HIV reverse transcriptase individually & in cocktail. Significantly, higher antibody response was attained in several strains of mice including low responder strains.

Bonnet monkeys were immunized with a cocktail vaccine employing the promising peptides identified . Work. was underway to overcome the carrier-induced immunosuppression observed during the course of clinical trials of PhCG in women immunized with carrier conjugated vaccines.

The work on upscaling the yield of hCG and oFSH at biofermentor level continued at IISc., Bangalore.

Oncology

Studies carried out at TIFR, Bangalore have shown changes in the expression and cellular localisation of Notch proteins in the transition from cervical intraepithelial lesion (CIN) III to tumours. NOTCH Staining is not detected in CIN I/II lesions and show clear widespread strong nuclear staining in tumours with a weak cytoplasmic signal. In CIN III lesions, principally membrane and cytoplasmic staining is detected. The experiments on the NOTCH pathway along with recent studies of sonic hedgehog signalling pathway in skin tumours are likely to offer new therapeutic strategies by designing inhibitors to disregulate developmental pathways.

Investigations carried out at the Institute of Life Sciences, Bhubaneswar have for the first time reported rearrangement of p53 gene in breast tumour, which might play role in the process of tumongenesis.

Transgenics

Efforts are being made to establish a transgenic mouse facility at CCMB, Hyderabad and use transgenic mouse models to study the regulation of the lamin A gene during embryonic development. The microinjection technique for injection of DNA into the male pronucleus of a fertilised egg has been standardised. When 90 injected embryos were transferred to six mice, 20 live births were obtained. In initial studies, tyrosinase gene was injected for easy identification of transgenic mice. Newborn mice were screened for the appearance of black patches against the normal white coat. A lamin A gene targeting vector was constructed for carrying out homologous recombination experiments in embryonic stem cells. Experiments were on to carry out gene targeting into these cultured embryonic stem cells. Techniques were standardised to isolate morulae from pregnant mice. More than 50% of the morulae developed into blastocysts. A tissue culture and morulae model for exploring the effects of generating an a errant lamina network by using antisense gene constructs is being set up using the tet on/off system for inducible expression. This would be useful in designing mutant lamin genes for studies in transgenic animals.

Drug delivery system

In a study carried out at AIIMS, New Delhi, antibacterial drug, (ciprofloxacin) was entrapped in positively charged liposomes.The liposomal encapsulation of ciprofloxacin increased corneal penetration and enhanced antimicrobial efficacy in Staph aureus induced corneal ulcer in rabbits. Six times lesser concentration of ciprofloxacin was found to be equally effective as conventionally used ciprofloxacin eye drops (0.31 %) in the treatment of bacterial corneal ulcers. The liposomal encapsulation of ciprofloxacin appears to be a useful adjunct in the management of bacterial corneal ulcers. Two systems namely, microspheres and gel implant were developed at the College of Pharmaceutical Sciences, Manipal, employing Poly (lactic-co-glycolic acid) (PLGA) as a biodegradable, injectable and long acting formulation for delivery of diclofenac sodium for effective treatment of arthritis. The formulations gave reproducible results with respect to both pharmacodynamics as well as pharmacokinetics and appeared to be stable with respect to size/drug content/drug release pattern with the. recommended storage condition. The PLGA microspheres seems to be better candidates for further scaling up as they exhibited superior control over drug release, stability and low toxicity profile besides easy manufacturing.

Anti-leprosy immunomodulator and its use for immunoprophylaxis

Based on safety & efficacy data generated at NII and the recommendations of the D.B.T., the Drug Controller General of India granted permission to M/s Cadila Laborarartories, Ahmedabad for manufacture of trial batches of M.w vaccine for testing and analysis by Central Drugs Laboratory, Kasauli (H.P.). The manufacture of this vaccine would be supervised by a team of scientists and technicians from the institute and Cadila Laboratories in the initial phase.

Immunoprophylactic trial has been underway in apparently healthy household contacts (HHCs) of index multi and paucibacillary leprosy cases. Approximately 24,000 healthy leprosy patients close contacts were given vaccine/placebo under codes. All the vaccinated contacts are being followed up. The first follow up survey of contacts (Aug.1993-March 1996) was completed as per schedule. The second mid-term follow up survey was launched in April, 1996 and by end of Feb, 1998, the survey of all the villages was completed. Confirmation of diagnosis of the newly detected cases among contacts was taken up. The second survey was completed in April '98. Analysis of field trial data is currently underway. The efficacy of this vaccine for immunoporophylasis would be known after the completion of the third resurvey.

Human genetics and genome analysis

Genetic diseases have posed a serious threat to the health of the Indian population.

This has led to an increased demand for genetic counselling and screening tests both for carrier detection and also identifying pregnancy at risk. The department has implemented a programme with the objectives of (a) to develop basic capabilities and strength; (b) to take up some application oriented projects to reduce the burden of genetic disorders in the country.

In addition to fourteen genetic clinics established for providing molecular diagnosis and counselling for common genetic disorders prevalent in the country, a programme on functional genomics has been implemented at CBT, Delhi. Molecular genetics in schrizophrenia and bipolar diseases at NIMHANS, Bangalore and Molecular Genetics for the diagnosis of haematological disorders including bone marrow transplantation and molecular genetic diagnosis for thalassemia, haemophilia, Glanzman's thrombasthenia at CMC, Vellore have been studied.

A Winter School on Human Genetics involving concepts, paradigms and methods was organised at the Indian Institute of Chemical Biology, Calcutta. The School was aimed at imparting training in the concepts, paradigms and principles underlying the methodology used in human genetics research. It was organised to provide the necessary background to the students to pursue careers in human genetics. About 60 students participated from various intitutions/universities of the country.

Genetic clinic cum counselling units

The unit at AIIMS, New Delhi, focused on thalassemia and Duchenne muscular dystrophy (DMD) and enrolled 151 thalassemic families and offered prenatal diagnosis to 134 families. Fetal status was found to be normal in 45, trait found in 71 and 18 were affected with thalassemia. Of the 45 families suspected for DMD, the dy'strophin gene mutation was found in 24 affected children. Prenatal diagnosis was offered to 9 families. A total of 63 families comprising 217 individuals were screened for haemophilia A and 8 families comprising 27 individuals were screened for haemophilia B. The unit also carried out cytogenetic and molecular studies for Fragile X syndrome and Albinism and Congenital Adrenal Hyperplasia. The genetic diagnosis cum counselling unit established at VIMS, Calcutta is provided prenatal testing to prospective bride and groom. In addition, molecular diagnostic services were provided to 76 subjects suspected for thalassemia. Major deletion was noticed in IVS-Int5 region and codon 26.

The work on molecular characterization and first trimester prenatal diagnosis of Beta thalassemia syndromes was carried out at the Institute of Immunohaematology, Mumbai. Molecular diagnostics to first trimister pregnant women for Beta thalassaernia has been provided by the centre. The diagnostics consisted of screening of 5 common mutation by PCR screening for rare mutation by ARMS & screening for new mutation by DGGE. Of the 177 unrelated heterozygotes screened, 79.6% cases had the 6 common Beta thalassemia mutations. The remaining cases had rare mutations.

Genetic counselling and prenatal diagnosis was offered to 56 families and 13 fetuses were found to be affected. The couples decided to terminate the pregnancies in these cases. Variable Number of Tandem Repeat (VNTR) analysis was also established to look for maternal contamination in CVS samples. Two VNTR loci (Apo B and ACT BP 2) were first selected on the basis of their heterozgosity. Fourteen families where the chorionic villus sample was found to be affected were initially tested. Six families (43%) were informative with Apo B while 8 (57%) were non-informative. These 8 families were then tested for the ACT BP 2 locus where 4 were informative. All informative families did not show any maternal contamination in the chorionic villus samples.

Further, the investigators have set up the Reverse Dot Blot Hybridization Protocol and applied it successfully to screening of the 5 common Indian Beta thalassemia mutations along with 2 abnormal hemoglobins Hb S and Hb E. The protocol has been tested by analysing 500 samples and it was found to be very specific and sensitive. The membrane strips with the blotted oligoprobes stable for a period upto 6 months would be supplied to Institutes wanting to set up this procedure for molecular characterization of the common Beta thalassemia mutations.

Carrier detection of haemophilia A and B families was initiated. Twenty females were diagnosed as obligatory carriers for haemophilia A by family pedigree analysis alone. Out of 28 possible carriers thirteen were diagnosed as carriers. Twelve families which included 62 subjects were screened for hemophilia B carrier status by the RFLP method. Screening for Glanzman's thrombosthemia (GT), & Von Willebrand Disease was also done.

The unit at Mahavir Hospital, Hyderabad examined, 208 patients of mental retardation and 93 patients for trisomy Twenty one had trisomy and 2 cases of 45 XO with mental retardation were diagnosed. Six families with a suspicion of Y-linked mental retardation were studied and investigated. Syndromic microcephaly was seen in 8 cases. 30 cases of suspected cystic fibrosis were studied.

The Genetic Unit established at BJ Vadia Hospital, M-umbai, examined 318 family members referred from various parts of country including Maharashtra for various genetic disorders.

Out of 1804 individuals tested 302 were thalassemia carriers, 44 had thalassaemia major, 69 suffered from iron deficiency and 120 individuals showed other haemoglobinopathies viz increased HbF, S carrier, S Thal, S Homozygote, E Thal, HbE, HbD, D Thal, HbQ and Q Thal. Proper counselling was given to all these individuals.

Parents of thalassaemia major children were also informed about inductive screening of sibs and cousins. 190 thalassaemia carriers (couples at high risk) were screened for28 mutations using ARMS technique.

Functional genomics

A major project was implemented on functional genomics with the objectives; (i) developing technology to assess functional genomics and (ii) identify genetic diseases associated with anticipation phenomena and repetitive DNA expansion with special reference to neurological and psychiatric disorders. Considerable progress was achieved on genomic instability, trinucleotide repeat expansion and neuroclegerative disorders. Underthe programme, a fast and efficient method has been standardised for isolation of DNA from 10 ml. During the year, a formal MOU has been signed on Functional Genomics with National Institute of Mental Health & Neuroscience, Banglore and Neuroscience Centre, All India Institute of Medical Sciences, New Delhi for collaborative effort.

Genome diversity

Considerable progress has been achieved in the project on Genomic Diversity in Indian Populations implemented by human genetics groups at the Indian Statistical Institute, Indian Institute of Chemical Biology and Saha Institute of Nuclear Physics, Calcutta. Investigators collected DNA samples from 12 ethnic populations inhabiting eastern and northern India for genotyping 25 highly polymorphic DNA markers. The data analysed so far revealed that:

(a) Subsequent to migration, following a population expansion, of modern humans (Homo sapiens sapiens) from out-of-Af rica about 100,000 years ago, one wave of migration entered India about 60,000-50,000 years ago. The group of modern humans that entered India, underwent a significant popula tion expansion within India. This conclusion has been drawn by studying the nature and extent of polymorphism with respect to eight human-specific Alu insertion / deletion polymorphisms. The extent of genomic diversity at these loci in the Indian populations exceeds that of African populations.

(b) South-east Asia has been peopled by individuals migrating from India, followed by the Austronesian language migration from southern China (which occurred between 6000 and 2500 years ago). A global comparison of the frequencies of haplotypes at two mtDNA RFLP sited (Ddel at nol 0394 and Alul at ntl 0397) has indicated that the Austro-Asiatic speaking tribals (e.g., Santal, Lodha) may be the original inhabitants of India. The mtDNA haplotype sharing and frequencies of STR markers indicate that genetic affinities of Indian caste populations do not correlate well with social rank.

Vaccines research and development

Bharat Immunologicals and Biologicals Corporation Limited, Bulandshahr (BIBCOL)

The company has become operational since January 1996 and is actively formulating Oral Polio Vaccine (OPV) from imported bulk and supplying to the National Immunisation Programme.

During the year, the company has formulated 100 million doses of OPV, the target for reaching full installed capacity utilisation and supplied to the National Immunization Programme. There is more than 500% increase in sales turnover.

A WHO team inspected the BIBCOL facilities as a prelude to grant of WHO-GMP certificate by National Control authorities. The team considered that BIBCOL has created the production facility as per GMP specifications and the facility is suitable for production of various vaccines and immunobiologicals. This visit was followed by a formal visit by a team constituted by Drugs Controller General of India for grant of WHO-GMP accreditation.

A diversification plan of BIBCOL for production of BCG, Measles and Tetanus toxoid vaccines in order to generate additional revenue has been approved.

Indo-US vaccine action programme

The theme of the programme is to focus research on new improved vaccines, immunodiagnostics and other biologicals. This programme has now entered in its third phase. Three meetings of the reconstituted Apex Committee were organised in order to discuss the policy matters and to consider 20 new preproposals. The project management and processing procedures were revised with specified time frames for more effective and interactive management. A workshop on "Emerging and Re-emerging Infectious Diseases" was held at NIH, Bethesda, USA on 5th October, 1998. The emphasis was on two major diseases viz., HIV/ AIDS and tuberculosis. In the HIV/AIDS area, 'presentations were made on the approaches towards vaccine development and overall scenario including epidemiology, transmission of disease, relevance of subtypes for candidate vaccine. In tuberculosis, the approaches towards vaccine development and the problem of multi drug resistance were discussed.

The 12th meeting of the Joint Working Group was held on 6-7 October'98 in Washington, DC, USA. The progress of the ongoing projects in the areas of rotavirus, RSV, hepatitis and tuberculosis was reviewed. Future areas of research and for workshops on Group A Streptococcus infection, DNA vaccines, therapeutic vaccines and experimental animal models simulating human diseases were finalised.

There has been very significant progress in some areas under Indo-US VAP.

Leishmaniasis

The leishmaniasis project at JNU, New Delhi has focused on two putative genes, orf F and orfG, of L.donovani. These genes are located on chromosome 35 in the LD1 region that is amplified in a large proportion of isolates. Preliminary data shows a correlation between increased copy number and higher expression of these genes with drug resitance observed in clinical subjects. A rapid, sensitive, specific and non-invasive method for diagnosis of kala-azar (visceral leishmaniasis) is being developed. The diagnostic reagent is based on use of recombinant ORF F or ORF G proteins.

Tuberculosis

A devR gene-based PCR assay method for diagnosis of tuberculosis has been developed at AIIMS, New Delhi. The dev gene is differentially expressed by virulent strains (H37RV) of Mtuberculosis. A patent application has been filed for a process to produce and express devR protein'. The luciferase gene has been engineered into a bacteriophage that infects M. tuberculosis in a collaboration involving Albert Einstein University and the Tuberculosis Research Centre in Madras. This tool has shown promise in the detection of antibiotic resistant tuberculosis. The tuberculosis group at IISc in Bangalore has investigated several antigens (10, 30, 38, 65 and 70 kD) and assessed their effect on peripheral blood mononuclear cell obtained from tuberculosis and matched controls (healthy contacts). Of these, the 10kDa elicited good T cell proliferation in both patients and healthy individuals.

Hepatitis

Two potential hepatitis C diagnostic assay methods have been developed at the Rajiv Gandhi Center for Biotechnology, in Trivandrum, and the Deccan Medical College in collaboration with the University of Colorado. They are based on PCR and ELISA technologies. The stability of the peptide for ELISA is being worked out to produce a commercially viable product. The facility to obtain soluble surface antigen from Hepatitis B virus from serum has been established.

Rotavirus

Neonatal rotavirus infection with strain 11 6E has been shown to be immunogenic and protective in hospital-born babies at AIIMS. The tissue cultured strain has now undergone phase I clinical trials in adults and children in Cincinnati, US. In a study at the IISc., Bangalore, another strain, designated as 1321, was identified as a vaccine candidate. The preclinical evaluation and Phase I trials of this candidate have been conducted in the US along with the rotaviral strain from AIIMS. Steps have been initiated to conduct phase I clinical trials in India.

Other areas

The malaria mission resulted in the development of twelve new preproposais which have been reviewed. Several of the collaborators have been invited to submit full proposals for consideration. Additionally, 17 new preproposals generated in the areas of HIV/AIDS, cholera, rabies etc. are under processing.

Edible vaccines

Expression of antigens to be used as vaccines in transgenic plants provides an inexpensive source for these immunotherapeutic molecules. Various such antigens have been ,expressed successfully in plants. Keeping in view the priority area of edible vaccines, the department implemented three projects in this area.

The project implemented as a consortium project at Delhi University South Campus, CBT, NII, New Delhi and IMTECH, Chandigarh made significant progress to develop edible plant vaccine against diarrhoea by expressing antigens of Vibrio cholerae in tomato which could be consumed raw in the form of fruit. The details are as follows:

Tomato transformation has been standardized using Agrobacterium mediated method. Vectors pBI121 and pCAMBIA2301 carrying Beta glucuroniclase (GUS) driven by 35S promoter of cauliflower mosaic virus were transferred to Agrobacterium and used for transformation of tomato cotyledons. The explants, which could regenerate in the presence of the antibiotic used, were assayed for the activity of GUS and found positive.

Various vectors have been constructed for expression of cholera toxin B subunit CTX-B gene in plants. Gene encoding CTX-B subunit was amplified using polymerase chain reaction (PCR). The primers were designed to incorporate Kozak sequence of 5' end and encloplasmic reticulum retention signal at 3' end. The amplified product was cloned in nUC18. The cassette for ctx B was cloned into pCAMBIA to prepare the vector pCAMBIACTB. This vector had GUS gene driven by 35S as an additional feature. A fragment carrying E8 fruit ripening stage-specific promoter was excised from vector pEsmutRN 2.0(-) and cloned into same sites in pBluescriptSK to create vector pE8SK.

A fragment carrying E8 promoter was excised and cloned at the same sites in vector pCAMBIACTB to create vector pCAMBIAE 8CTB. Agrobacterium cultures transformed with these strains are being used for transformation of tomato and tobacco plants. In addition, tcpA has also been cloned in pUC vector for further genetic engineering.

Animal biotechnology

The various projects implemented are structured towards bridging gap areas in research, productivity and production enhancement in livestock and also development of processes and products like diagnostics and vaccines. The projects cutting across a number of sub-areas in animal biotechnology have registered good progress and generated a number of research leads towards -commercialisation.

Transgenics

A total of 82 positive transgenic founder mice have been produced using different constructs. Seven transgenic lines have been developed. Transgenic mice using hepatitis B virus X gene have been developed in order to see the mechanism of hepatocellular carcinoma. Hepatitis B is one of the most infectious viral diseases of human beings and causes a wide spectrum of liver diseases. Transgenic animals using fragile x gene have been developed to observe the mechanism of x fragile syndrome leading to mental retardation. Transgenic mice have been produced by injecting 1.9 kb linear construct of neomycin resistant gene under the control of pPGK promoter. These may be used as a source of primary feeder cells for growing embryonic stem cells in order to maintain their totipotency and to see the effect of neomycin resistant gene widely used for human gene therapy.

In another project, towards producing mice for over expressing mutant p53 gene, the p 53 gene has been screened in patients with oral cancer by PCR-SSCP analysis and by direct DNA sequencing. Two specific mutations have been identified in addition to six other known mutations. All these eight mutations have been generated by antibiotic selection in an in vitro mutagenic system.

Efforts are underway towards targeted deletion of casein gene in mouse. So far, kappa casein and alpha casein gene have been cloned and the map of these genomic regions have been prepared. Gene targeting vectors for targeting kappa casein gene have been constructed and construction of alpha casein gene vector is in progress.

Embryo transfer technology and related areas

Homologous adioimmunoassay and ELISA for pituitary hormones have been developed, standardised and evaluated. The buffalo FSH subunit coding full length cDNA clone has been expressed and the gene product identified. Monoclonal antibodies have been produced against buffalo prolactin and other hormones. Antibodies to buffalo hormones were produced and identified by immunocy-tochemistry. Recombinant ovine growth (rOGH) hormone has been expressed in two different expression vectors and a high level of yield has been obtained. This has also been produced through high cell density fermenter. The recombinant hormone is purified and its biological activity is being assessed. The embryo sexing method when field validated till now turned out to be correct in 49 out of the 50 calves born.

Techniques for superovulation and nonsurgical embryo collection techniques in camel have been standardised. Embryo transfer adopting non-surgical method was accomplished and two pregnancies established. Folliculogenesis was observed in non-breeding season and early post-partum period. These findings lead to an easy and practical way to reduce the calving interval in camel.

Vaccine

Rabies vaccine for animals using laboratory rabies strain PV-11 seed virus has been produced. The potency of the bulk vaccine was found to be 3.6 IU by NIH test approved by WHO. The vaccine is being subjected to sterility, identity, toxicity and potency tests in laboratory mice rabbits and guinea pigs. Recombinant protective antigen of anthrax (rPA) was purified and found to be have a molecular weight of 83 kDA.. This antigen was found to be biologically as well as functionally active and on par with the native PA purified from B.anthracis. This may be used to develop an effective recombinant vaccine against anthrax. Recombinant dog zona pellucida peptides have also been developed and a process to grow these in a batch fermenter has been optimized. This will be helpful in controlling stray dog population.

Diagnostics

Immunodiagnostic tests for trypanosomiasis including double immunodiffusion test, card agglutination test (CAT) and enzyme linked immunosorbent assay (ELISA) have been standardised and evaluated using serum from experimental as well as natural cases of trypanosomiasis in camel, buffalo, and cattle. The Ag-ELISA test developed in the project was also evaluated using serum samples obtained from various research institutes. The efficacy of Ag-ELISA test was between 75 -80% underfield conditions.

Production of monoclonal antibodies against PPR a disease in cattle etc. has been undertaken and the virus is being propagated in a verocell line. A PCR method was standardised by amplifying the parvoviral DNA from live and inactivated tissue culture viruses. An expected PCR amplified fragment of 241 bp was seen in positive cases. PCR based detection of EHV-1 was also standardised using Pneumabort "K" vaccine as a positive control. EHV-1 virus is being propagated in BHK-21 cell line and this has been confirmed by PCR test.

Nutrition

The department has given special attention to this area keeping in view the non-availability of quality feed. A brain storming session was held on bio-conversion of agro-byproducts; lignocellulose degradation for animal feeds. The following areas were identified for further investigation: (a) reactor design for solid state fermentation and the associated processes for large scale bioconversion of lignocellulose residues to animal feed. (b) selection and improvement of lignin degrading microorganism (c) rumen manipulation (d) genetic manipulation of microbes for enhanced ligninase expression. Investigators working under the area have been asked to submit the proposals

Demonstration

Small goat units (5+1) were provided to earthquake affected victims in the Latur region belonging to below poverty line families. This provided an opportunity for self employment. The 84 beneficiaries selected were imparted practical training of goat keeping. Other small and marginal farmers and landless agricultural labourers; evinced interest in adopting this vocation. Under the Leather Technology Mission, 19 carcass utilisation plants have been commissioned and another 6 are under different stages of establishment. This programme has directly benefited the weaker sections of society

Under the technology transfer-cum-demonstration on poultry layers at TANUVAS, the hen day egg production in various demonstrations farms increased from 260 to 275. Feed efficiency varied from 1.75 to 1.80. The cost of production of feed has been reduced fiom Rs. 6400 to Rs. 5650/tonnes of layer mash. Layer house mortality has also been reduced to below 10%.

In another demonstration project, broiler performance has gone up and the weight of the broilers increased from 1.8 to 1.9 kg in two weeks. Feed conversion ratio reduced from 2.2 to 1.8/2 due to proper and scientific management . Mortality was found to be reduced significantly. In a project at DARL, Pithoragarh efforts are being made to produced physiologically adapted broiler stocks for cold climate. Attempts were also made to utilise some locally available feed to reduce feed cost in the region.

Aquaculture and marine biotechnology

Frontier areas of focus have been transgenesis and molecular biology. Some interesting leads were generated towards process and product development.

Feed development

At CIBA, indigenous prawn feed production technology was developed using locally available raw materials. Three grades of feeds namely starter, grower and finisher, with protein levels of 42%, 38% and 35% respectively were produced for Penaeus monodon and P.indicus. The feeds were tested in yard experiments as well as in farmers growout ponds. Both tiger prawn and white prawn showed excellent growth with an average FCR ranging from 1.6 to 2.0: The feeds are comparable with commercial feeds. The pilot scale production of feeds was successfully carried out using a commercial pellet mill. The technology package is being transferred to entrepreneurs. The feed is suitable for semi-intensive and extensive culture of tiger prawn and white prawn. The cost is about Rs. 30/ kg.

CFTRI has worked out a low cost feed based on poultry/fish offal wastes. The waste is utilised as a substitute for fish meal. The fermentation based process appears promising and the product is under evaluation. Development of a technology for effective utilisation of silkworm pupae for aquaculture feeds is underway. The pelleted feed containing silkworm pupae (SWP) silage when fed to broiler chicken upto 8 weeks revealed that the silage feed consumption was 5.3% lower and live weight gain was 0.5% higher than fish meal control diet. The FCR was 2.14 for silage feed compared to 2.26 for fishmeal control feed. A process patent for the preparation of fermented silkworm pupae silage useful as an ingredient in animal feeds has been filed. Studies on development of rancidity in SWP during fermentation and its control as well as nutritive quality evaluation of fermented SWP silage by feeding fish in collaboration with CIFA, Bhubaneshwar are in progress.

At CIFA, Bhubaneshwar, studies on the role of hormones in growth and survival of cat fish and their fingerlings were taken up. The studies showed that the treatment of catfish larvae with estradiol before the commencement of first feeding resulted in production of fingerlings with significantly higher growth rate. There was not much difference in the weight gain of the fry in various groups except those treated with testosterone, which gained weight at a slower rate. The balanced diet for catla fry and catfish have been formulated by supplementing critical essential amino acids such as lysine and methionine. The experimental feed enriched with vitamins and minerals having 32% crude protein and high levels of lysine and methionine and cystine have shown higher growth rate and survival of catla fry and fingerlings. Good growth and maturity was reported in catfish brood fish fed with a diet having 30% fish meal with plant ingredients enriched with vitamins and minerals.

Synthetic prostaglandins

At NCL, Pune, synthetic analogues of prostaglandins was carried out. The synthesis of 5, 6 dihydro analogues of prosolvin was completed and the synthesis of 4,5 (cis) olefin analogues were in progress. Prostaglandins were tested individually and in combination with dopamine antagonist, domperidone, Ca++ or primed with pituitary gland extract and the results were comparable. Various doses (10-100 ug) of PGF2a, carboprost and cloprostenol were tried and about 30 experiments were conducted and their effect on major carp breeding was observed. Cloprostenol at 75 mcg/kg showed luteolytic effect. The studies on dose manipulation and screening of other prostaglandin analogues will be taken up during the breeding season of Indian major carp.

Genetics

At CCMB and MKU, genomic libraries of Catla catla, Labeo rohita and Clarias batrachus were constructed. Rainbow trout growth hormone gene has been integrated in catfish. Presumptive transgenic catfish on analysis with southern blot analysis confirmed genetic integration. Molecular cloning of fish growth hormone cDNA has been achieved and recombinant clones developed in Indian major carp rohu (Labeo rohita) and catfish (Heteropneustes fossilis).

The isolation of high molecular weight DNA and fractionation of genomic DNA was completed at JNU. A cDNA library was constructed using lambda vector by following conventional cDNA cloning strategy The primary cDNA library was amplified and screened. The inserts of all the clones positively hybridised with specific probe. The PCR amplified and cDNA library inserts were found to be identical i.e. 1.2 kb. This has indicated the nucleotide sequence of the rohu GH cDNA. At JNU, attempts were underway to construct genomic DNA library of Indian major carps. Success was achieved in sequencing the DNA encoding for specific proteins of spleen and interesting results were noted in many of the clones. Further efforts are on to generate indigenous gene constructs to produce transgenic fish.

At CMFRI, through the project on genetic manipulation of seaweeds by cell culture and somatic hybridization a national facility for parasexual fusion and genetic modification of the genetic content of commercial seaweeds has been established. Tissue culture of agar yielding seaweeds was taken up and the thallus of agar yielding seaweed, Gracilaria edulis maintained in the laboratory. Treatment with 2-4-D and Kinetin induced callus and subsequently resulted in multiple 'shoot' initiation in the explants of G.edulis, in vitro. Cell fusion experiments were attempted using the cell fusion system and varying the length and frequency of electric pulses towards standardization of this technique and to understand the optimum requirement for the isolation of seaweed protoplasts.

Biomolecules/bioactive compounds

In order to ascertain the presence of antifouling compounds, the work on evaluation of Indian horshoe crab (Tachypleus gigas) was initiated at NIO. The animals collected on different occasions were evaluated for the abundance of micro and macro-ectocommensal population. This indicated that micro and macro-ectocommensal population on female crab is comparatively less than that on male horseshoe crab. Screening of extracts obtained from bacteria isolated from female horseshoe crab with fouling bacteria indicated that bacteria colonizing the horseshoe crab have the potential of producing metabolites which can prevent further epibiosis. Evaluation of different extracts against fouling diatoms and larvae is underway.

Studies on synergism with molluscicides of plant origin against harmful snails were undertaken at Gorakhpur University. The observations indicated that piperonyl butoxide (PB & MGK-264) increased the efficacy of neem oil, garlic powder, Polianthus bulb, ginger oleoresin and Trachyspermum ammi seed powder. These combinations were found to kill harmful snails as well as make them sterile even at sublethal concentrations.

At CSMCRI, Bhavanagar, studies were carried out on neuropeptides of cyanobacteria from Arabian sea. Potent toxin producers like Oscillatoria, Synechocysts, Anabaena, Pseudoanabaena were isolated. Experiments to study the effect of light intensity at different temperatures on production of biomass of unialgal cultures were carried out. The isolates of Oscillatoria and Synechocysts were cultured under control conditions to obtain sufficient unialgal biomass and the toxicity was tested in lyophilized samples. Good growth of Synechocystis was observed in a nitrogen deficient medium.

At Cochin University, the isolates of ammonia and nitrite oxidising bacteria from marine, brackish and freshwater were mass cultured and immobilised for developing bioreactors for nitrifying water. This was developed to eliminate toxic ammonia from the rearing water without interrupting routine hatchery management. Six consortia of ammonia oxidisers and nitrite oxidisers for non-penaeid hatchery system were identified and found potent enough to oxidise ammonia and nitrite at a rapid rate at pH ranging from 7-8.

The bioreactors designed can be connected to a spent storage tank for nitrification and subsequent reuse of water. Further, this can be put into operation for nitrifying the incoming water before being used for larval rearing. These reactors are being taken up for field trial.

Disease diagnostics and vaccine development

At Bharathidasan University, studies were carried out to prevent the infection of Aeromonas and Pseudomonas by immunoprophylactic measures in cultured freshwater fishes like catla, rohu and mrigal. The bacterins were prepared from virulent strains of Aeromonas hydrophila. Different forms of bacterins were studied for their immunogenicity and protective efficacy. The studies reveal that polyvalent antigens are capable of eliciting a better immune response. The involvement of IgM class of antibody has been confirmed by the 2-mercaptoenthanol sensitivity test besides revealing that the antibodies produced in the immunised fish are antigen specific. There was specific immune response with A.hydrophila vaccine. A suitable protocol has been developed for conducting field trials.

Under the multi-centric project implemented at Madras University and College of Fisheries, Mangalore, work on genome and antigen characterization of white spot baculovirus of shrimp was taken up for the development of diagnostics. The occurrence of white spot baculovirus (WSBV) has been shown to be the causative agent responsible for mass mortalities in juveniles and sub-adults of the cultured Indian penaeid shrimps, P.monodon and P.indicus and both ultrastructural and experimental evidence supported these findings. Data on the sequence of the Indian strain of WSBV is being generated to develop DNA based diagnostic kit.

The work on the development of monoclonal antibodies for diagnosis, serotyping and antigen characterisation of antigen of white spot virus was taken up. Infected shrimp and crab were collected from Karnataka and Andhra Pradesh coastal sites and the virus isolated and purified. An ELISA has been developed for measuring antibody titre in immunised mice and for screening of hybridoma clones. Several hybridoma clones were produced and used for fusion with SP2 myeloma cells. 10 ELISA positive clones were obtained. These were further minicloned and characterised.

Mission mode project on prawn culture

At CIFA, Bhubaneshwar, under the technology project on semi-intensive prawn aquaculture a hatchery, feed mill and prawn farm have been established. The complex is functional in growout and production activities. The facility has been established to develop broodstocks of giant freshwater prawn (Macrobrachium rosenbergii). This facilitated production of seed almost round the year, which is a significant achievement in prawn aquaculture. About 65 batches of larvae were hatched out during February-November, 1998 and reared successfully in the semi-closed hatchery system. The larvae were reared with newly developed larval and post larval diets. About 1.5 million seed were produced and 0.1 million seed was utilised for stocking in the project ponds and remaining supplied to the farmers for production of marketable prawns. In a growout system, the prawns were fed with newly evolved improved .growout diet in the pellet form produced in the feed mill. A total of 670 kg of prawns was harvested in 7 months from these 4 ponds (1.675 t/ha). Nutritionally balanced, cost effective, environmentally sound diets for hatchery and grow out phases of prawn aquaculture have been developed. Feeds produced are being sold to farmers.

The technologies developed have been transferred through training programmes to the interested farmers and entrepreneurs in different states. Ten progressive farmers of different regions of Orissa have taken the technology; also in M.P., U.P., Bihar and West Bengal.

At NIO, Goa, studies were taken up to find out the influence of salinity and pH on growth of Penaeus merguiensis. The results suggest that the growth performance of juvenile P.merguiensis can be improved by increasing the salinity in the farm. The suitable pH was between 7.5 and 8.5. The study recommended that the cultivation of P.merguiensis can be taken up during the summer months along the West Coast when salinity in the farm is high and brooders are available in large numbers. This would help in crop rotation, reduce pressure on wild brooders of P monodon and may also reduce the recurrence of WSBV infection.

The growth and survival of hatchery reared Macrobrachium rosenbergii were studied at different salinities. Though this species can survive and grow in low saline brackishwater areas, the best growth performance occurs in freshwater medium. Thus this species can be considered as a candidate species for polyculture in brackishwater areas. R&D in oil palm and coconut

The work on reproductive biology of oil palm (Elaeis guineensis) continued jointly at University of Delhi, Delhi and Bangalore University, Bangalore. Pollination biology studies were conducted in the plantations of Oswal Oil Palm Ltd., Bhadrawati (Karnataka). The pollen grains in the air were found to be limited to 18-20 meters from the pollen source, beyond which pollen would become a limiting factor for effective pollination.

The problem of low pollen availability is accentuated in plantations when most of the trees are in female phase. Under such situations stored pollen grains can be used for assisted pollination. It is possible to store oil palm pollen grains for more than one year at -20°C with 80% viability. A new culture medium which gives constant and satisfactory results has been standardised to assess the viability of stored pollen. Stored pollen grains can be sprayed on female infloresence with the aid of a crude automizer to achieve pollination. Studies on the structure of the pistil and details of pollen germination and pollen tube growth have been carried out.

Ten different coconut accessions were selected for preliminary study, on DNA fingerprinting at Central Plantation Crops Research Institute (CPCRI), Kasaragod. These accessions were selected on the basis of their desirable characteristics and their wide use in hybridization programme. Partial genomic library of coconut was constructed in E.coli DHS strain by cloning 1-2 kb Eco RI fragment of West Coast Tall (WCT) genomic DNA into plasmids; and were obtained on selection medium. Colony hybridization using non-radioactive labelling method confirmed the recombinant nature of clones. The dot blot analysis for estimation of copy number of these clones is under progress. West Coast Tall (WCT) and Chowghat Orange Dwarf (COD) DNA were restricted with 10 different restriction enzymes with a view to identify the informative probe-enzyme combination. The hybridization of these southern blots is underway. Attempts are also on to standardize the hybridization with non-radioactive labelled probes.

4

Biotech Product/Process Development

Tissue culture pilot plant/micropropagation technology park

The Two Tissue Culture Pilot Plants achieved their targeted production and field evaluation continued. In order to effectively transfer the proven technology to entrepreneurs, utilizing the existing infrastructure and expertise of the Pilot Plants, two Micropropagation Technology Park (MTP) - Pilot Plants were supported.

The MTPs are serving as a platform for transfer of proven technologies, which would include providing the required infrastructure, know-how training etc. Field data for the demonstration of tissue culture raised forest trees is being collected and analysed. Studies have also been taken up for development/refinement of tissue culture protocols of economically important species - especially horticultural crops.

Large scale production of the important tree species continued and over 40 lakh plantlets planted in an area of approx. 3500 ha. for field demonstration. The field data recorded indicated better performance of the tissue culture raised plants vis-a-vis the control. A preliminary cost benefit analysis indicated about 5 times higher return in the case of tissue culture raised plants.

Micropropagation technology park - NCL, Pune

Protocols were developed and upscaled for large scale micropropagation of different varieties of banana, sugarcane, turmeric and ginger. A single step process was standardized for micropropagation of sugarcane, turmeric and ginger. A single step process was standardized for micropropagation of sugarcane, replacing the normal two step process. Two thousand tissue culture raised plants of economically important varieties of Banana viz. Basarai and Srimati were field planted in a farmer's field near Pune to get first hand information on field performance with respect to growth, yield, time of first harvesting etc.

Micropropagation technology was developed and upscaled for three economically important varieties of Phragmites viz. P.karka, P.communis and P.australis. Phragmites is a common seed belonging to the family Graminae. P.australis is used for the treatment of many industrial wastes by the method called "The Root Zone" treatment. Five thousand tissue culture raised plants of P.australis were supplied to a private company situated in Pune. The technology on micropropagation of teak was transferred to International Plant Laboratories Ltd. (IPL), Baltonsborough, UK. Hands on training on micropropagation of teak protocol was imparted to a representative from IPL based on the agreement made between NCL and IPL.

The technology has been well adopted at IPL and has successfully completed its agreement period. Technologies for three forest tree species and economically important horticultural and plantation crops are also being transferred to the Industry. In addition to transfer of technology for commercialization, the MTP is also providing a complete technology package on a turn key basis to State Government Research

Institutes/Universities. This includes setting up of the laboratory, species protocols and training. A major component of the MTP activities is training, being provided at all levels — scientists, technicians and students.

Micropropagation technology park -Teri, New Delhi

While continuing with the mass propagation of tree species, a large number of tissue cultured plants of various forest species were produced at the MTP These plants were distributed to different forest departments and private growers for field trials as well as routine plantations. 50 clones of E.tereticornis were studied. Out of the various clones that were tested, three clones (No. 348, 360 and 2116) proved to be significantly superior at half the rotation age as compared to the conventionally raised control plants. Over 1.4 lakh plants of E.tereticornis and about 24,000 plants of E.camaldulensis were despatched from MTP Production of Dendrocalamus strictus through somatic embryogenesis progressed well.

The main problem associated with D.strictus protocol is its high sensitivity to media ingredients, sub-culturing time and the ability of technicians to distinguish and separate out embryogenic calli from non-embryogenic calli. To simplify the production process, a micropropagation protocol by auxiliary branching method using seedling was worked out. 4.1 lakh plants of P.deltoides were despatched from MTP facilities. Field results suggest that the cuttings derived from tissue cultured plants have a better root system and are more vigorous. This might be due to rejuvenation of clones under in vitro conditions. In a field trial being carried out at National Research Centre for Agroforestry, Jhansi two genotypes of A.pendula multiplied through tissue culture have shown a mean annual increment in height of over 1 m. Considering the fact that A.pendula is a very slow growing and recalcitrant species, this gain in height is very significant.

The existing productivity levels of most of our fruit crops are among the lowest in-the world. This problem is severe in crops that have been perpetually propagated vegetatively and have accumulated several diseases. To improve the quality of the planting material, a number of horticultural species were taken up. Nearly 22,000 tissue culture plants of banana were distributed to various growers who are likely to be benefited both by the disease-free nature of the planting stock as well as the superiority of the clones. The two varieties of banana presently being multiplied are Robusta and Dwarf Cavendish. Test results of tissue culture raised plants in the field indicate clonal uniformity and comparatively higher yields. Mass propagation of strawberry was undertaken. During 1997-98 over 85,000 plants were distributed to various growers for commercial use. In 1998, over 1,00,000 strawberry plants were distributed to growers from MTP. Mycorrhizal associates for strawberry were isolated. Tissue culture propagated plants are supplemented with mycorrhizae at the nursery stage.

In order to popularize tissue cultured plants, a nursery meet and a landscapers meet was organised during this year. Nearly 50 nursery men and landscapers from leading nurseries in Delhi, Noida and Faridabad participated. They were apprised of the benefits/advantages of tissue cultured plants over conventionally raised plants. During the meet, the nursery owners shared their views about the technology.

Technologies for fire forest and horticultural species were under transfer to the industry for commercialization. Training was provided to scientists, technicians and students.

Total area covered under forest trees

Species Approximate	No. of Plants Despatched	Recommended spacing (m x m)	area (ha)
Anogeissus pendula	4,42,094	3 x 3	397.92
Anogeissus latifolia	1,17,458	3 x 3	105.72
Dendrocalamus strictus	91,493	5 x 5	228.73
Eucalyptus spp.	13,05,022	3 x 2	783.32
Populus deltoides	12,46,490	5 x 3	1871.60
Miscellaneous	1,0,729	—	—
Total	32,13,286	3387.29	—

Tissue culture large cardamom–product plan

The demonstration project on evaluation of the performance of tissue cultured plantlets of large cardamom (Amomum subulatum) vis-a-vis open pollinated seedings in planters' field in Sikkim (52.5 ha) and West Bengal (17.5 ha) continued. During 1998 planting season, an area of 12.25 ha in 49 units was field planted as per details given below:

Zones	Clones	No. of units planted	Total area (ha)
North Sikkim	SBLC-47	3	0.75
	SBLC-47A	3	0.75
East Sikkim	SBLC-47	10	2.50
	SBLC-47A	11	2.75
Darjeeling	SBLC-47	5	1.28
	SBLC-47A	17	4.25
	Total	49	12.25

A total of about 1,24,000 tissue culture plantlets and 40,000 open pollinated (OP) seedlings are being maintained in four nurseries which will be field planted in about 140 units during 1999 planting season. Multiplication of four elite clones through tissue culture and raising of OP seedlings for field planting during the year 2000 are in progress. Three training programmes were organised for the beneficiaries of the project and also to those who have shown interest in taking up planting during the next season. More than 100 farmers participated in the above training programmes.

Tissue culture vanilla—product plan

The project envisages evaluation of the performance of tissue culture plantlets of vanilla (Vanilla planifolia) vis-a-vis stem cuttings in planters' field over an area of 150 ha in the states of Kerala (60 ha), Karnataka (60 ha) and Tamil Nadu (30 ha). An area of 39.25 ha during the last two planting seasons - 1996 (5.50ha) and 1997 (33.75 ha) was planted. During the 1998 season, an area of 44 ha covering 176 units was planted in three states. The details of statewise coverage is given below in the table. The balance target area in the project will be covered during the 1999 planting season. Field nurseries comprising tissue culture plantlets of MCV-1, MCV-2 and MCV-3 were established at various centres located in Kerala, Karnataka and Tamil Nadu and 56,320 tissue cultured plantlets and corresponding stem cuttings (14,080) supplied for planting in the farmers' farms during 1998 season. Field visits were made for providing technical guidance and to record growth parameters.

The observations made from the plots of 1996 and 1997 planting revealed that stem cuttings show initially better performance in vine length than tissue cultured plantlets. The number of nodes and leaves were more in tissue cultured plantlets of 1997 planting in Trivandrum, Idukki and Wynadu zones of Kerala. Four training programmes on cultivation and processing of vanilla have also been conducted during the year at different zones (Idukki, Wynadu, Trivandrum and Calicut) identified in the project. In all, 216 beneficiaries / farmers participated.

Biotechnology-based programme for SC/ST population

About 35 project have been implemented with a view to providing training, demonstrations and extension activities.

Aromatic and medicinal plants: The Itanagar branch of RRL, Jorhat implemented a project on "Promotion and cultivation of aromatic plants and production of essential oils for the benefit of tribal population of Arunachal Pradesh". Its main objective is to motivate local people through training and demonstration to take up organised cultivation of potential aromatic plants in Arunachal Pradesh. 224 local tribal people were trained on cultivation and processing of Citronella, Lemongrass and Patchouli.

The planting material of citronella has been grown in 9 ha. area and about 1.7 lakhs Citronella seedlings have been distributed to beneficiaries belonging to villages of Arunachal Pradesh. In addition, a nursery of 4000 seedlings of patchouli was raised for distributing planting material free of cost to the tribals. These efforts have resulted in cultivation of aromatic plants in more than 50 ha. area at 5 different locations. The institute is also setting up 4 processing units for essential oil extraction at 4 locations. In an another project at Krishi Vigyan Kendra (KVK), Pal, dist. Jalgaon (MS) nurseries of Citronella, Lemongrass, Palmrosa, Ashwagandha, Isabgol, Safed Musali and Costus has an area of 5 ha. and planting material/seed distributed to 270 farmers who raised crops of medicinal and aromatic plants at their 32 ha. land. The project has helped the farmers to increase their farm income 2-4 times. More than 1000 people have benefited through training, field demonstrations and cultivation of aromatic/medicinal plants. A distillation unit has also been established for Citronella and Lemongrass.

The Central Institute for Aromatic and Medicinal Plants, Lucknow introduced cultivation of rose and geranium and their distillation raised a nursery of 3000 rose and 2500 geranium plants at its Purara farm near Baijnath in Dist. Bageswar for supplying planting material to the SC/ST farmers. The institution conducted training courses and apprised 19 farmers, on economic details, the methods of cultivation, marketing etc. of rose and geranium and other supporting crops like palmrosa, tagetes, lemon-grass through lectures and live demonstrations at Purara farm. The IHBT, Palampur, has encouraged local SC/ST farmers to cultivate the Tagetes miuta and Rosa demascena and extraction of their essential oils at commercial levels. A multi purpose direct fired essential oil distillation unit of 4 quintal capacity was installed at village Jhiri in dist. Mandi has been formally handed over to the village Panchayat Jhiri, and it is now being used by the villagers.

During November, 1998, 50 kg of Tagetes minuta oil worth Rs. 1.00 lakh was produced by this unit. Another multi-purpose 1.5 quintal capacity field distillation unit for distillation of fine grade oils was fabricated and being installed at Dharamsala dist. Kangra. Chlorophytum borivilianum (Safed musli) is an important medicinal plant comparable to Korean Zinseng. Gyan Bharti Trust, Udaipur has undertaken a project for procuring musli tubers from identified sources, multiplying the same at its Tapovan Ashram premises and lay out demonstrations on fields of tribal farmers after imparting training in its cultivation practices. The Trust conducted 20 demonstrations in fields of the trained tribal farmers.

The Ayurved Gramoudyog Sodh Sansthan, Jodhpur raised Withania somnifera and Cassia angustifolia plants in 21 ha. land belonging to SC/ST farmers. It has also raised a nursery of nearly 500 plants of Commiphora wightii which would be transferred in fields in next 2-3 months. Grama Nava Nirman Samithi, Hyderabad implemented a project on cultivation and distillation of aromatic plants viz., Palmarosa, Citronella & Mentha for the benefit of SC/ST women. Navalbhau Pratisthan, Navalnagar dist. Dhule (MS) has also undertaken a project on aromatic and medicinal plants.

Floriculture: The Central Agricultural University, Imphal implemented a project for training SC/ST youths of Manipur in orchid production. It has developed a protocol for micropropagation of popular tropical Dendrobium spp. and trained about 80 unemployed SC/ST youth for 10 days on commercial cultivation of hybrid orchids. The university developed 5 hybrids involving local spp. Renanthera, Vanda and Cymbidium. Efforts are underway to develop hybrids from the local orchid spp. which have qualities of cuff lower orchids and are at the verge of extinction.

Guwahati University took up project on application of in vitro propagation techniques in multiplication of cultivars of Chrysanthemum and Gladiolus for large scale planting, training of SC/ ST rural youth and field demonstration to demonstrate floriculture as a source of self employment and income generation.

Mushroom Cultivation: The M.S. Swaminathan Research Foundation Community Agrobiodiversity Centre, Puthoorvaya in Wayanad dist. in Kerala surveyed the district for the distribution pattern of mushrooms and trained 25 SC/ST youths of the selected villages on Mushroom cultivation, post-harvest technology and development of value added products. The trainees were also taken to nearby agricultural research institutes and imparted skill in spawn production. The centre also collected few mushrooms used in traditional medicinal system for treatment of Jaundice, ear ache, inflamation, dehydration etc.

The Centre for Rural Development and Technology IIT, New Delhi imparted training in growing edible mushroom to about 100 persons from two villages in Gurgaon and Rohtak dist. of Haryana. During the last two seasons, about 1000 Kg mushroom was produced by the beneficiaries as a kitchen garden activity for their consumption and as a cottage industry on cooperative basis for marketing. In a project on Demonstration of mushroom cultivation for the benefit of SC/ST in Eastern U.P., 90 persons from 3 selected villages of dist. Faizabad were involved in mushroom cultivation and they were acquainted with the economics and nutritional value of mushrooms and recipe preparations. Most of them started cultivation of Pleurotus sajor caju in their own houses.

Vermiculture and Vermicomposting: The Gandhigram Rural Institute, Gandhigram (TN) made efforts to popularize vermicomposting alongwith sericulture (moriculture & silkworm rearing) through field demonstration and training as revenue generation programme. The institute trained 120 persons from 25 villages. These persons have already set up 10 vermiculture and 6 sericulture units, which are functioning successfully and also encouraged a large of farmers to venture in this area.

Krishi Vigyan Kendra (KVK), Nanded (MS) has trained 100 farmers from nearby 10 villages on the vermicompost production through bioconversion of agro-residues, and its use in agricultural and horticultural crops. Most of these farmers were reported to produce and use vermicompost in their fields. A vermicomposting biofertilizer production-cum-training project is also being implemented at Kohima in Nagaland. Under this project, 100 unemployed youths were trained on different aspects of vermicompost production, and its application demonstrated in potato crop.

Quail Farming: The Regional Research Laboratory (RRL) Jammu continued its demonstration project on disease free and better quality quail broiler production for meat for the benefit of tribals to help the poor tribal masses' Around 360 persons belonging to 3 dists. namely Jammu, Kathua and Udhampur were trained on quail production covering brooding, rearing, feeding schedule, fabrication of cheaper cages and litter system from locally available raw material. The project resulted in the establishment of 32 small production units (100-200 birds each) by the beneficiaries in 14 villages in the 3 dists. From these small units each beneficiary got a profit of Rs. 400 - Rs. 800/- per lot and training for better care and management of Japanese quails (Coturnix coturnix japonica).

Biological Control of Plant Pest and Diseases : The Tamil Nadu Agricultural University trained 130 farmers in pest and disease identification, collection of crop pests for the production of biopesticides, laboratory host Corcyra rearing for the production of egg parasitoid, Trichogramma chilonis, production of botanical pesticides, antiviral principles and nuclear polyhedrosis viruses of Spodoptera litura and Helicoverpa armigera. In addition, 174 farmers were trained in a one day programme to create awareness on the hazards of chemical pesticides and benefits of biopesticides in Integrated Pest Management (I PM). The project covered a total of 7 villages of Madurai and Virubhunager dists. in Tamil Nadu.

Botanical pesticides from neem, Pongamia, Vitex, Ipomea, Jatropha, sps. etc. were used in brinjal, bhindi, tomato and redgram for the control of pests and diseases. In rice fields, sprays were given with non-edible oils like neem, Pongamia and Madhuca at 3% individually and in combination at reduced rates, and compared with one insecticide and untreated control. The rice diseases and pests controlled by these methods were demonstrated.

NPVs B.t and fungal pathogens of insect pests, viz. BeauYeria bassiana, Paecilomyces spp., Verticillium lecanni, etc. were used in cotton, vegetables, pulses and oilseeds. The egg parasitoid, Trichogramma chilonis was used in the management of lepidoptcran pests of cotton, vegetables, oilseeds, etc. Pheromone traps were used for monitoring and control of Helico-erpa armigera and Spodoptera litura in cotton, vegetables and pulses. The TNAU covered a total of 22 ha. crop area of tomato, brinjal, bhindi, redgram and groundnut under the project for field demonstration on the use of various biological control agents and biopesticides.

KVK, Parbhani (MS) produced biological control agents viz., Trichogramma chilonis (parasite), Chrysoperla cameia (predator) and Nuclear Polyhedrosis Virus (antomopathogen) on laboratory scale. A total of 82 It. HaNPV, 55 lakhs Trichogramma and 10 lakhs Chrysoperla were produced and used in IPM of pigeonpea, cotton as well as chickpea. KVK has conducted field demonstrations on the use of various bioagents covering HaNPV on 82 ha., Trichogramma on 37 ha. and Chrysoperla on 20 ha. A one month training was conducted for 9 persons on the production biological control agents. Shri Dhaneswari Manav Vikas Mandel, Kalamb dist. Osmanabad (MS) also has trained around 600 persons from the targeted groups on the production of HaNPV, Trichogramma card production, production of

Cryptolemus, neem powder and urea coating with neem product. It has conducted field demonstrations on the use of these biological agents in IPM in Jawar & Cotton crops at 12 farmers' plots which were visited by about 1000 farmers from nearby areas.

Aquaculture: Oriental Research Foundation, Bhopal implemented an aquaculture project to increase employment and improving economic status of weaker sections in Hoshangabad dist. in M.P. The facilities for fish seed rearing available with Central Institute of Fisheries Education, Powarkheda were utilized under the project. Seeds of major carps were reared upto the size of 50 mm fingerling at Chandrapura and Powarkheda farms, and healthy free seed supplied to 20 co-operative societies working at various perennial and seasonal tanks in different dists. of the state. The seed was also stocked in Khoripura, Dewas and Goharganj tanks.

A total of 1,64,000 fingerlings were stocked in these tanks and about 16 tonnes of fish harvested and 50 people were benefited as each of them earned about Rs. 6,600 to Rs. 10,000 per year. KVK, Karda dist. Washim (MS) continued its demonstration project on aquaculture in the tribal areas. It procured fish seed of Indian major carp, grass carp, silver carp and common carp, and stocked in the nursery pond at Karda for transferring to 10 selected seasonal and penile ponds. In a series of training courses conducted on different aspects of the fish and prawn culture, 80 persons were trained.

Assistance was provided to the persons trained in the previous year to start their fish farming activities. With these KVK efforts fish production could be raised upto the level of 3000-3500 kg/ha/yr. with the application of scientific and technical know-how, against the yield of 500-600 kg/ha/yr. with traditional practices. The St. Anthony College, Shillong took up a project on the production of fish seed and rearing of major carps and catfish. The project will cover induced breeding, rearing and training. It is expected that the project would help in improving the financial status of the fish farmers of the region.

Health Care: All India Inst. of Medical Sciences, Sir Ganga Ram Hospital, New Delhi with the District Collectorate, Department of Tribal Development and Health, Wayanad and the Foundation for Fetal Research, Chennai initiated a control programme for sickle cell disease in tribal population of Kerala. The first phase of the screening of the tribals was started in September, 1998 with daily visits to the villages, and haemoglobin electrophoresis at two base laboratories are currently in progress. About 15,000 subjects were covered. The ultimate goal of the project is to use biotechnological tools to develop and execute a community control programme for this dreaded disease.

Indian Women Scientists' Association and Institute of Immuno-haematology, Mumbai continued working on the project for training and education of tribal women for improving their health and economic standards. 10 tribal villages of Ahmednagar district, each having the population of 500-1500 tribals were selected, and 10 semi-illiterate women one each from the villages were trained in workshops held at Rajur and Bhandardhara. In the workshops, information on aspects such as gastro-intestinal diseases, skin diseases, respiratory infection, tuberculosis, tetanus, malaria, vitamin deficiencies, snake bite, purification of drinking water, immunisation, nutrition etc. was given in simple language with the help of posters. Vivekananda Institute of Medical Science, Calcutta continued the study on the use of biotechnology dietary derived supplements in improving health status of SC population of three villages in West Bengal. The study has covered 3 adjacent villages of South 24-Pragna dist. of West Bengal. During the surveys, it was found that 62 children out of total 229 and 79 mothers out of 151 had sign and symptoms of Vitamin-A deficiency. Of them, 14 children and 26 mothers were found with histological evidence of Vitamin-A deficiency as evident from examination of their conjuctival swabs. It was observed that in case of children after giving Spirulina preparation (500 mg twice daily x one month) the specimen of their conjuctival swabs became normal, and in case of mothers also the swab reverted to normal after one course of Spirulina (1 g twice daily X one month).

Vivekananda Institute of Medical Sciences has also taken up recently another project on studies of genetic disorders to provide counselling with special reference to haemoglobinopathies in the tribal population of Tripura. The project is focused on screening of the population to assess the extent of genetic diseases (HbE betathelisinia) among the tribals and educate them in gene related diseases.

Biotechnology-based programme for women and rural development

The Task Force met twice recommended fifteen new projects and reviewed the ongoing ones.

Food processing: Under The project proposal entitled "Storage and preservation technologies for agriculture produce of U.P hills", plants for horticultural importance were identified keeping in mind the agro-climatic data of area, land specific information, people based information, present availability of fruits and vegetables, list of conventional and non-conventional fruits, seasonal availability of different fruits and traditional method of preservation of fruits/vegetables. Two training programmes were organised and around fifty women were trained for setting up their units for processed food products using the local horticultural produce.

In another project entitled "Empowering women through entrepreneurship development training", the first training programmes was conducted for 15 unemployed women graduates. The intensive training course included lectures on entrepreneurship development, marketing, setting up a small enterprise, procurement of working capital, loan from bank and other agencies, raw materials for food processing industry, aspects of finance, steps on setting up of industry, legal aspects, hygiene at work place & maintenance of equipments. The hands on training were given for two weeks. These trained women were taken to various units. Some of them are in the process of setting up their own enterprises.

Waste Land development : To cultivate Emblica in 'Usar' soil of U.P. seeds of Emblica officinalis and training were provided to the beneficiaries. The beneficiaries were allotted the nursery trees to keep the plants viable and growing. Eighteen training programmes were arranged including one major camp. The trainees have also been taught about the various properties of 'Usar' soil.

Waste Management: In Vermicomposting and Mushroom cultivation to utilize waste material, selected rural women/ families were trained at their respective places on different aspects of two technologies through lectures and demonstrations, site visits and distribution of popular literatures. The families are being provided the requisite material and guidance for technology implementation and marketing of the produce. Six public contact programmes on Vermicomposting and Pleurotus (Mushroom) cultivation were organised.

Floriculture: Two projects were supported on tissue

culture assisted floriculture in selected village panchayats of Kerala at TBGRI and Federation of Floriculturist of India (FIF), Trivandrum and "Micropropagation of ornamental plants of Attipra panchayat" at Kerala University. These projects deal with tissue culture of Orchids, Anthurium and other ornamental flowers. TBGRI has already trained 25 beneficiaries from Venganoor and 10 from Sreekaryam Panchayts. Orchid and Anthurium cultures from selected hybrids of commercial value were initiated and multiplied. About 50 plants are already established in the green house. Two training programmes have been organized by Kerala University twenty women were trained in micropropagation of ornamental flowers.

Sericulture : During the first phase of projects, techniques for rearing of silkworms species 5dfls of CB (PM x KA) and two hybrids KA x NB4D2 OR NB7 x NB18 were perfected. Beneficiaries from non-traditional areas were identified. Demonstration units at beneficiaries' land are being set up.

Medicinal plants: To prepare an inventory on medicinal herbs of Garhwal Himalayas, a project is being supported for collecting and compilation of information on herbs in the villages of three districts Dehradun, Chamoli and Rudraprayag. Information has been compiled on the socio-economic status of villages, health status of the region, prevalent diseases of the villagers, market value of different herbs, abundance of herbs available in the region in different seasons.

Based on market demand, nursery preparation for Mentha arvensis (Pudina), Withania somnifera (Ashwagandha), Rawolfia serpentina (Sarpgandha), Potentilla fulgeum (Bajradanti), Sarpetina (Sarpgandha), Piccrorhiza cusava (Kutki), Centella asiatica (Brahmi), Euphorbia thymifolia (Chopalu) has been started.

Human Health, Genetic Disorders and Counselling : The project on " Role of Biotechnology awareness in prevention of genetic disorders among rural women", is under operation at Sanjay Gandhi Post-Graduate Institute (SGPGI), Lucknow. Surveys have been conducted to identify genetic disorders in the villages. Blood samples were collected and being analysed by trained nurses/ mid-wives and counselling to the affected families are being provided.

Biotechnology Based Product and Process Development: Development and transfer of the process know-how for mosquitoes and household pests repellents/ herbal formulations for women welfare" is being pursued by CIMAP, Lucknow. The products are floor mopping emulsion, mosquito repellent agarbatti & dhup batti. Unemployed women and youth of 3 blocks of Bakshi Ka Talab have been selected for training in cultivation and product development.

Environment Protection and Awareness: One project is being implemented to provide training to the rural women in the environmental protection through bio-monitoring of water pollution and other associated problems. The Biosensor technology developed at Vishvabharti University, West Bengal was adopted for rural application. Regular visits to the villages, were also conducted to develop awareness and motivation for the use of biotechnological tool for monitoring the level of contamination through pesticides in their agriculture land and water bodies.

Golden Jubilee Women Biotechnology Park: "Golden Jubilee Women Biotechnology Park" at Kelambakkam, Chennai was inaugurated by Honourable President of India on July 29, 1998 for celebrating Golden Jubilee Year of country's independence.

The park aims to provide opportunities for professionally qualified women to take a career of remunerative self-employment through the organization of environment friendly biotechnological enterprises. The park will be designed on the principle of decentralised production supported by appropriate centralised services to promote a series of high tech biotechnology based enterprises aiming to capture a number of niche markets in the areas of Agri-biotech, Food biotech, Medical biotech etc. The R&D institutions, the corporate sector and the financial institutions would assist the women entrepreneurs in achieving the objectives of the Park. The Park will serve as a model to foster the technological and economic empowerment of women. Twenty acres of land have been provided by the Tamil Nadu Government at Kelambakkam, Chennai for the park. Eight prospective entrepreneurs have been selected to begin with for producing ornamental fish, Collagen, Vitamin and Mineral Premixes, Entero rapid biochemical testing system, Tissue culture/ Micro propagation of Plants, Bioconversion of waste into organic manure, Spices mixture and Spirulina.

"A Colloquium On Biotechnology for Women : A Vision for 21st Century": To celebrate International Women Year a Colloquium was organised at Nil, New Delhi 7th November, 1998, was inaugurated by Prof. Archana Sharma. The 7th November, 1998 being the birth day of Madam Curie, the first woman scientist who bagged two Nobel Prizes was selected. About 130 scientists and technologists actively participated and deliberated in the areas like agriculture, health, environment, industry, basic sciences and human resource development. Important views were expressed on technological empowerment of women using suitable biotechnology.

Model Biovillage Project (Mocha-Gorser, Porbandar Gujarat): A model Biovillage project was formally announced by the Hon'ble Minister for Science &

Technology Dr. M.M. Joshi during the inauguration of S&T exhibition on 3rd August 1998 at the National Stadium, New Delhi. This was one of the events planned by the Department of Biotechnology to commemorate the Golden Jubilee of India's Independence.

The selection of the site was done keeping in view the significance that this is the birthplace of the Father of the Nation. The lead agency Central Salt and Marine Chemical Research Institute, Bhavnagar coordinated with various other agencies to launch the program. The other collaborative agency for this project are Meteorological Department, Porbandar; Gujarat Agricultural University, Junagarh; National Research Center for Groundnut, Junagarh; Regional Centers of Central Leather Research Institute, Ahmedabad; National Environmental Engineering Research Institute, Ahmedabad; Birla VXL Industrial Ltd., Porbandar, Dist. Panchayat. The activities undertaken at the site are managed through the Panchayat of Mocha-Gorser.

The project has progressed well and sites were selected for desalination plant, wasteland plantation, carcass disposal-cum-training center and marine algae cultivation. Nursery for wasteland plantation (Salvadora, Jojoba, Jatropha) has been raised and ready for plantation in wasteland plot of the project village; Desalination plant is ready and installed in January 1999 at project village. Blue-print for carcass disposal-cum-training center is ready Farmers Training was organised for use and production of Biofertilizers and Biopesticides. About 30 farmers took training at Gujarat Agricultural University Campus, Junagarh for 2 days (10-11 Dec. 1998).

Biotech process engineering and industrial biotechnology

A number of projects directed towards product and process development have been supported.

Role of interfacial concentrations in reverse micellar biotechnology: Working on the role of the interfacial concentrations in reverse micellar, the investigating group at IICT, Hyderabad observed that the interfacial basicities of cationic reversed micelles are remarkably less than that of normal aqueous cationic micelles. Such interfacial basicities of reversed micelles are likely to be one of the key factors controlling the catalytic efficiencies of biocatalysts located in the interfacial region of the reversed micelles such as lipase. An experimental protocol for probing the local molar concentrations of water and bromide counter-ions present inside the water pool of a cationic reversed micellar system was developed. A novel chemical method was developed for sensing the remarkable exo-surface basicities of cationic liposomes.

Microbial production of plant growth regulators: The significant achievements in the project at NCL, Pune are isolation of actinomycetes and azotobacter strains producing plant growth regulators. Extraction methods for isolation of cytokinin-like products from culture broth were standardized. Bioassay methods for detection of cytokinin-like activity in crude broth, crude extract and prep TLC fractions were also standardized. It is observed that a considerable number of actinomycetes and azotobacter isolates are found to produce cytokinin-like activity in minute quantities.

Scale up of A.rhizogenes mediated transformed hairy root cultures: Experiments conducted at CIMAP, Lucknow in bench top fermentor showed that the stagnation or clumping of hairy root mass at certain regions of the fermentor resulted in inadequate mixing which limited the growth of hairy roots. Experiments conducted on the culture of hairy roots in the fermentor led to the conclusion that the bio-reactor needs certain modifications. These modifications in the bio-reactor yielded 1.65 to 1.78 times higher bio-mass when compared with the yield of previous experiments.

Extraction of Penicillin-G from fermentation broth: The work was carried out at NCL, Pune. The solvent extraction of Penicillin-G from aqueous broth was optimized by using amine extractants. The extraction was optimized for pH 7.0 and high recoveries got. The back extraction of solvents, which initially posed a big problem was optimized in a single stage recovery. Other conditions optimized for the amine extractions were pH, temperature, ionic concentration and relative concentrations of the penicillin, amine extractant. The penicillin was extracted from aqueous phase using a membrane extraction device, developed at NCL, Pune. More than 70% extraction efficiency was obtained using a recycle operation.

Characterization of human breast tumour associated antigen: Human breast tumour associated antigen (BTAA) was purified from 28 breast tumour tissues at NCL, Calcutta. Three DEAE fractions (HF1, HF2 and HF3) were obtained and presence of the tumour associated antigen in the fraction was determined by screening the breast cancer patients sera against the DEAE fractions. It was observed that the female breast cancer patients presented antibodies against HF1 whereas male breast cancer patients had antibodies against HF3. BTAA purified from the HF1 by HPLC was of 85 kDa and HF3 was 72 kDa protein. The BTAA is being used for screening of sera samples obtained from breast cancer patients.

Optimization of methods of biosynthesis of plant lipoxygenase based bioactive lipids: In a study at the University of Hyderabad, Lipoxygenase (LOX) activity levels were measured in different plant parts of varied species. Highest LOX activity was observed in rapidly growing seedlings of green gram, followed by pigeon peas and other species of leguminaceae. Potato tubers also recorded significant production of LOX. LOXs from pigeonpeas, greengram and potato tubers were purified by employing conventional chromatographic as well as HPLC techniques. Different substratas resulted in different lipoxygenase product profiles in green gram/ pigeon pea. The purified lipoxygenase products were tested for their anti-fungal effects on the wilt fungus. Preliminary results indicated that the LOX metabolites are highly effective in inhibition of growth of the fungus.

Scale up of hairy root cultures in specially designed bioreactor and down stream processing for the production of high value phytochemicals: Hairy root cultures of Beta vulgaris for production of betalaines, Tagetes patula for production of thiophene were established at CFTRI, Mysore and experiments conducted to study the influence of polyamines and microbial elicitors on the growth of hairy root cultures. Several kinetic parameters which influence large scale cultivation in bioreactors were studied at shake flask level focusing mainly on the aspects such as growth curve, bio-mass maxima, kinetics of nutrient depletion, effect of inoculum density, effect of larger volumes and product accumulation. A prototype bioreactor was designed.

Bioreactor design: role of hydrodynamic shear on enzymes: Investigations were taken up at UDCT, Mumbai on the measurement of turbulent flow in stirred bio-reactor using Laser Doppler Anemometers (LDA), design of impellers, Computational Fluid Dynamics (CFD), etc. About 40 different impellers have been fabricated and the fields generated by these impellers measured using LDA. A combination of experimental LDA measurements and CFD simulations have been enabled prediction of the impeller characteristics like flow numbers and power numbers. It was also observed that different impellers offer different stresses even when compared on the basis of equal power consumption per unit mass. A combination of LDA measurements and CFD simulations thus offer a possibility to compare different impeller designs which may lead to development of optimum impeller geometry which would offer less hydrodynamic shear, yet maintain good oxygen transfer rates.

Mass inoculum production of Ceriporiopsis subvermispora and Phanerochaete chrysosporium for bio-bleaching and bio-pulping: The work at University of Delhi involved morphological characterization of C.subvermispora on different media, effect of physical factors on sporulation in minimal medium, effect of nutritional factors on sporulation, effect of various stress media on sporulation etc. Based on the results, conditions were standardized for inducing maximum sporulation in C.subvermispora. Methods were also standardized for separation of viable spores.

Development of high flex-life polyurethane for use in cardiovascular devices: The main objective of the investigation at SCT, Trivandrum is to develop blood compatible and biodurable (high flex-life) polyurethane for use in cardiovascular devices. Hydrophobic polyurethane-urea HFL18-PU9 was prepared using discyclohexyl methane disocyanate, hydroxy terminated polybutadience and hexamethylene diamine and subjected to accelerated chemical degradation and accelerated flexural fatigue tests. Accelerated chemical degradation tests, weight loss determination tests, accelerated flexural fatigue tests were conducted. It was found that the candidate polyurethane HFL18-PU9 survived 720 million cycles of flexing without weight loss, which is equivalent to 18 years of survival in human being. The studies reveal that the polyurethane HFL18-PU9 has the potential application for use in cardiovascular devices.

Food biotechnology

Value addition to foods, development and presentation technologies and packaging of foods, biosafety have been the areas of focus.

Production of low cholesterol egg: At CFTRI, Mysore supercritical carbon dioxide extraction technique was followed to reduce the cholesterol in liquid egg and spray dried egg powder. Isopropanol treatment helped in breaking the lipoprotein binding and facilitated extraction of cholesterol in liquid egg by supercritical carbon dioxide technique. This method was found to remove cholesterol from liquid egg. The recovery of cholesterol was high (90.0%) in spray dried whole egg powder (without isopropanol treatment). Phospholipids were not observed to be affected.

Biodegradable ecofriendly packaging films: In vivo biodegradation studies chitosan and cross-linked chitosan films was carried out at CFTRI, Mysore in soil collected from four different locations and at different RH values. The soil samples were cleaned and films of size 2X4 cms. were weighed and buried inside the soil at both constant and varying RH values. From the percent weight recorded regularly, type-4 soil showed 22 and 49% weight doss, respectively for chitosan and cross-linked chitosan films after 7 days. After 2 weeks, complete disintegration of films in soil types 1 and 4 was observed but C in soil types 2 and 3 it was moderate.

At RH of 25% and above, crosslinked chitosan film was observed to be degraded completely, whereas the chitosan film was only partially (12.5%) degraded. 50% RH it was found to be completely degraded. Cross-linked chitosan film required comparatively less moisture to undergo degradation in vivo in the soil. Both cellulose and starch based films being very hydrophilic, were observed to be degraded and disintegrated in less than 48 hr. Significant shelf life extension at ambient and cold storage temperature was observed by use of coating formulations in various fruits.

Culture and cultivation of seaweed for food: Studies were conducted at CSMCRI, Bhavanagar. The germplam of Porphyra (nine species) and Monostroma (one species) occurring on the Indian coast was studied and maintained in laboratory cultures which were optimized for growing all the species of Porphyra and Monostroma. The studies on the life cycle of all seaweeds were completed in the laboratory cultures. The biochemical analyses (ash, protein, carbohydrates, total carbon and nitrogen) including mineral (Na, Ca and K) and trace elemental constituents of all the species, which occur abundantly, were carried out. Studies on organic nutrients like amino acids, lipids and fatty acids are in progress. Attempts are under way to conduct field cultivation of above-mentioned seaweeds on pilot scale. It is expected to develop cultivation technology package as well as process for making seaweed foods from Indian plants.

Development of process for flavours & food additives: Various strains of Trichoderma viride were screened for 6 pentyl -alpha-pyrone (6pp) which is a secondary metabolite at CFTRI, Mysore. Optimization of cultural and nutritional parameters was carried out under submerged fermentation conditions. The highest level of 6pp obtained was in the range of 400-500mg/l. Solid substrata like defatted coconut gratings, wheat bran etc., though supported good mycelia growth showed predominance of methyl ketone production with no production of 6pp. A process at the lab scale level has been developed for the production of 6-pentyl - alpha-pyrone. Procedures were standardized for producing flavour nucleotides by the in-vivo digestion of nucleic acid contents of the food grade yeast by exogenously added enzyme. Reaction conditions have also been optimized for the conversion of d-lemonene to racemic carvyl acetate with 65% yield using microbial lipases and for the enzymatic preparation of important terpene esters. Development of a process for Xanthan gum by fermentation: The bench scale data obtained in shake flasks were successfully scaled-up to 50-L scale in a pilot fermenter at CFTRI, Mysore. Xanthan yield of 60-70 g/ 100 g of sugar supplied was obtained in 72 hours.

The media was optimized to replace the expensive organic nitrogen source with inexpensive ammonium nitrate and corn steep liquor. The complex problem of mass transfer and agitation of high viscosity was tackled by appropriate impeller design. The xanthan product obtained compared favourably with the commercial sample. The product was applied successfully in selected foods such as fruit squashes, extruded products, traditional foods like, Idli etc. Toxicity testing studies showed no adverse effects. The process has been demonstrated and an Indian industry has agreed to be a partner for the development towards commercialization of the process know-how.

Microbial Bio-transformation of Terpenes of High valued Food Flavours : Two fungal cultures, Penicillium Sp. and Aspergillus Sp. showing potential for biotransformation of terpenoids to high valued food flavourings were selected after screening at CFTRI, Mysore. The Penicillium sp. was observed to convert with high efficiency, limonene to carveol under the optimized conditions. Cultural conditions were optimized for conversion of alpha-pinene to verbenol and verbenone by Aspergillus sp. The yield observed was 1.2 mg of verbenol from 20 mg of alpha pinene.

Strain improvement attempts were made by subjecting the fungal cultures to UV irradiation and treatment with ethyl methane sulphonate and colchicine. Some of the variants showed marked morphological differences which were reflected in the product yield. An

Aspergillus variant caused biotransformation of alpha-pinene with a yield of 4.56 mg% of verbenol and a UV derived Penicillium variant caused formation of 3.7 mg % verbenol which amounted to about 15 and 8 fold increases respectively in the yield of products.

Based on the results of laboratory studies, large scale trials on the verbenol formation by Aspergillus sp. and its UV variant were carried out in 2 litre fermentors and a yield of 3 mg% and 5.3%, respectively was obtained.

Biotechnology research for food safety: The project jointly supported by the Department of Biotechnology and Ministry of Food Processing Industries at CFTRI has obtained significant leads in the following areas:

(a) Safety analysis of genetically engineered plants of food value: Genetically engineered Brassica was evaluated for safety of the oil. The animal experiments for 90 days by feeding with normal and genetically engineered Brassica oil at 5 and 7.5 % did not induce any mortality or abnormal changes in albino rats. The toxicity studies (both acute and subacute) with Brassica seed oil cake are underway.

(b) Development of ELISA based detection kit for pesticides of importance in foods: Validation of thiram kit for poultry feed raw materials and poultry feed was done by spiking maize, bengal gram, green gram, ragi and jowar with thiram. No interference occurred in any one of the above extracts and thus further clean up of the sample was not required. However, the locally available poultry feed samples spiked with thiram and extracted with extraction solvent of the kit, interfered with thiram analysis. The extract was passed through an ad sorbent system to remove interfering substances before thiram analysis.

(c) Development of rapid detection techniques for Aflatoxin B1 based on ELISA: Several maize samples were analysed for Aflatoxin estimation in the range of 10-200 ppb by immuno-dot blot method. The values were found to be in agreement with the TLC method of estimation, a conventional method widely used.

(d) Development of a biosensor for the detection of organophosphorous (OP) pesticide: Studies were conducted by using both spectrophotometer and biosensor methods to find the optimum pH for the immobilized AchE enzyme activity. Studies revealed that the immobilized enzyme exhibited maximum activity at pH 7.5. Studies were conducted to optimize the molarity of buffer with immoblized enzyme for maximum activity and it was found that percentage inhibition did not change with the molarity of the buffer used. A signal conditioning and data acquisition system is under way to analyse OP-pesticides. The response range was kept between 0 -10 volts. Validation of the biosensor for detection of OP pesticides in food samples is underway.

(e) Biomarkers of toxicity: Metal induced testicular toxicity was studied in rat; gerbil and mice under metal (Cd, Ni, and Pb) induced lipid peroxidation. Rats were found to be the most susceptible followed by gerbil and mice. Modulatory effect of taurine, quercetin on cadmium induced lipid peroxidation was studied in vitro. Both taurine and quercetin significantly abolished metal induced lipid peroxidation (LPO) with quercetin being more effective than taurine. Various hydroxyl scavengers viz., mannitol, histidine, sodium azide reduced the degree of LPO significantly suggesting involvement of hydroxyl radicals. Cadmium induced lipid peroxidation in testicular cells was studied, Cd was found to induce concentration related increase in lipid peroxidation. Mercaptosuccinate (glutathione peroxidase inhibitor) and 3 - aminotriazole (catalase inhibitor) resulted in a marked increase in LPO.

Processing of juices from exotic & minor fruits: The work was taken up at UDCT, Mumbai. Fruits were analysed for proximate constituents acidity, pH, ascorbic acid, anthocyanin pigments, tannin & pectin contents, Analysis of the flavour profiles -of the fruits is under process. Parameters for inactivation of major enzymes like polyphenol oxidase, peroxidase & catalase from these fruits have been optimized. Assays of enzymes important to fruit processing viz. Polygalacturonase, polymethyl galacturonatelyase, pectinmethyl - esterase, polygalacturonase, polymethyl galacturonase, cellulase, xylanase & amylase were standardized.

Deseeding of amla seeds was conducted using traditional method & compared with enzymatic deseeding. Pectinex 3XL was- found to be the best with respect to deseeding, vitamin C retention, & juice yield.

Large scale production of betalains by hairy root cultures of Beta vulgaris: Hairy root cultures of Beta vulgaris were established by transformation of B.vulgaris using Agrobacterium rhizogenes clone TR 105 at CIMAP Lucknow. From the established clones, three elite were selected on the basis of their pigment production, rapid growth in phytohormone free media and stability of biomass and pigment production for 62 generations (15 days as one generation). One clone produced predominantly yellow coloured betaxanthins, while the other predominantly the red violet betacyanins and the third one orange red colour (mixture of betaxanthin and betacyanins). The pigment content was observed to be increased three folds in a suitable medium.

Enhancement of Yields and Diversification of Growth Substratas for Production of Pleuroutus (Oyster Mushroom): A single step oil seed cake supplementation of the rice straw substrata after complete colonization by the mushroom mycelium was observed to double the mushroom yield and its protein content at CFTRI, Mysore. The OSC - M (mushrooms raised on rice straw supplemented with oil seed cake) decreased the carbohydrate content by 50% of RS - M (mushrooms raised on rice straw). There was a desired softening of the OSC - M accompanied by reduction in total dietary fibre (TDF) by 45%. These produce nutritionally upgraded modified mushrooms with intense flavour and desired softening of texture.

Confirmatory trials on the use of coffee pulp as an effective growth substrata for production of oyster mushroom were conducted. The yields were observed to be at par with that on rice straw. These were found to be rich in proteins and free amino acids. Production of oyster mushrooms on coir waste and sunflower plant residue was standardized and is relevant as a rural based technology.

Screening and identification of edible tribal belt mushroom species of Madhya Pradesh and protocols for large scale production: The study was taken up at R.D. University, Jabalpur. Extensive periodical survey of various tribal and forest belts of Madhya Pradesh, resulted in the collection of 140 mushroom spedmens including 33 edible forms. Ethnomycological studies conducted during survey revealed that certain species of mushrooms are used for medicinal and edible purposes by making various types of recipes. Further studies on in-vitro cultivation of selected mushroom species are underway.

Biotechnological development of shelf stable probiotic cultures containing dairy food: These studies were undertaken at Gujarat Agriculture University, Anand. Promising cultures of lactobacilli and bifidobacteria of human and other origin were isolated; low cost buttermilk/whey-cereal blends with good nutritional value and acceptable organoleptic quality were formulated. Comparison of milk, buttermilk and whey blends was done and finally six blends each from different groups were selected for spray drying.

Genetics of amylase production in thermophilic fungi and strain improvement : Thermomyces lanuginosus a thermophilic fungus of immense biotechnological importance for the production of thermostable amylases was taken up at GND University, Amritsar for strain improvement. Through repeated mutation, protoplast fusion and transformation a strain that was catabolite repression resistant, partially constitutive and hyperamylase producing was developed. A total of 10,300 mutants were derived by mutagenesis of aleurospores/protoplasts of T.lanuginosus and screened for amylase production using plate assay The developed strains were observed to be stable. Further optimization of the production parameters and strain validation is being carried out at the fermentor level.

Development of low cost nutritious food supplement(s) using biotechnological approaches: Four low cost food supplements (a) soft chikki (b) suruchi meetha (c) nutro-crispo and (d) sweet and salty providing more than 400 K cal and costing less than Rs. 5/- per 100 g packets were developed by NDDB, Anand at CFTRI, Mysore and which were validated by NIN, Hyderabad for their organoleptic & nuritional properties. These products were released by Honorable Prime Minister Atal Behari Vajpayee to the school going children on 14th November 1998.

Microbial biotechnology

Restoration of Coal and Manganese Mine Spoil Dump through an Integrated Biotechnological Approach: An Integrated Biotechnological Approach (IBA) developed at

NEERI involves design of suitable pit size, amendment of mine spoil with organic material (pressmud, ETP sludge) and soil, isolation and multiplication of site specific strains of Azotobacter and Rhizobium and mycorrhizal fungi, screening of most suitable plant species, inoculation of selected species with specialised cultures of endomycorrhizal fungi and nitrogen fixing bacteria like Azotobacter for nonleguminous and Rhizobium for leguminous plant species. Biorestoration studies were carried out at Durgapur coal mine under Western Coalfields Limited (WCL) and Gumgaon and Dongribuzurg mines under Manganese Ore India (MOIL) on 1 hectare area at each site with plantation of about 2,500 trees of high ecological and economical importance. 7,500 trees at three sites included high value timber trees like teak, shishum, shiwan, neem, fruit trees like mango, chickoo, amala, custard apple, ber and other ecologically important species like bamboo, cassia, acacia etc.

The overall impact of IBA is that it provides food, fodder, timber wood and clean environment which improves the living conditions and socioeconomic status of the local population.

Studies on the proteases of Bacillus thuringiensis: At Osmania University, Hyderabad, the endogenous protease activated crystal toxin from Bacillus thuringiensis subsp. Kurstaki was purified. The purified toxin was homogenous, as demonstrated by two-dimensional polyacrylamide gel electrophoresis and contained 1.38 moles neutral sugar and 9 moles sialic acid per mg protein. Amino terminal amino acid sequence data revealed that the toxin is a cleavage product of 132 kDa protoxin with glutamic acid-30 of the deduced amino acid sequence of the crystal protein.

The intracellular proteases in sporulated Bacillus thuringiensis subsp. Kurstaki were studied to identify the endogenous proteases involved in the activation of protoxin. The proteases obtained with 30% ammonium sulphate saturation were analysed by both gelatine zymography and azocasein hydrolysis.

The three proteases were heat-stable at 65°C while the 69kDa proteases were active upto 75°C. Intracellular protease-deficient mutants (ethyl methanesulfonate mutagenesis) could not generate the active toxin suggesting the existence of a specific enzyme affecting the conversion of protoxin to toxin.

Cloning and expression of haemoglobin gene: Cephamycin C belongs to betalactam group, produced by Streptomyces clavuligerus and is used as a basic drug for the synthesis of cefoxitin, cefmetazole, cefotetan etc., which are extensively used in preventing post-operative infections caused by resistant bacteria. The project at Osmania University, Hyderabad aimed at genetic manipulation of S.clavuligerus to improve the efficiency of trapping (Sequester) oxygen under reduced oxygen tension by cloning and expression of heterologous bacterial haemoglobin gene from vitreoscilla in cephamycin C producer strain of S.clavuligerus.

Two promising isolates were obtained which belong to Vitreoscilla stercoraria and exhibit interesting features with respect to heme protein expression. The two promising isolates were designated as PS 15 and PS 24. The two isolates have shown higher cellular heme protein and its expression was dependent on oxygen levels. Under oxygen limiting or oxygen poor conditions (hypoxic conditions) the production of heme protein was significant than the culture grown under highly aerated conditions.

Cloning and molecular characterization of thermostable inulinase gene from thermophilic actinomycetes: The studies were undertaken at GND

University at Amritsar. In order to search for novel microbial source: of thermostable inulinase soil and root sample from rhizosphere of dahlia (Dahlia pinnata) and chicory (Cichorium intybus) plants collected from 15 different locations in Punjab were screened for inulin hydrolysing activity. Of the forty strains isolated, two actinomycetes and two fungal strains viz., Aspergillus fumigatus and Pencillium purpurogenum showed considerable extracellular inulinase activity. The two fungal strains were deposited with MTCC, IMTECH , Chandigarh.

Biochemical, genetic and molecular analysis of nitrophenols degradation by microorganisms: Several organisms capable of utilizing p-nitrophenol (PNP) as the sole source of carbon energy were isolated by enrichment technique at IMTECH, Chandigarh. Following biochemical characterization, two organisms, viz. Arthrobacter protophornase RKJ100 and Pseudomonas cepacia RKJ200 were chosen for further work. Both organisms degrade PNP via an oxidative route as indicated by the accumulation of nitrite molecules in the culture medium. Studies indicated that degradation occur via hydroquinone formation as shown by TLC and GC; hydroquinone is further degraded via the b-ketoadipate pathway. Results have demonstrated that a plasmid of approximately 50 kilobase pairs is responsible for carrying genes for PNP degradation in P.cepacia RKJ200.

The P.cepacia RKJ200 is also capable of utilising 4-nitrocatechol as sole source of carbon, nitrogen and energy and is degraded via an oxidative route.

Bio-treatment of refractory gold ores and concentrates : The main focus of the research at IISc., Bangalore has been the design and development of a laboratory scale continuous reactor system for biotreatment. Among four different samples investigated, G.R. Halli concentrate, which found to be highly sulphitic (50% pyrite & arsenopyrite) was chosen for continuous trials. A strain of Thiobacillus ferrooxidans TfH6 isolated, characterized and activated in previous studies was used. A 17L bioreactor system has been designed and fabricated. Several experiments on bioleaching of the concentrate have been conducted to develop a blueprint for design and operation of the demonstration plant at Hutti.

The bioleaching of concentrate was carried out at 20% pulp density and it was found that the microorganisms were not completely active at this density. Therefore, experiments were conducted with microbial culture, grown for 48 hours in 9K medium. The steady state was found to reach after 8 days and 30% of the iron and 50% of the sulphur present initially in the concentrate was found to be oxidized. The gold extraction efficiency was 70-75%. The untreated concentrate showed only about 40% gold extraction efficiency. These results clearly indicate the beneficial effects of biotreatment of refractory gold ores. Efforts are being made to enhance the extraction.

Anti-microbial drugs from Cyanobacteria: At the University of Madras, a marine cyanobacterium (Spirulina subsalsa BDU 40303) with potent antibacterial compound was identified which can be used even against Pseudomonas. A marine cyanobacterium (Oscillatoria laetivitens BDU 20801) with anti-Candida activity was identified and the partially purified compound was highly effective. Purification and identification of the active compound is in final stages. A marine cyanobacteriurn (Phormidium valderianum BDU 30501) with potent antiviral activity against HBV, HSV and HIV has been identified. Partial purification resulted in enhanced activity against different viruses with different fractions noted, indicating the presence of more than one antiviral compound.

A survey of North Andaman Islands conducted by

Bharathidasan University has resulted in the enumeration of 70 species of marine Cyanobacteria belonging to 25 genera and 10 families. This reveals the rich biodiversity of marine cyanobacteria in this area. The centre now has marine cyanobacteria of 268 strains belonging to 70 species 25 genera, and 10 families. Phormidium valderianum BDU 20041 was identified to be a good biotransformant. It has transformed ferulic acid (a product of lignin degradation) to vanillic acid (an aromatic alcohol used as food additives. This was confirmed by GC-MS studies. Likewise, cholesterol transformation to several products has been worked out in P.valderianum BDU 30501 and O.subtilissima. BDU 92183. Identification of these by products is underway.

A surfactant producing strain was identified. Its stability was found to be better than commercial surfactants such as sodium dodecyl sulphate, (SDS) and Tween 80. The mode of chromium uptake by cyanobacteria was found to be an active process. The metal gets detoxicated to trivalent chromium and enzyme glutathione-Stranferase also aids in reducing the toxicity. This finding helps to improve the bioaccumulation capacity of organism and its use in effluent treatment is being attempted. Study on the effect of stabilisers and inhibitors with different b.lactam substratas with P valderianum BDU 30501 has aided in the identification of the enzyme as a cephalosporinase.

Molecular breeding of polycyclic aromatic hydrocarbon degrading bacteria: A bacterial strain Alcaligenes odorans, capable of degrading a wide range of PAH compounds was selected at TERI, New Delhi. The carbon starved cells of the selected bacterium A.odorans could take up about 13% of total [^{14}C] - Pyrene, of which 11% [^{14} C] Pyrene were retained within the cell biomass and 3% [^{14}C].-pyrene was liberated as $^{14}CO_2$ in 120 minutes.

Assays for the known enzymes involved in PAH

degradation revealed that Alcaligenes odorans also has catechol 2,3 dioxygenase, an enzyme primarily responsible for ring cleavage in aromatic degradation. The observation clearly shows that A.odorans cleaves each of the four rings that are present in pyrene to generate catechol, which can thus be channelised into degradation pathway that generate intermediates for the Kreb's cycle - the principal energy generating pathway.

Having obtained an efficient PAH degrader, which also has the capacity to degrade a variety of alkanes, the larger objective of the project has been to develop a technology that can effectively reclaim crude oil/oily sludge. In order to monitor the survivability of the bacterial isolate that are released into contaminated soil, molecular markers have been developed using bacterial repeat sequences. These repeat sequences yield highly reproducible and species specific fingerprints. Experimental trials are underway wherein Alcaligenes odorans are isolated and identified from crude oil contaminated microcosm using PCR fingerprinting.

Development of GE Phosphate solubilising Pseudomonas: Pseudomonas fluorescens is a well-characterised plant growth promoting rhizobacterium that can effectively colonise a wide variety of plants under diverse environmental conditions. The objective of the project at M.S. University, Baroda is to genetically modify this organism so as to enable it to solubilize mineral phosphates, thus imparting yet another property beneficial to the plants that it colonises. Normally P.fluorescens strains do not secrete organic acids in sufficient quantities to release phosphorous from soil phosphates. Analysis of acid production using methyl red indicator plates with different concentrations of buffer showed that this organism fails to acidify the medium when buffered Tris HCL pH 8.0 at 70mM or above is added. By transforming P fluorescens with a vector carrying the ppc gene encoding phosphoenol pyruvate carboxylase from Anacystis nidulans, clones obtained show acid production at 100 mM buffer concentration. These modified strains can grow on medium containing rock phosphate as the sole phosphorous source and bring about reduction of pH from 8.0 to 5.0. Results indicate the transformant to be more effective at phosphorous solubilization than the parent strain. The efficacy of the modified strains in plant growth enhancement is under study.

Application of thermophillic microbes for improved leaching of copper: The studies were taken up at IICB, Calcutta. The copper ores of eastern region, mainly of the Ghatshila area of Bihar, are normally composed of chalcopyrite, and as such are not good substratas for bioleaching by mesophilic bacteria. However, leaching of these ores with acidic ferric sulphate solution in the presence of silver ion as catalyst suggests that these ores are amenable to hydrometallurgical processes, and can be extracted through application of microbes. Studies on the chalcopyrite rich copper ores of Ghatshila region with thermoacidophilic archaeal strains show that leaching may be achieved with an A.brierleyi strain which could leach more than 16% of copper within 30 days from 5% (w/v) suspensions ores at 65%C. Leaching of copper increased steadily after 15 days of incubation, and the increasing tendency of leaching was maintained even after one month.

The results suggest that leaching should be continued for a longer period of time to get more dissolved copper from ores. Apart from A.brierleyi, other archaeal strains were reported to have bioextractive properties. A surda concentrate was tested for amenability to leaching with the A.brierleyi strain. After 45 days, the strain could leach as much as 3.85% of total copper from a 5% (w/v) concentrate suspension.Cloning of dehydrogenase gene and construction of genetically engineered organism for L-ascorbic acid production: A breakthrough has been achieved at RRL, Jammu. Gluconobacter oxydans block mutant capable of producing free gluconic acid has been developed by Tn5 transpogenesis and the mutant has potential commercial importance. Glucose dehydrogenase a gene from G.oxydans was transferred in Pseudomonas species through conjugation using pML 122 as the vector. A fast growing clone showing high specific activities of GDH and GADH enzymes was selected. Fermentation studies on the clone revealed 40% increase in the productivity of 2-keto-gluconate- a penultimate intermediate of isoascorbic acid (Isovitamin C) used as antioxidant for the preservation of food products.

Process development of alkaline proteases: The investigations were carried out at IMTECH, Chandigarh. The isolated alkalophilic Bacillus sphaericus was observed to produce an alkaline protease, using a relatively less expensive production medium, which seems to have good industrial potential for a variety of applications. This enzyme was observed to be optimally active at 50-55°C and a pH of 10.5. The optimum temperature was found to increase to 60°C in presence of Ca++-The enzyme was found to be quite stable at a wide range of pH values (7.5-11.0). Salt precipitated powdered enzyme preparation was found to be quite stable for 18 months at 37°C.

Iron Control in Hydrometalurgical Leach Liquor using Thiobacillus: Iron oxidation studies were carried out at RRL, Bhubaneshwar in a specially designed bioreactor. Fe(II) concentration was varied from 1 to 10 gpl in the growth medium. The lag phase continued from 8-10 hours and at 10 gpl the oxidation rate was maximum i.e. 500 mg/l.hr. Fe(III) concentration was varied from 0.5 to 4 gpl. It was observed that, higher ferric concentration had a negative effect on the growth and activity of Thiobacillus ferrocxidans. The medium of the pH was varied from 1.25

to 2.5. An increase in the oxidation rate was observed from pH 1.25 to pH 2.0 and thereafter it decreased. At pH 2.0 the maximum rate of oxidation was observed to be 132 mg/l/hr. Biomass concentration was varied from 10^3 to 10^{13} cells/ml. At maximum biomass concentration the rate of oxidation was maximum i.e. 477 mg/l/hr. Generation time was observed to vary from 2 to 16 hours depending on the oxidation parameter.

Fermentative Production of Lipase and Immobilization of the Pure enzyme: Studies were undertaken at Jadhavpur University, Calcutta. A lipase producing Corynebacterium strain was isolated from spoiled coconut. A highyielding strain m_{13} was isolated by induced mutation using N.T.G. Optimum assay conditions for enzyme (substrata olive oil emulsion) were temperature 60°C, time 10 min, pH 8.0, $CaCl_2$, Conc.110 mM.

Microbial Synthesis of Inulinases: Inulin sources have recently received interest as renewable raw-material for the production of fructose syrup and ethanol. The study was taken up at RRL, Trivandrum. Eighty four strains were isolated from rhizosphere soil samples around the dahlia tubers on synthetic medium containing inulin as a carbon source, for the production of extracellular inulinase. Among the isolates, six different mesophilic cultures were selected for further studies and finally one of them was taken for detailed characterisation. This was identified as Staphylococcus sp. The microbial culture synthesised inulinase that was active on inulin and was extra-cellular in nature. Solid state fermentation was carried out for the production of inulinase from a bacterial strain of Staphylococcus sp. RRL1 and a yeast strain of Kluyveromyces marxianus ATCC 52466. Both the cultures grew well in a wheat bran medium.

Novel Alkaline Thermostable Lipase: Purification, Characterization and Gene Cloning: An extracellular thermostable alkaline lipase was produced by a thermophilic Bacillus strain J33. An agrowaste by-product (Wheat bran 1%) enhances the lipase production by 3-4 folds in comparison to the nutrient broth (1 %). The enzyme was purified to 175 folds with 15.6% recovery by ammonium sulphate & Phenyl Sepharose column chromato-graphy. Polyclonal antibody was raised against this lipase with other lipases from thermophilic and mesophilic microorganisms. For cloning the gene, a genomic library has been constructed in cosmid vector (pHC 79). The colonies (positive clones) started giving clear zones after 15 days incubation at 4°C. Two positive clones have been isolated and checked further by western blotting. After confirmation the clones are being used for subcloning the lipase gene.

Microbial production of Biodegradable plastics: At RRL, Jorhat over hundred bacterial strains were isolated from soil samples and tested for their ability to accumulate PHA. Three strains isolated from an oil contaminated site were found to accumulate considerable PHB (polyhydroxybutyrate) under nitrogen limitation condition. Effect of temperature, carbon and nitrogen sources on PHB production were studied and PHB isolation procedure standardised. Isolate number RLJ 071 when cultivated at 42°C for 28 hours in 10% sucrose containing nitrogen limitation medium, produced cells having 68% PHB content. PHB isolated by sodium hypochlorite-chloroform dispersion method was in white crystalline powder form having a melting point of 180°C.

Development of Bioabsorble Polymers: The objective of the project at IIT Delhi is to develop biosoluble materials for clinical applications. The most important biomedical applications of biodegradable polymers are in the areas of controlled drug delivery systems; implants for fracture repairs, ligament reconstruction, surgical dressings, dental repairs, contact lenses, vascular graft and organ regeneration. Thus, a variety of homopolymers having these repeat units was initially synthesized in different molecular weight range. Their chemical structure and physical properties were evaluated. A new series of block copolymers were prepared from polylysine and polyaspartic acid which were subsequently characterized. Long term animal studies in several different species are required for further utilization of these materials as class III and/or implant grade materials.

Degradation of Pesticides by facultative anaerobes: Two strains of Micrococcus sp. harbouring plasmids (5 kb, 62 Kb) degraded malathion and chlorpyriphos. Degradation studies with plasmid cured derivatives of the strains suggested involvement of plasmid to be degradation of malathion and chlorpyriphos. Interspecies protoplast fusion between the strains resulted in cointegrate formation of the two plasmids as evident from comparison of electrophoretic mobility of plasmid DNA of the fusant and the parent strains. The resulting fusant was resistant to 3, 5 -dinitrosalicylic acid and sodium azide (300 and 200 ppm respectively) against which cells of parent strains were sensitive. Enhancement of endosulfan degradation by the fusant was also observed (about 10-12%).

Production of thermostable Proteases and Lipases in thermophiles: A gram negative spore forming rod was isolated at Punjab University and was identified to be Bacillus sp. IS-20. This was subjected to substrata improvement with chemical and physical mutagenic agents. One of the mutants SS-3 gave increased enzyme yield and was selected for subsequent studies. The enzyme was found to be quite stable at broad pH and temperature range and was compatible with various detergent preparations.

Another isolate Bacillus sp. RSJ-1 giving the best lipase at a pH of 9.0 and a temperature of 50°C was selected. The organism: was subjected to mutagenesis by Ultraviolet irradiation and ethyl methyl sulphonate and one of the mutants with enhanced enzyme yield was selected. The lipase production was optimized by using various carbon nitrogen source as well as environmental parameters.

Enhancement of microbial protein production through genetically engineered Bacterial Haemoglobin: The study was under taken at IMTECH Chandigarh. In response to oxygen deprivation, a unique haemoglobin like protein (VHb), displaying relatively high rate of oxygen dissociation, is produced by a gramnegative, aerobic bacterium, Vitreoscilla. Gene (vgb) encoding for this bacterial haemoglobin has been cloned and overexpressed in E.coli under the native oxygen-sensitive promoter of vgb, gene. Four site-directed mutants of VHb were generated by introducing specific changes at E7 residue of VHb through vgb gene manipulations. SDS-PAGE analysis of recombinant E.coli carrying the mutant VHb indicated that Hb constitutes 5-8% of total cellular protein. To get primary indication in the oxygen binding characteristics of these mutants, relative change of oxygenated form of various VHb mutants into reduced form with respect to time was determined. These mutants were found to have significant differences with respect to their oxygen binding kinetics as compared to wild type VHb protein.

Genetic Transformation of Filamentous Fungi: The work was carried out at IISc Bangalore. A fungus has been demonstrated to be capable of secreting up to 20-30 grams of protein per litre of culture medium. The fungus Neursopora crassa is an attractive model organism because background information on its genetics and physiology is available. A noteworthy aspect of this work was the preparation of enzyme for isolation of protoplasts. Soil samples, amended with fungal cell wall material, were incubated in moist conditions for several days to enrich the resident population of organisms capable of utilizing fungal cell wall as carbon source. A species of Trichoderma secreted cell wall lytic activity when grown in optimized media.

The "home-made preparations of the lytic enzyme released protoplasts from germinating conidia of wild-type and several auxotrophic strains N.crassa; the protoplast releasing activity being comparable to that of the expensive, commercial enzymes. The transformants were selected on the basis of complementation of recessive auxotropic mutant genes. The uninucleate microconidia could serve as recipient cells for transforming DNA, circumventing the difficulty of purifying the transformed nucleus. Even when mutinucleate protoplasts were used for transformation, prior incorporation of the mcm gene into the host strain (by crossing) allowed the primary (heterokaryotic) tranformant to bud out microconidia which could be plated on selective medium to recover the individual transformation products. The transformants were selected in a medium supplemented with inositol alone. Colonies of primary transformants were grown to conidiation. The multinucleate (heterokaryotic) conidia, containing mixtures of untransformed (his) and transformed (his+) nuclei, were allowed to germinate in shake cultures at 22°C. Under these conditions the mcm gene was expressed and the culture selectively produced microconidia by microcycle microconidiogenesis. Southern analysis of transformants showed that the plasmid sequences were integrated randomly in different nuclei.

Microbial Diversity: A national network R&D programme is being launched for biotechnological exploitation of microbes including extremophiles for industrial applications, wherein microbial diversity aspect shall also be dealt with. The programme would envisage exploring the microbial flora of the country from different regions, their collection, identification and indexing. A number of centres are to be established in different locations which would be networked so that the scientists could have access to the database of culture collections available at all the centres. This national endeavour is important keeping in new that India has acceeded to PCT from 8 th Dec. ,1998 and is now member of the Paris Convention "Union".

Intellectual property rights, bioproducts and biosafety

Intellectual property rights

The department this year reconstituted the Patent Screening Committee to facilitate researchers to file their patents in India and abroad for the processes/ technologies emanating out of biotechnology research. As per the recommendations of the Scientific Advisory Committee, the department is bearing the entire expenditure for patenting of research leads submitted by the applicants whether the project has been funded by the Department or the lead has been obtained through their institutional or other grants.

During the year the Patent Screening Committee cleared 8 applications. Applications from research institutions from CSIR were also allowed to file joint patent applications with DBT through CSIR mechanism. NRDC has been helping in the process of patenting in India and abroad. So far, 48 applications have been received by the department out of which 31 applications have been filed in India and abroad. This year 3 Indian patents and 2 US patents have been sealed for DBT in joint collaboration with the host institutions. The other applications are under various stages of processing or for consideration by the Patent Screening Committee.

Bioproducts

The department, in close collaboration with Department of Electronics has funded two projects on electroporation equipment development and on microwave disinfection of hospital wastes. Projects are also being funded for the development of projects and services in association with the industry. In the joint projects with the Department of electronics, industry has also participated in the development of technologies. The project on technology perfection and transfer of agglutination based detection of HIV-I & II antibodies in human blood has reached a stage when the prototype kit would be ready for multi-centric trials in comparison with other imported HIV detection kits.

The packaging material for the kit has been standardised and efforts are on for the preparation of indigenous standard sera panels. The technology for the monoclonal antibodies for phage coat proteins gIIIp and gVIIIp, which were transferred to M/s Pharmacia Biotech, USA have been launched formally by M/S Amersham Pharmacia Biotech in December, 1998. The products are HRP/anti-M13 monoclonal conjugates. These antibodies would be useful to the researchers using Phase Display Technology worldwide.

Biosafety regulations

The Department of Biotechnology actively implemented the rules and procedures contained in the Notification No. 1037(E) dated 5.12.1989 under the Environment Protection Act, (EPA) 1986, issued by the Ministry of Environment & Forests, to monitor the Recombinant DNA Research work in India. In accordance with the Notification, the Department had brought out "Revised Guidelines for Research in Transgenic Plants & Guidelines for Toxicity and Allergenicity Evaluation of Transgenic Seeds, Plants and Plant Parts" in August, 1998.

The Guidelines include a complete design of a contained green house suitable for conducting research with transgenic plants. Besides, it provides the basis for generating food safety information on transgenic plants and plant parts. In addition to the above, the Department has been nominating its representatives Institutional Biosafety Committees (IBSCs) to have vigilance on the research activities in Genetically Modified Organisms (GMOs) and guiding research institutions on the safety aspects of GMOs.

In order to bring about public awareness on the safety issues emanating from the use of GMOs, the Department had conducted seminars at five places at Delhi, Calcutta, Hyderabad, Pune and Bangalore on Biosafety Guidelines to widely disseminate information on safety and benefits among the scientists who are working in this area.

(i) Institutional Biosafety Committees: Currently, 125 IBSCs are functional at research institutions, university departments and at private industries in the country where recombinant DNA work is being carried out.

(ii) Review Committee on Genetic Manipulation. The Department had reconstituted the RCGM by inducting more members form diverse areas of applications including agriculture, drugs & pharmaceuticals, industry and environment management. The members inducted have been raised to 16 from the earlier 9 members. During the year, two meetings of the newly constituted committee were convened and several field experiments in small plots were permitted for generation of data on transgenic plants in different agroclimatic conditions in the country. The target transgenic crops were brassica, cotton, tobacco, brinjal, cabbage, cauliflower and tomato. The scope of activity of the RCGM members was also enlarged within the provisions of the law by creating a Monitoring-cum-Evaluation Committee to independently work and assist the RCGM in technical evaluation of limited field trials on transgenic plants in open environment. This technical committee met twice and guidelines for evaluation of the transgenic plants in open environment are being developed. On the basis of the evaluation of research conducted by M/s Bharat Biotech India Ltd., Hyderabad on recombinant Hepatitis B vaccine produced in yeast, as examined by its IBSC and the research results scrutinised by the RCGM, the latter had recommended the proposal to the Genetic Engineering Approval Committee (GEAC) of the Ministry of Environment & Forests for clearance of the product under EPA for manufacture and use in the country. Subsequently on approval, the product was launched by the Company.

5

Human Resource Development

An integrated programme of Human Resource Development covering teaching, training, rewards and incentries and popularisation of biotechnology programmes has been implemented in more than 40 research and academic institutions in the country covering practically all the states except Haryana and North West region. Effect in on to cover these regions also with an appropriate teaching/ training projects. The emphasis was on generation adequate of human resources trained in the multi-disciplinary and knowledge intensive field of biotechnology, essential to implement various projects. There were structured to meet the trained manpower requirement for the promotion of biotechnology and its applications in the country. The details of the various schemes are as follows:

Post-graduate, post-doctoral and post M.D./M.S. programme

The department continued its support to post-graduate courses at M.Sc./ M.Tech. levels in selected universities/ institutions. These courses are :

— 6 M.Sc. courses in general Biotechnology.

— M.Sc. courses in Agricultural Biotechnology.

— 1 M.Sc. course in Medical Biotechnology

— 1 M.Sc. course in Marine Biotechnology.

— 4 M.Tech./M.Sc. (Tech.) in Biochemical engineering, Bioprocess technology and Biotechnology.

The total intake of students to the above courses was around 450 per year. An in-depth evaluation of the implementation of the PG/PD. programmes was made in the course coordinators meeting held at IIT, Mumbai on 1.9.98. In addition, a two year post-doctoral research-cum-training programmes at 4 institutions and a one year Post MD/MS training course in medical Biotechnology were supported. During the current year one year diploma course in Medical Biotechnology at Utkal University, Bhubaneshwar, 4 new M.Sc. Biotechnology' courses viz. at Jammu University, Jammu; Birsa Agricultural University, Ranchi; Gujarat University, Ahmedabad and Mysore University, Mysore were taken up for support.

Financial assistance in terms of a one time grant has been provided to Sri Venkateswara University, Tirupati which has started a PG course in Biotechnology. A Placement Cell established with the financial assistance of the Department in BCIL, New Delhi to facilitate the students in finding jobs in industries has started functioning and has already placed a few students in biotech industries.

Biotechnology associateships

The programme provides an opportunity to scientists for undertaking advanced research in frontier areas of biotechnology in leading research institutions in the country and abroad. Two kinds of associateships, namely, National Associateship and Overseas Associateship are awarded every year.

National associateship: The national associateship is awarded to scientists to conduct research in leading national institutions engaged in biotechnological research activities for a period of 9-24 months. The scheme also has a provision for training in an overseas laboratory for a period of three months for those associates who had availed the associateship for a minimum period of nine months in national laboratories. For the year 1997-98, 14 scientists were selected for training in national laboratories and 5 scientists selected for overseas training in premier research institutions. The scheme was reviewed and certain modifications have been incorporated for its effective implementation. It is proposed to award around 20 associateships for the year 1998-99.

Overseas associateship: The overseas associateship is awarded under two categories, namely, long-term and short-term associateships for a period of one year and 3 to 6 months respectively. For the year 1997-98, 26 scientists were selected, 11 for long term and 15 for short term awards. It is proposed to award around 25 associateships for the current year.

Training programmes

Short-term training courses for mid-career scientists: The department supported Short-term training courses have been supported for 2 to 3 weeks duration in universities and research institutions having facilities and expertise in the areas of Biotechnology to impart hands-on training on emerging research techniques in various specialised disciplines of biotechnology.

Mid-career scientists, faculty members of university departments, post-doctoral research fellows, research associates attend these courses and the knowledge gained by them would facilitate in pursuing their R&D programmes as also in undertaking new research initiatives in their parent institutions. On an average 12 to 15 participants attend each course. During the year, 18 short-term training courses have been approved in various areas of biotechnology and 8 courses were conducted. Around 110 scientists were trained.

Technician training: Keeping in view the utility and the requirement of trained technicians for biotechnological research and industrial activities in the country, supported technician training programmes of two categories, namely, short-term (2-3 months) and long-term (one year) have received support. A proposal for conducting a long-term technician training diploma course and one short term training course is being approved. Post M.Sc. and M.Tech. training in industries: The objective of this scheme is to orient the Biotechnology post graduates to the needs of biotech industries. Students passing out of the post-graduate courses in biotechnology are selected and placed for training in various biotech based industries for a period of 6 months. This scheme is being implemented through the Biotech consortium India Ltd. (BCIL), New Delhi. During the year around 25 students were selected for training in various biotech industries in the country.

Visiting scientist from abroad programme

Under the scheme, eminent scientists working in the frontier areas of biotechnology in research laboratories abroad are invited for a period up to 3 months to research institutions/universities in India to initiate collaborative research programmes or conduct training courses or to participate in teaching activities. The scheme enables the sharing of the current state of knowledge in the frontier areas of Biotechnology. During the year, one scientist from USA visited JNU,-New Delhi for a period of about one month.

Biology scholarship and national biocience awards

The biology scholarships are awarded to the top students

in biology at the CBSE 10+2 level examination in order to encourage them to take up biology as their career. It is proposed to award 15 scholarships to the students among the top 40 in the CBSE 10+2 examination on the occasion of the National Science Day. Each student will be given a lumpsum cash award of Rs. 15,000/-, a gold plated medal and a certificate of merit.

A scheme has been approved for instituting 10 National Bioscience Awards for scientists below the age of 45 years, who have made outstanding research contributions in biology and biotechnology. This was announced by the Ministry of S & T & HRD during the 86th session of the Indian Science Congress at Chennai on 3rd Jun., 1999. was taken up.

Popularisation of biotechnology

This was done through, biotechnology publications, popular lecturers by experts, support to National Science Day celebrations, films and exhibitions aimed at popularising biotechnology and its applications among students and general public.

Biotechnology publications: A programme with a view to disseminating the basic concepts, potentials and recent developments in biotechnology among the students and general public was implemented through the National Institute of Science communication (NISCOM), New Delhi. Popular articles on biotechnology were published regularly in the Science Reporter and Vigyan Pragati.

Hindi versions of three books which were published earlier in English under vistas of biotechnology series have been brought. Under 'Foundations of biotechnology series', five more books are being brought out. An illustrated dictionary of biotechnology was compiled.

Popular lecturers by experts: The objective of this scheme is to create awareness of recent developments and potentials of biotechnology among students and general public through popular lectures by experts in biotechnology. A series of three lectures each on various topics is sponsored by the department in academic and research institutions in the country. Out of the three lectures in a series, at least one lecture is delivered in the regional language or in Hindi.

Apart from the various areas of biotechnology, topics such as bioethics, patenting and IPR issues concerning biotechnology were identified for organising popular lectures with a view to promoting the public understanding of these issues. During the year, around 15 proposals for organising popular lecture series would be supported.

Exhibitions: The department organised a major exhibition on the theme "Genetics" at Teen Murti House, New Delhi during November 14-30, 1998. This was a major attractions for students who visited in very large numbers. Apart from this, DBT participated in the following exhibitions:

— G-15 Exhibition, Cairo, Egypt: 14-17th May, 1998.

— Science and Technology exhibition at KP College ground, Allahabad: 17-20th June, 1998.

— India's vision for the future at India Gate, New Delhi: 1-16th August, 1998.,

— Science and Cultural Expo '1998 at Joka, South 24 Parganas, West Bengal: 5-13th September, 1998.

— Indian Science Congress exhibition at Anna University, Chennai : 3-8th January, 1999 -More than 3 lakhs students visited.

— Swadeshi Mela at Pragati Maidan, New Delhi: 25-30th January, 1999.

— G-15 Exhibition, Jamaica 9-14th February, 1999.

National Science Day: The department provides grant for the celebration of National Science Day by the institutions conducting DBT sponsored PG/PD. programmes in biotechnology. Activities such as open houses, exhibitions, debates, essay competitions, quiz programmes etc. on various topics of biotechnology are organised.

Seminars/symposia/conferences

Financial support was provided for holding national/ international seminars/symposia/ conferences/ workshops relevant to biotechnology by universities, research institutions and recognised registered societies. During the year, financial assistance was provided for holding around 80 seminars/symposia/conferences.

The department coordinated the holding of the 10th International Congress of Immunology in New Delhi during November 1-6, 1998. The department took active part in the 86th session of the Indian Science Congress held in Chennai during January 3-7, 1999 with the focal theme, "New Bioscience: Opportunities and challenges as we move into the next millennium".

Under the travel support scheme, financial assistance was provided to about 10 scientists actively associated with the activities/programmes of the department, for participation in major international conferences held abroad.

6

Centres of Excellence and Biotech Facilities

The Centres/Facilities/Programmes were reviewed by an Apex Committee and the Task Force on Bioinformatics and Infrastructure. Interaction with the industry, publicity of services and supplies, in-house R&D and database development have been the major activities.

Repositories

The overall objective of this scheme is to promote establishment of repositories for conservation/ preservation of living organisms including microbes both useful and harmful in agriculture, human health, animal husbandry and bio-industry. These repositories would also serve as referral centres.

Microbial Type Culture Collection (MTCC) at IMTECH, Chandigarh: The major objectives of the facility is : to serve as a depository of microbes including patented cultures as well as genetically manipulated organisms; maintain and preserve micro-organisms and to make efforts to develop newer and more efficient methods of preservation; act as an agency for the distribution of authentic strains to research laboratories and industries; prepare a comprehensive collection of Indian micro-flora and engage in research to determine potential use of these organisms for industrial and other applications; conduct training courses in microbiology and interact with other international centres.

MTCC has nearly 3,500 microbial cultures in its collection, the facility supplied 103 actinomycetes, 815 bacteria, 312 fungi, 71 plasmids, and 118 yeast to different research laboratories. A significant development during this year is the increase in supply of microbial cultures to industrial clients. Most of the pharmaceutical and biotech companies regularly procure cultures from MTCC. MTCC publications are also in demand and 25 manuals of "Bacterial Genetics", 18 manuals of "Actinomycetes" and 7 "Bacterial Genetics Kits" have been supplied. Eighty three unknown microbial cultures have been identified. A brochure on MTCC has been printed and mailed to about 1500 clients. Facility for storing patent cultures is ready with about 70 patented cultures mostly from IMTECH scientists. MTCC is a member of World Federation of Culture Collection (WFCC) and is registered with the World Data Centre for Micro-organisms.

National Centre for Conservation and Utilisation of Blue-Green Algae (NCCUBGA), Indian Agriculture Research Institute, New Delhi: The germplasm collection has about 600 unialgal cultures of blue-green algae consisting of unicellular, colonial and filamentous forms. These cultures are regularly sub-cultured and maintained. Besides maintaining BGA cultures, 6 species of Azolla are also maintained in laboratory and field conditions throughout the year.

A study carried out to examine the effectiveness of BGA for the specific application of solubilizing phosphorus from BOF (Basic Oxygen Furnace) slag from steel plant revealed that organism showed marginal to very good growth on this non -conventional Phosphorousnutrient source. Organisms like Westiellopsis prolifica, Calothrix brevissima and Nostoc calcicola besides showing good growth, were also able to colonise the moist BOF slag granules. Studies conducted to examine the response of microalgae to flouride showed that the tested algae remained unaffected upto 25ppm flouride. Chlorococcum humicola proved to be more tolerant than Anabaena khannae. Anabaena khannae showed better scavenging ability, perhaps due to the presence of polysaccharide sheath.

About 4.5 tonnes of soil based algal inoculum were produced and supplied to the farmers and research workers. The newly developed straw based and clay based BGA biofertilizer was also produced and supplied for experimental field trials. The clay based algal biofertilizer was tested for its efficiency and shelf life. The material could be easily stored for two and a half years under ambient conditions without any loss in viability. A training programme on 'Mass Production of Microalgae' was organised from September 14-19, 1998.

National Facility for Marine Cynobacterial Germplasm Collection, Bharathidasan University, Tiruchirapalli: The centre had 268 cyanobacteria strains belonging to 70 species, 25 genera and 10 families. Survey of North Andaman Islands has resulted in the enumeration of 70 more species of Marine Cyanobacteria belonging to 25 genera and 10 families revealing rich biodiversity of these organisms in this area. Phormidium valderianum was identified to be a good biotransformant of ferulic acid (a product of lignin degradation) to vanillic. Likewise, cholesterol transformation to several products have been worked out in P.valderianum (BDU 30501) and O.subtillissima. (BDU 92183). Identification of these by-products is underway.

A surfactant producing strain was also identified with stability better than commercial surfactants. Chemical characterisation of the compound is underway.

The mode of chromium uptake by cyanobacteria was found to be an active process. This finding helps to improve the bioaccumulation capacity of organisms. Its use in effluent treatment is being attempted. Study on the effect of stabilisers and inhibitors with different beta lactam substratas with P.valderianum has aided in the identification of the enzyme as a cephalsoporinase. A non-nitrogen fixing cyanobacteria proved to be a promising strain for the decolourisation of melanoidin pigment - a natural recalcitrant polymer of distillery effluent.

National Facility for Plant Tissue Repository (NFPTCR), IARI Campus, New Delhi: About 900 accessions of various priority crops (banana, sweet potato, Alocasia, Dioscorea, ginger, turmeric, Actinidia chinensis, Piper, Allium, medicinal and aromatic plants etc.,) were maintained under short- to medium-term for 424 months, in the culture room at 25°C and at low temperature, depending on the species. Amongst new accessions introduced/established in the repository are those of ginger (21), Curcuma (19), tarto (5), Mentha (12), Pelargonium (1) and Eremostachys (2).

Cryopreservation experiments were conducted on seeds and embryonic axes of Quercus to test their storability at different temperatures. Embryonic axes of seeds of different varieties of jackfruit were subjected to varying rates of drying and freezing for cryopreservation purposes. In all, 1243 accessions of orthodox seed spp. and 100 of recalcitrant spp. have been successfully cryopreserved

In vitro exchange, multiplication and training services were extended to workers on request basis. A total of 48 accessions of banana were multiplied and supplied to various research centres of the country such as NRC on Banana, Trichy (37), Dharwad University,

Karnataka (9) and a private company in Ellur, Andhra Pradesh (2). These were requested for field evaluation and R&D work. Training on tissue culture methods was imparted to students from Bhagalpur and Meerut Universities.

Under R&D programme, micro-propagation protocol is being standardised in several new species like Elettaria, Vanila, planifolia, D.rotundata and wild Allium species. Using leaf explants, direct regeneration protocol has been standardised in Piper colubrium and P.hapnum. Shoot tips of Dioscorea floribunda and D.wallichi could be successfully cryopreserved using vitrification, with high frequency of survival and regeneration.

Repository on Filarial Parasites and Reagents at Mahatma Gandhi Institute of Medical Sciences (MGIMS) Sevagram, About 300 filarial sera belonging to different groups i.e. Microfilaraemia, Acute, Chronic and Occult clinical cases from different endemic zones viz., Vidarbha, Raipur, Calicut, Bhubaneshwar and Rourkela have been collected. Filaria sera samples were supplied to various research groups. Training on enzyme immunoassays for detection of filarial antibody and antigen was provided to staff from Institute for Vector Control and Zoonoses, Hosur. SEVA FILACHEK, ELISA was useful in immunomonitoring of filarial patients for appropriate period of DEC treatment for clinical relief and cure. The bulk kits were supplied to the Institute for Vector Control and Zonoses, Hosur, NICD Centre, Calicut and Medical College, Mangalore for screening and monitoring filarial cases. FPLC purification filarial antigen yielded 3 diagnostically important antigen fractions

Repository on Medicinal and Aromatic Plant Materials at CIMAP, Lucknow: About 150 accessions and 200 species of medicinal and aromatic plants were incorporated in the herbarium. In vitro conservation of about 40 germplasm accessions belonging to 10 different plant species (e.g. Artemisia, Catharanthus, Duboisia, Papaver, Panax etc.) was achieved. A library of isolated pure compounds including marker phytochemical constituents of the various medicinal and aromatic plants has been developed and their structure confirmed through spectral analysis.

A rapid, simple and sensitive reverse phase HPLC method for the simultaneous determination of pharmacologically important sesquiterpene artemisinin together with arteannuin-B and artemisinic acid in Artemisia annua plant has been developed. A rapid and simple reverse phase HPLC method has been developed for the quantitative determination of asiaticoside from Centella asiatica. A very simple method was developed for qualitative assessment of adulteration in rose oil by FT-IR spectroscopy. A repository of 2D fingerprint densitograms of different plant extracts has been established. The chloroform extracts of Moringa fruit showed strong activity against bacteria causing infectious diseases. Several plant compounds with anti-deterrent and anti-feeding activities were identified.

Programme support and centres of excellence

Programme support in high priority areas of biology: IISc., Bangalore

Infectious Diseases: In Mycobacterium tuberculosis, four genes and related promotors have been cloned and characterised. A type-1 topoisomerase has been purified to homogeneity Sp. from Mycobacterium smegmatis and characterised. The mycobacterial enzyme has no zinc finger motif. M.tuberculosis enzyme (partially purified) also exhibited similar characteristics distinct from those of E.coli enzyme. There is a potential to exploit the unique properties of the enzyme to develop it as a molecular target against mycobacterial infections. The results of studies on DNA strand exchange by Rec A indicate that invasion of the newly formed heteroduplex DNA by the displaced ssDNA may contribute to inefficient homologous recombination in mycobacteria. Analysis of reactivities of antigens expressed from 40 unique genes previously identified using a genomic expression library of M.tuberculosis (field isolate) has revealed that seven of these antigens react with patients' sera whereas antibodies to killed mycobacteria did not recognise most of the antigens expressed in the library. The result suggests differential presentation to the host immune system of the same antigens derived from live and killed mycobacteria. The nucleotide sequences of the genes for the seven antigens revealed that all represented hitherto unreported genes of M.tuberculosis.

PPRV H is a hemagglutinin-neuraminidase (HN), a property exhibited only by Pestedes Petits Ruminants Virus (PPRV) and not by Rinderpest virus. The fusion protein F of PPRV is also unique among morbilli viruses in exhibiting fusion activity, without being assisted by H protein. Using recombinant DNA techniques, the functional domains of HN and F have been mapped. Furthermore, using extensive phylogenetic analysis of cloned sequence, it was shown that the Indian isolates of PPRV are distributed among three lineage groups.

Drug and Molecular Design: Studies on enzyme targets and inhibitors form an important component of the programme. The inhibitory action of synthetic peptides and mutations on the dimerisation of L.casei thymidylate synthase has been characterized using physico-chemical and crystallographic approaches. The crystal structure of a complex of E.Coli urase DNA glycosylase with a proteinacious inhibitor has been determined. Through mutational analysis, the basis has been laid for a detailed structure-function study of EcoP1 and EcoP 151 restriction enzymes.

In efforts involving membrane receptors and channels and carbohydrate binding proteins, signal transduction through guanyl cyclase receptor and its role in toxin-mediated diarrhoea were studied using a variety of approaches. It was established that fenvalerate interacts with the channel form of gramacidin. The interaction of alkaloid toxins and blockers with voltage gated sodium channels were investigated. Structure-function correlations for garlic lectin and allinase have been established. The crystal structure of garlic and basic winged bean lectins have been determined.

The crystal structure of physalis mottle virus has been determined. A method for accurately predicting the temperature of maximal stability of proteins from structure or sequence, has been developed. Models for 3,4 and 5 standard B-sheet structures have been designed and synthesised and the NMR structure of the 4 stranded sheet has been determined.

Gene targeting, genetic disorders and genetic diversity

The polymorphic microsatellite $(CA)_n$ markers of Diacama ceylonese have been cloned and characterized. The novel DNA binding properties of meiosis specific HOP1, a component of yeast synaptonemal complex has been elucidated.

The full length cDNAs for two different MADS box genes for rice OSMADS1 and OSMADS2 have been cloned and their temporal and spatial RNA expression patterns studied in the developing rice inflorescence. DNA isolated from the members of 3 families of an endogenous group was used to asses the level of autozygosity in these samples using X-chromosome markers. DD-RTPCR analysis of RNA from first trimester (FTD) and term placenta revealed several differentially expressed genes.

One of them was exclusively expressed in FTP and was identified as T-Plastin which is known to be involved in neoplastic growth. A 6.5 kb DNA containing cucumber chloroplast tRNA^{Ile} and tRNA^{Ala} genes has been sequenced Identification of signal transduction pathways of phytohormones using the cucumber system has been initiated. Signal transduction pathway of cytokinin may involve Ca^{2+} mediation.

Molecular analysis of PAH gene in 3 families manifesting PKU has been done and detects in the coding region were identified. Blastomere biopsy from cleavage-stage rodent embryo is being standardized.

The molecular analysis of the bglto genes in different members of the Shigella genes shows considerable rearrangement at the genomic level. Deregulation of post transcriptional destabilization pathways of PDGF-BmRNA mediated by the 3' UTR primarily contributes to the activation of PDGF-BmRNA in a variety of tumour cells. A eukaryotic promoter linked to a G-free casette was targeted to rat liver by receptor mediated gene delivery and the transcripts detected by dot-blot and RT-PCR analysis. Thus the same promoter constructs can now be examined in in vitro transcription assays as well as by in vivo gene targeting.

Biotech facilities

Animal house facilities

CDRI, Lucknow. The breeding unit of this facility maintained nearly 34,000 animals comprising 25 different strains. It supplied 57,244 animals within the institute for use in various projects and 3,054 animals were supplied to 28 different organisations throughout India and Nepal.

Three new inbred strains of mice (Bal b/ c, SJL/j and NZB/j) were produced. A new strain of white hamster was developed.

A total of 2563 samples from different animals, pellets, bedding materials and water were screened for microbiological monitoring and 2552 samples for parasitological monitoring. Radiological, haematological and parasitological monitoring of 163 monkeys of the institute and 36 monkeys of AIIMS, New Delhi were done.

Three cell lines were maintained and 3 new ones were procured. Newly developed white hamster was further characterised using biochemical markers. Rhesus babies born through breeding were successfully weaned.

NIN, Hyderabad: A total of 43,000 animals were bred and 33,809 were supplied. A total of Rs. 21.24 lakhs was generated as income. The characterisation of WNIN/Ob (obese rats with euglycemia) and WNIN-GR-Ob (obese rats with impaired glucose tolerance) was completed. On the applied aspect, the WNIN/GR-Ob rats seems to be an excellent model on diet induced diabetes. Preliminary data on the therapeutic effect of curry leaves using these rats was encouraging as the animals showed 40-60 percent reduction of blood glucose levels on short term treatment.

The preliminary data available on the unique wild white rat detected in the facility was compared to albino rats. These rats are not albinos as they showed the presence of tyrosinase, a key enzyme for melanin conversion, which is absent in the Wistar strain of rats which is an albino.

Centre for genetic engineering and strain manipulation at Madurai Kamaraj University, Madurai

Research and development activities of the centre are

aimed at production of biological products and process optimization using prokaryotic system. It also envisages development of improved strains of bacteria by gene manipulation. Production of antitumour antibiotic daunorubicin was started by incorporating indigenous technology. The expensive production process has been changed in order to bring down the cost of production. It has been shown that the antibiotic daunorubicin could be produced by growing Streptomyces peucetius in phoshate buffered media containing sesame oil cake (SOC) as carbon source in 100 litre pilot scale production facility. Daunorubicin yield increased 5.4 fold in SOC medium, compared to maltose containing medium. The technique is being perfected for commercial production.

Daunorubicin producing strain of Streptomyces grows in chitin as a carbon source and produces extracellular chitinase enzyme. The enzyme has been purified to homogeneity by ion exchange chromatography and gel filtration chromatography. N-terminal amino acid sequence shows homology to Streptomyces lividans chitinase. Cloning of the chitinase gene is progress. Chitinase genes are used in various applications including insect control. Genetic instability in Streptomyces is characterized by deletion and amplification of the genome. The extent of deletion in spontaneous Cml^s Arg^+ mutants of Streptomyces lividans was found to be about 600kb inferring that the genome of the organism exists both as linear chromosome and circular DNA.

National facility for Biochemical Engineering Research and Process Development Centre (BERPDC) at IMTECH, Chandigarh

The facility was utilised for in-house projects for streptokinase fermentation, hydantoinase production and production of lipase, naringinase, DNA polymerase etc. This has provided both scientific interaction and benefits to other research groups. During the year, the fermentation and downstream processing facilities of this center were utilized by different agencies for optimisation of a process to concentrate industrial waste having high COD using reverse osmosis system; for optimisation of fermentation process parameters for the production of phytase by Aspergillus niger; for production of cellmass for enzyme isolation and for scaling up the process for secondary metabolite production.

The centre organised a Workshop on Industrial Fermentation and Downstream Processing from 2-13th March, 1998. It was attended by 15 participants from all over India and was self-financing.

National facility for biological and organic mass spectrometry, IICT, Hyderabad

A National facility for Biological and Organic Mass Spectrometry along with Matrix Assisted Laser Desorption lonisation (MALD/ TOF) facility was established through joint funding by DBT and DST at the Indian Institute of Chemical Technology, Hyderabad for use by researchers in structure determination of various biological molecules.

7

Biotechnology Information System Network

Large amount of DNA sequence data and other biological research data involving micro sequencing of proteins, 2-D gel patterns of proteins and polypeptides, metabolic pathways, physical and genetic maps of the organisms, cell line information, and microbial strain data, etc. have revolutionized the field of bioinformatics. Projects such as Species-2000, global plant check list, information on release of organisms in environment, and Animal Virus Information, etc. are producing hard data at the species level in multimedia format. The rate of growth of biological data is estimated to be more than 200 million base pairs per year.

The database content itself is doubling in size approximately every year. This enormous growth of biological data and its availability-in the major international databases is serving as a source of knowledge to life scientists. The whole paradigm shift in molecular biology towards data intensive research in search of useful genes, is basically due to the fact that the genetic data is becoming the major driving force in drug discovery, protein engineering, design of new molecules, and other related areas. The large store of biological data holds the promise to serve as the "Discovery Super Highway" for innovations in biotechnology through a process of analysis and transformation of molecular and structural data into biological knowledge.

Bioinformatics has acquired great importance due to its applications in the Genome projects. The target of decoding the three billion base pairs of the human DNA has become achievable only through the use of various innovative techniques and methods evolved by bioinformatics scientists. Bioinformatics has become an essential component of biotechnology based product and process development. The process of drug design and development is expensive and time consuming. The application of the tools and techniques of bioinformatics has resulted in the reduction of cost in the development of drugs. This aspect has a tremendous impact on the society. If a newly discovered drug is life saving, the gains are not only in terms of financial savings but also in, saving lives.

Biotechnology Information Systems (BTIS)—A national bioinformatics network

India was one of the first countries that had taken steps in establishing a nation wide Bioinformation System. The Department had taken this major leap forward after carrying out both micro and macro level planning with a mission to make India a leader in Bioinformatics. The Biotechnology Information System (BTIS) Programme was launched to harness the scientific knowledge in various inter-disciplinary areas of biotechnology. The programme is comprised of a distributed database and network system namely Biotechnology Information System Network (BTISnet). Under the BTISnet, 10 Distributed Centres and 38 sub-centres have been established in universities and institutes engaged in active research in the area of biotechnology.

In the current year, 15 new sub-centres were established in various universities and research institutes which were running major biotechnology programmes and projects. As a consequence of these initiatives, computer literacy and awareness among Bio-scientists has grown significantly. Large number of public domain databases with regular updates, in the area of molecular biology and genetic engineering have become available to scientists in India. NICNET provided the initial connectivity to all these centres through V-SAT. Internet connection became available through NICNET and ERNET, making the bioinformatics centres and sub-centres, hubs of activities related to data access, data analysis and modelling. Major databanks such as Animal Virus Information System, have been developed in the country.

Software tools for sequence, analysis, on work stations were developed in the country in the form of software packages and made available at a low cost to various universities, colleges and research institutes. India became a node on the Microbial Strain Data Network, Hybridoma Data Bank, EMBnet and Asian Pacific Countries Bioinformatics Network. Under the FARM programme, India was chosen to be the nodal country to provide training and coordination of the Information network for agricultural scientists in eight countries belonging to South East Asia. Shortage of manpower in this new area has been tackled by conducting a large number of short term courses by several centres and long term courses at two selected centres— University of Pune and Madurai Kamaraj University.

DBT with the help of NIC is updating connectivity by providing V-SATs of 64/128 KBPS bandwidth to selected centres. The network has established links among scientists in organizations involved in R&D and manufacturing activities in biotechnology. Since its establishment, the BTISnet is providing a single major information resource in the country covering several inter-disciplinary areas of biotechnology. The network has also established linkages with various national and international information networks through the modern computer and communication systems by implementing several network services such as e-mail, discussion groups on the Internet and other internet based facilities for access to worldwide resources in biotechnology.

The network approach has been very useful in the successful implementation of the project, as it has established a link between diverse groups of scientists working in various interdisciplinary areas of biotechnology. The network encouraged sharing of knowledge and greater interaction amongst the scientific community irrespective of their geographical locations in the country.

Services

The BTIS Network and its constituent centres are providing the following services:

(a) Handling and management of biological data, including its organization, control, linkages, analysis etc.,

(b) Communication among people, projects, and institutions engaged in the biological research and applications. The communication may include e-mail, file transfer, remote login, computer conferencing, electronic bulletin boards, or establishment of web based information resources,

(c) Organization, access, search and retrieval of biological information, documents, and literature and

(d) Analysis and interpretation of biological data through computational approaches including visualization, mathematical modeling, and development of algorithms for highly parallel processing of complex biological structures.

BTIS secretariat

The BTIS secretariat, positioned at the Bioinformatics Division at DBT, is the coordinating and developing organization of the Department of Biotechnology. It is entrusted with the following functions.

1. Coordination of existing information facilities and services to evolve a National Biotechnology Information System in the field of biotechnology.
2. System design and further development of the system.
3. To evolve a national bio-information policy.
4. Evolving standards and guidelines.
5. Organization of new information centres and assistance to existing units.
6. Support for development of information analysis tools and databanks.
7. Support to training programmes.
8. Support to R&D programmes on bioinformatics.
9. Public relations work and information promotion.
10. Advisory services and consultancy.
11. Collaboration with international agencies.
12. Advising the Government on collaboration with other countries in the field of bioinformatics.
13. Advising on the IPR issues related to Biological Databases
14. Control of Annual BTIS budget.

Apex Biotechnology Information Centre (BTIC)

The Apex Centre at DBT is responsible for coordinating, organizing and providing information services at national level covering a wide range of subjects in large sectors of national endeavour in biotechnology. It is coordinating the activities of other Distributed Information Centres and plans to provide a nation-wide communication network between the DICs and other Sub-Centres. It also coordinates linkages and cooperation with external sources in bioinformatics including documentation and information centres abroad.

The BTIC has the mandate to continuously assess information requirements in biotechnology and organize creation of necessary computer and communication infrastructure to provide bioinformatics support to the national community of users spread across the country.

It has endeavoured to establish national databases in the country in collaboration with several national and international agencies and has encouraged bilateral and international collaboration in bioinformatics. It has also initiated major research projects in bioinformatics for creating synergy for developmental activities in bioinformatics.

It promotes standards for databases, data exchange and nomenclature for molecular biology data in order to facilitate sharing of such data amongst laboratories on a national and international scale.

BTIC is processing the development of a web-site to provide a window to all the bioinformatics resources in the country and would provide appropriate linkages with all the centres established under this programme.

Distributed Information Centres (DICs)

Nine DICs have been established with the task of providing subject/discipline-oriented information to all institutions belonging to the branch and other institutions and individual users interested in a particular subject related to biotechnology. These are listed below:

Genetic engineering

1 . Indian Institute of Science, Bangalore

2. Madurai Kamraj University, Madurai

3. Bose Institute, Calcutta

4. Jawaharlal Nehru University, New Delhi.

Animal cell culture and virology

5. University of Poona, Pune.

Plant tissue culture, photosynthesis and plant molecular biology

6. Indian Agricultural Research Institute, New Delhi.

Oncogenes, reproduction physiology, cell transformation, nucleic acid and protein sequences

7. Centre for Cellular & Molecular Biology Hyderabad.

Immunology

8. National Institute of Immunology, New Delhi.

Protein modeling and protein engineering

9. Institute of Microbial Technology, Chandigarh.

Distributed information sub-centres

A large number of R&D institutions and universities form a chain of distributed Sub-Centres set up in geographic locations affiliated to each DIC in their respective area. Thus, the distributed Sub-Centres provide an added dimension of access and diffusion of information across the network.

Twenty-three sub-centres have already been established at the following locations:

Location	Area of Specialization
Aligarh Muslim University, Aligarh macromolecular conformation	Protein & Nucleic Acid Sequences,
All India Institute of Medical Sciences,	Medical Biotechnology
New Delhi Anna University, Chennai	Production of Biologicals and Bioprocess Engineering.
Assam Agricultural University, Jorhat	Agricultural Biotechnology
Banaras Hindu University, Varanasi	Environmental&Agricultural Biotechnology
BERC, IIT Delhi, New Delhi	Biochemical Engineering & Biotech.
Biotech Consortium India Ltd. (BCIL), New Delhi	Commercial' Biotechnology
Calcutta University, Calcutta	Microbial Biotechnology and Medical Biotechnology
Cancer Research Institute, Bombay	Cancer Research and Cell Biology
Central Drug Research Institute, Lucknow	Drugs & Pharmaceuticals
Central Institute of Freshwater Aquaculture, Aquaculture, Bhubaneswar	Aquaculture

Devi Ahilya Vishwavidyalaya, Indore	Enzyme purification and Plant Molecular Biology
Guru Nanak Dev University, Amritsar	Plant Biotechnology
Indian Veterinary Research Institute, Izatnagar	Veterinary Biotechnology
Kerala Agricultural University, Thrissur	Agricultural Biotechnology
M.S. University Baroda, Baroda	Microbial Technology & Genetic Engineering
National Dairy Research Institute, Karnal	Dairy Science & Biotechnology
National Environmental Engineering Res. Institute, Nagpur	Environmental Biotechnology
National Institute of Oceanography, Goa	Marine Biotechnology
Pondicherry University, Pondicherry	Plant and Animal Biotechnology
Tamilnadu Agricultural University, Coimbatore	Plant Molecular Biology
Tamilnadu Veterinary & Animal Sciences Univ., Madras	Veterinary, Animal & Fisheries Biotechnology
University of Delhi (South Campus), New Delhi	Membrane Biology

New initiatives

Establishment of New Bioinformatics Centres: Fifteen new bioinformatics centres are being established this year at the following locations:

— Himachal Pradesh University, Shimla, Himachal Pradesh.

— Mahatma Gandhi Institute of Medical Sciences, Wardha, Maharashtra.

— North Eastern Hill University, Shillong, Meghalaya.

— Birla Institute of Scientific Research, Jaipur, Rajasthan.

— —Punjab Agricultural University, Ludhiana, Punjab.

— Bharathidasan University, Tiruchirappalli, Tamil Nadu.

— Indian Institute of Technology, Kharagpur, West Bengal.

— Banasthali Vidyapeeth, Banasthali, Rajasthan.

— Central Institute of Medicinal & Aromatic Plants, Lucknow, Uttar Pradesh.

— Central Sericulture Research & Training Institute, Mysore, Karnataka.

— Dr.Y.S.Parmar University of Horticulture & Forestry, Solan, Himachal Pradesh.

— Tropical Botanic Garden & Research Institute, Tiruvananthapuram, Kerala.

— Regional Research Laboratory, Jammu, Jammu & Kashmir.

— G. B. Pant University of Agriculture & Technology, Pantnagar, Uttar Pradesh.

— M. S. Swaminathan Research Foundation, Chennai, Tamil Nadu.

Augmentation of Infrastructure facilities at the existing Sub-DICs: Augmentation of Bioinformatics Infrastructure facilities has been carried out for some of centres to cope up with the increasing demand and technology trends in Information Technology (IT). All existing Sub-DICs under BTIS have been provided computer server for networking.

National Node of EMBnet at CDFD: The mirror site of EMBL was established last year at CDFD, Hyderabad. This EMBnet node at CDFD achieved the status of national node from its previous status of the associate node of EMBnet.

R&D Projects: New R&D Projects in Bioinformatics were initiated to build up capacity in database management, software and development of tools for analysis of biological data. The projects have been initiated in the areas of molecular modelling tools for biologically active domains, neural networks for epitope and paratope designing and a database of biotechnology industries and institutions in SAARC countries

CODATA '98: The International Conference and General Assembly meeting of CODATA '98 was held in Delhi, India for the first time in recognition of the country's strength in various interdisciplinary aspects of bioinformatics. CODATA '98 has been organised with the active participation of BTIS centres. Over 20 countries participated in this event.

Local Area Network (LAN): State-of-the-art Local Area Network (LAN) was established by the Apex Centre in DBT to provide full Internet services to all scientific officers of the department. More than 70 nodes have been interconnected through this LAN. All officers and sections were provided computers, which were networked through LAN. Full INTERNET access facility is available on several nodes of the LAN. The LAN is a switch-based technology with a dedicated high-speed connection to each node.

Computerisation in DBT: In keeping with the national mandate for developing efficiency through computerisation, the NIC Computer Cell undertook the following major activities during the year in close co-ordination with BTIC and other scientific divisions.

— Conversion of major operational software in the department like Project Management System, Biofertiliser System Budget and Expenditure and Payroll to make them Y2K compliant so that year 2000 will not be a hinderance to execute these packages.

— Upgradation of the Project Registry Software to provide additional queries and reports. A bi-lingual acknowledgement facility has been implemented on pre-printed stationary to promote the usage of Hindi.

— Modification of the payroll software to incorporate recommendations of the 5th pay commission.

— Initiation of computerisation of certain administrative activities as per the directives of Cabinet.

— Development of a database on Institutional Biosafety Committee (IBSC) with a view to monitor the recommendations of IBSCs and their implementation in consultation with Genetic Engineering Advisory Committee (GEAC)

— Development of an Information System on Mission Mode Project on Technology Development and Demonstration of Biofertilisers.

National facilities on interactive graphics and molecular modelling

Five biocomputing facilities under the umbrella of "National Facilities on Interactive Graphics and Molecular Modelling" have been established with the task of providing computational support to scientists working in the area of molecular structure modelling, 3D structures, active site modelling, crystal structures, conformational analysis, protein and DNA structures and interactions, homology studies and like. These biocomputing centres are located at the following institutions:

1. Indian Institute of Science, Bangalore
2. CCMB, Hyderabad
3. MKU, Madurai
4. University of Poona, Pune
5. Bose Institute, Calcutta

A new facility for molecular modelling has been set up at JNU, New Delhi, as a core facility to support biocomputational requirements of the university. The scientists at the university have developed automatic methods for comparing macromolecular structure and identifying regions that, are structurally similar.

They are also engaged in research in related areas in the construction of databases, modeling of structures for molecular recognition and drug design. Therefore, a powerful computational facility suitable for visualization of molecules and their structures was a well-timed programme. The facility at JNU is being used for the following:

Database searching of protein data bank for structural similarity studies, classification of Brookehaven structural database into homologous protein structural families, multiple structural alignment of proteins, homology modelling of protein structures, generation of mutation data matrix based on structural alignment, docking algorithm for molecular recognition, identification of similar active sites in any given protein family and drug design.

Human resource development in bioinformatics

Advanced Diploma Course in Bioinformatics At MKU, Madurai; University of Pune, Pune: DBT has initiated long term academic courses in bioinformatics leading to the award of an advanced diploma in bioinformatics. The courses are being conducted at Madurai Kamaraj University, Madurai and University of Poona, Pune. There has been a sudden spurt in the demand of such professionals by small size gene-hunting companies. Many of the larger pharmaceutical companies are now seeing real value in gene mapping and sequence data and have started attracting experts from academia. These courses are designed to impart knowledge in the inter-disciplinary aspects of bioinformatics covering basics of molecular biology and computer science. In the light of these developments, the efforts started by DBT are likely to lead towards generation of employment opportunities.

Training/Workshops/Long term Courses in Bioinformatics : Apex bioinformatics centre has brought out a National Training Calendar of the training programmes conducted by various centres and sub-centres. A number of workshops and training programmes were conducted under the BTIS programme on the use of computers and databanks in modern biology and biotechnology Considering the importance of the subject, some institutions and university departments have introduced a formal course of training in bioinformatics as a 3- credit one-semester course in their existing post-graduate programmes in biotechnology. DBT has initiated a long-term academic course in bioinformatics leading to the award of an advanced diploma in bioinformatics. The course is being conducted by Madurai Kamaraj University, Madurai. A similar course has been started at the University of Poona.

Dissemination of information usage resources

BTIS resources are now being used by about ten thousand scientists from all parts of the country. The services include analysis of biological data, bibliographic references to published literature in biotechnology (including patents data), software development for computationally intensive problems in biology such as molecular modelling, genome analysis, protein engineering for rational drug design, etc. The centres have started their own newsletters and other SDI services, which have become very popular.

8

International Collaboration Programmes

There has been a steady increase in the number of International Cooperation programmes in biotechnology with both the developed and developing countries. The ongoing bilateral programmes have been with Germany, Poland, Russia, Sri Lanka, Switzerland, Sweden, UK and USA while programmes of cooperation with Cuba, France, Japan, Israel, Italy, Tunisia and Vietnam are being finalised. New initiatives have been taken with Australia, Brazil, Hungary, Khazakistan, Korea, Norway, Mexico, Netherland, Romania, Slovenia, Singapore and Thailand. Multilateral programmes are also being strengthened amongst the SAARC, G-15 and ASEAN countries.

Bilateral collaborations

Ongoing collaborations

The Second Meeting of the Indo-German Committee on Science & Technology held at Ooty on April 28-29, 1998, identified biotechnology as an important emerging area for cooperation between the two countries. To step up the level of cooperation it was agreed to enter into a MOU between DBT and GBF for which thrust areas of cooperation have been identified. A draft agreement has already been exchanged. The Committee also agreed to consider setting up a Technological and Incubator Centre for Technology Development and Technology Transfer in

Biotechnology to take up product and process development in biologicals and diagnostics, transfer of technology arrangements and start up companies. The concept paper on the centre and details would be discussed at next meeting.

Under Indo-FRG Agreement in S&T, five joint projects implemented between 1988-90, were completed during the year 1994-95. During the year, three projects have been implemented namely:

Indo-German Cooperation in the field of human genome research and medical genetics at GNDU, Amritsar and Institute of Human Genetics, Berlin, Germany: The research on various families of congenital cataract have resulted in localisation of the gene for cerulean cataract with sutural opacities in one family. The breakthrough came in the case of a large autosomal dominant, 5-generation, congenital cataract family with more than 30 affected individuals. Screening was done for 10 different important loci for congenital cataract on chromosomes. The gene was mapped on the long arm of chromosome 22 using microsatellite markers. Strong linkage was noted at the region close to B-crystallin gene cluster which code for important ens proteins. Further screening of these genes suggested a CAG TAG mutational changes which may have led to the creation of a stop codon and hence chain termination resulting in truncation of the protein by 51 amino acids. Genome wide screening in another large congenital cataract family is in progress.

One hundred and nine new cases investigated for genetic studies included 16 cases of Retinitis Pigmentosa, 65 cases of Congenital Cataract, 8 cases of Marfan's Syndrome, 14 cases of High Myopia and 6 cases of other eye disorders. The detailed medical history of all the patients was recorded and blood samples of 130 patients of the above mentioned categories have been collected and stored. The isolation of DNA from these samples is underway and preliminary analyses have been carried out on these patients.

An Assistant Geneticist was trained for three months at Microsatellite Centre, Institute of Human genetics, Humboldt University, Berlin in linkage analysis for various gene localisation studies. Three scientists including Prof. Karl Sperling, Director, Institute of Human Genetics, Humboldt University, Berlin, Germany visited the Centre for conducting joint training programmes and discuss strategies for future research. A site visit has been made to review the programme.

Growth/control, cell shape and tumorigenesis studies at Devi Ahilya Vishva Vidhyalaya, Indore and German Cancer Research Centre, Heidelberg: In Drosophila, a variety of tumour suppressor genes were identified as recessive mutations which induce tumorous growth in target organ/cell types such as the imaginal discs brain or blood cells. An important member of this class of genes in drosophila is the lethal giant larvae (IgI) tumour suppressor gene.

The German collaborator, Prof. Bernard Mechler had earlier cloned this gene and is further characterising it for various cellular functions. The Indian collaborator has been characterising the developmental role of this tumour-suppressor gene. Collaboration includes identifying new members of the genetic circuitry which partake in the IgI mediated tumour suppression. The experimental strategy adopted for investigation include genetic screens for new second site mutations which enhance or suppress the Igl mutant phenotype. Two mutagenesis screens are being used for this purpose. One of them is chemical mutagenesis while the other involves P-mutagenesis.

The mutagenized chromosome would be tested for their ability to enhance or suppress the phenotype of an engineered Igl allele, which carry a point mutation conferring it a temperature sensitive phenotype. This temperature-sensitive allele has been generated in the laboratory of the German collaborator and carries a known point mutation in the Igl coding domain. The mutagenized line which displays enhancement or suppressor of the lgl^{ts} phenotype would be further characterised to localise the genes of interest and eventually clone them. A conservative estimate shows that between 15-20 genes are likely to interact with Igl and be a part of the genetic pathway involved in IgI mediated tumour suppression.

Rapid detection of seafood associated pathogens using molecular techniques at College of Fisheries, Mangalore and University of Wurzburg,Wurzburg, Germany: The project commenced in September 1998. Work has been initiated on development and evaluation of PCR based methods for rapid detection of Salmonella contamination of seafoods. Hin and H-I genes are involved in the control of phase variation of Salmonella and are present in all motile Salmonella species including Styphi, S.paratyphi, S.typhimurium and S.enteritidis. Oligonucleotide primers were synthesised based on the nucleotide sequence of these genes and these primers are currently being evaluated for rapid detection of Salmonella species in seafoods. Prof. Dr. W.Goebel, the German counterpart in the project visited Mangalore in December 1998 and discussed the programme of research and gave two seminars on molecular approaches to detection of Listeria monocytogenes in clinical and food samples.

Indo-polish

As a follow up of the seven member Polish delegation

visit to India in April 1997, four new projects in the area of Medicinal and Aromatic Plants and Medical Biotechnology have been developed. One project has already been implemented while three projects have been peer reviewed and are pending clearances from the ministries concerned of the Government of India.

The projects implemented, include: "Withania somnifera: in vitro propagation, isolation and microbial transformation with anolides and evaluation of immunomodulatory properties and therapeutic potential" at Nil and the Department of Botany and Pharmaceutical Botany, Warsaw and Department of Pharmacolognosy, Medical Academy, Lubnin, Poland.

Three projects under consideration are: "Elaboration of effective chromatography methods of analysis for chemotaxonomic investigations of medicinal plants and micropreparative isolation of components of standards and elucidation of molecular structure" at TBGRI and Medical Academy, Lublin, Poland; "Bioproduction of Camptothecin and related Plant-Specific anti-cancer compounds using tissue cultures" at TBGRI and The Warsaw Medical Academy, Poland; and "The development of enzymatic process for the transformation of isoprenoids" at RRL, Jammu-Tawi and Polish Academy of Sciences, Poland.

Indo-Sri Lanka

As a follow up of a Joint Indo-Sri Lanka. At the Workshop of experts in biotechnology held at the National Institute of Immunology, New Delhi in January, 1998, ten specific projects in seven priority areas were identified for developing complete proposals. Two projects have already been implemented. The progress made in the projects is as under:

Non-cellulosic polysaccharides of lesser known

millets and grain legume and their physiological effects; Jawaharlal Nehru University, New Delhi and CISIR, Colombo: This multicentric project was initiated in May 1998 to identify selected non-cellulosic polysaccharides in food grains especially millets and grain legumes; use of physiological studies to identify active principles responsible for hypocholesterolemic and hypoglycemic effects; characterise key enzymes in the pathway of bioactive non-cellulosic polysaccharides; develop protocols for regeneration and transformation of millets and grain legumes; identification and cloning of genes for the key enzymes and development of transgenics for higher levels of bioactive principles. Preliminary analysis and estimation of beta-glucan from a few legumes for selecting the plant system have been conducted from germinated seeds of pea, mung bean, cicer, soybean and cajanus and in leaf tissue from pea, cicer and mung bean. Since cicer, mung bean and soybean were found to be rich in beta-glucan, these species were adopted for callus cultures. Attempts were also made to produce callus from pea and Cajanus to enhance beta-glucan content in these species. Seeds were surface sterilised with 0.1% $HgCl_2$ and inoculated in basal MS medium for germination in dark. Parts of five to seven day old seedlings were used as explants. Nodes, internodes, young leaves and mature cotyledons of soybean were inoculated in two different basal media (MS and 135) with BAP. Callusing was observed within 10-15 day with mature cotyledons. Callus is being inoculated in different media for analysis of beta-glucan. Suspension cultures are also being maintained to optimise conditions for induction of the enzyme.

Use of molecular and cytotaxonomic techniques to study Anopheles culicifacies complex and its relationship to malaria transmission in India and Sri Lanka at MRC, Delhi and IFS, Candy, Sri Lanka: Two surveys were carried out in Rameshwaram island of Ramanathapuram district, Tamil Nadu State, India. Examination of male mitotic chromosomes from neurogonial cells of IVth instar larvae of isofemale lines established from these collections revealed the existence of both acrocentric and submetacentric Y-chromosome karyotypes in A.culicifacies population. The male mitotic and meiotic preparations were documented. Mosquitoes from acro and submetacentric lines were stored for molecular analysis. The submetacentric form has been identified as species E in A.culicifacies complex, whereas the acrocentric forms is species B. The results have been communicated as a research paper entitled "Evidence for a new malaria vector species, species E within the Anopheles culicifacies complex".

H.E. Mr. Batty Weerakoon, Minister for Science and Technology, Sri Lanka visited the Department and discussed with the Hon'ble Minister of Science and Technology, areas for cooperation in Science and Technology. As a follow up, a draft on Programme of Cooperation to be signed between two countries in the area of biotechnology has been sent to Sri Lankan side for comments.

Indo-Sweden

Five projects were pursued under the Indo-Swedish Collaboration in Biotechnology. Two projects at IIT were terminated in June, 1996. Remaining three projects were evaluated by international experts and are in phase two extension, one each at CFTRI, Mysore, NCL, Pune and PROMED, Chennai. In addition, one new proposal entitled "Integrated Biotechnological Approach for the Rejuvenation of Heavy Metal Mine Spoil Dumps and Mine Lands" at NEERI, Nagpur, has been implemented.

Tree Tissue Culture at National Chemical Laboratory, Pune and Swedish University for Agricultural Sciences, Uppsala, Sweden: Tissue culture studies were conducted on economically important Indian pines. Auxiliary bud proliferation, rooting and hardening of plants have been achieved in Pinus caribaea and P.kesiya, using explants from mature trees. Similarly success has been obtained in regeneration of adventitious buds from mature embryos of Pinus roxburghii and P.wallichiana via organogenesis and induction of somatic embryogenesis from immature zygotic embryos of P.roxburghii. Studies were also conducted on scaling up of Picea cell lines in bioreactors.

During the visit of Indian scientists to Swedish University of Agricultural Sciences, Uppsala, Sweden, studies were carried out on biolistic transformation of Pinus roxburghii and Pinus contorta using cotyledons as the target system. Successful transformation and expression of reporter gene driven by the ubiquintin promoter was obtained even 23 days after gene bombardment. Work was also carried out on cryopreservation of meristems of teak (Tectona grandis L.) and success has been achieved in cryopreservation of meristems and their survival.

Further studies during phase II are being concentrated on developing protocol for auxiliary bud proliferation and regeneration of plantlets from mature plants of Pinus roxburghii, control of contamination, sprouting, multiplication and rooting of buds and plantlet regeneration by organogenesis in mature zygotic embryos. For somatic embryogenesis, embryogenic cell lines have been initiated in Pinus roxburghii from megagametophytes containing immature zygotic embryos. Maturation and conversion of embryos have also been achieved.

"Cultivation of Microorganisms and Production of Lactic Acid by Fermentation" at Central Food

Technological Research Institute, Mysore and University of Lund, Sweden: The treatment of polypropylene matrix with chitosan was found more effective than treatment with PEI. Optimum concentration of chitosan for matrix treatment was determine . Molasses being a cheap source of carbon, the work on production of lactic acid by fermentation from cane molasses was initiated using L.delbrueckii. Experiments led to the development of a process in which yeast extract from nutrient medium is eliminated. 100% conversion of 10% initial sugar in 72 h was possible (in 10L fermentor experiments). The experiments at 50L fermentor scale gave satisfactory yields indicating that scale-up may not be a problem. Experiments at 10L fermentor level with glucose and starch hydrolysate as carbon source gave comparable lactic acid yields. Downstream processing for producing lactic acid and calcium lactate through crystallization and evaporation of treated fermented broth was worked out.

Removal of biomass by adjusting pH and heating, carbon treatment and crystallization are being optimized. Downstream processing developed, gave good quality calcium lactate (98% purity) and lactic acid of 50% concentration.

The work on Ion-exchange resin application for downstream processing was continued. In addition to Indian FF-IP and Indian N-IP from Ion-exchange, two more Ion-exchange resins namely Tulsion A-27 MP and Tulsion A-36 from Thermax Ltd. were also evaluated. Adsorption isotherms for all four resins were determined while Tulsion A-36 gave adsorption capacity of 500 mg lactic acid per gram of dry resin (highest), Indian FF-IP gave absorption capacity of 407mg/g of dry resin (lowest). The results indicated that use of Ion-exchange resin at large scale may not be feasible due to large quantity of water required for washing the column and limited adsorption capacity.

L.plantarum was used for the production of lactic acid bacteriocins active against a number of pathogens and food spoilers. The bacteriocin called Plantaracin was purified and characterized. Plasmid curing experiments suggested that bacteriocin in L.plantarum is chromosomal bound and has a molecular weight of 2500d.

Natural & Recombinant Proteins/ Enzymes for use in practical application (Biosensors) at Centre for Protein Engineering & Biomedical Research, Voluntary Health Service, Madras and University of Lund, Sweden: New polymers have been developed for use as modifiers in the covalent modification of enzymes. This can stabilize the enzymes to make them suitable for applications for routine use such as 'biosensors'. The modifiers newly developed/studied include activated disaccharides (sucrose, maltose and lactose) and Polyethyleneimine (PEI) derivatives of the disaccharides and succinylated and glutarylated -PEI. In addition other modifiers prepared include maltodextrin—modified enzymes e.g. bovine trypsin. The results show that PEI—sucrose made with a ratio 1:10 gives the best modifier. However, the disaccharides were better stabilizers than the PEI-disaccharide derivatives. Similarly succinylated - PEI was only a moderate stabilizer and glutarylated PEI produces an immobilized enzyme with the enzyme precipitating out after modification.

Modified -graphite for use in fabricating biosensor / analytical probes are now being developed. Efforts are on to make the surface of graphite receptive to coupling enzymes. These surfaces will be made either hydrophobic or hydrophilic by adsorbing spacer molecules such as sugars, polysaccharides or aliphatic diacids. These spacer molecules will later be activated by a) oxidizing the sugars or b) carbodimide activation of the - COOH groups in the diacids.

Indo-Swiss

Phase-III collaborative activities are being pursued at 6 Institutions in the country upto March, 1999. Planning for implementation of a new phase of bilateral collaboration in the area of Agriculture and Environment has resulted in short-listing of proposals. The new projects will be implemented from June, 1999.

Indo-UK

"Genetic and Molecular Analysis of Anthracyclin Antibiotics" at Madurai Kamaraj University: Studies were carried out for production of antitumour antibacterial daunorubicin by incorporating indigenous technology. It is already shown that daunorubicin could be produced by growing Streptomyces peucetius in phosphate buffered media containing sesame oil cake (SOC) as carbon source in 100 litre pilot scale production facility. Cost of production came down to 0.26% of the cost of HEPES buffered medium containing maltose as carbon source. Daunorubicin yield increased 5.4 fold in SOC medium, compared to maltose containing medium. The technique is being perfected for commercial production. Daunorubicin producing strain of Streptomyces grow in chitin as carbon source and produces extracellular chitinase enzyme. The enzyme has been purified to homogeneity by ion exchange chromatography and gel filtration chromatography N-terminal amino acid sequence shows homology to Streptomyces lividans chitinase. Cloning of the chitinase gene is in progress. Genetic instability in Streptomyces is characterized by deletion and amplification of genome. Research in this area showed that the genome of the organism exists both as linear chromosome and circular DNA.

A Memorandum of Understanding was signed in London on February 9, 1998 between the Department of Biotechnology and the Biotechnology and Biology

Scientific Research Council, United Kingdom for cooperation in biotechnology.

During the visit of a three member team of experts to UK from April 21-24, 1998, discussions were held to develop specific projects in the areas of chromosomal analysis; avian genetics; vaccine technologies; immunology of transmission of malaria; quality control and characterisation studies related to animal cell cultures. Specific themes were identified for the joint workshop in the area of animal biotechnology proposed to be held in New Delhi. Four pre-proposals have been developed and are under consideration of BBSRC.

Indo-USA

During the official visit of H.E. Dr. Donna E. Shalala, Secretary of Health and Human Services, Government of USA to India in November-December, 1997, a Joint Statement was signed on Expansion of Indo-US Collaboration on Contraceptive and Reproductive Health Research.

The First Meeting of the Joint Working Group of the Indo-US Initiative on Contraception and Reproductive Health Research held at the Department on March 23-24, 1998, identified specific collaborative opportunities between the two countries in the areas of Reversible Male Contraceptive Methods; Long Acting Injectables for Women; Physical and Chemical Barrier Methods for Contraception and STD Prevention; Basic and Applied Research on Immuno Contraception. The Group also discussed administrative and policy issues relating to implementation of the programme which included solicitation of proposals, time tables, review and approval mechanisms, protection of human and animal subjects, publications and intellectual property rights, project monitoring and evaluation, fiscal accountability, scientific interaction and funding considerations. The formats for submission of joint pre-proposals and final proposals were agreed to and priority areas notified. More than 23 proposals have been received for consideration of the joint working group meeting scheduled for April, 1999.

In continuation of the ongoing project at NII, New Delhi, three new projects have been implemented at IRR, Bombay. The projects include:

(a) Evaluation of anti-fertility effect of FSH binding inhibitor (FSHBI).

(b) Development of an in vitro screening system for evaluating the potencies of progesterones developed for therapeutic and contraceptive applications.

(c) Molecular cloning and antifertility effect of 26 KDA epididymal sperm maturation antigens.

The progress made in the ongoing project at NII, New Delhi is as under :

Evaluation of the efficacy of recombinant bonnet monkey ZP3 and its corresponding synthetic peptides to regulate fertility in primates; National Institute of Immunology, New Delhi: Experiments were carried out to optimize the expression of the recombinant bonnet monkey ZP1 (rec-bmZP1), using different vectors systems. Expression of rec-bmZP1 was tightly regulated in SG13009 (pREP4) E.coli cells using pQE30 vector, where as a leaky expression was observed in the pRSET-A vector using BL21 (plysS) E.coli cells. However, lesser degree of the smaller molecular weight fragments were observed in case of rec-bmZP 1 expressed under T7 promoter using BL21 (plysS) cells. At the level of shake flask culture, 5 mg of recombinant protein could be isolated in a single step using metal affinity column from 1 litre of culture broth. The antibodies raised in female rabbits against rec-bmZP1 conjugated to diptheria toxoid (DT) recognized native bonnet monkey as well as human zonae. Human eggs treated with these antibodies, in vitro, showed a significant decrease in number of sperm bound and number of sperm penetrated as compared to preimmune serum treated oocytes. The efficacy of rec-bmZPI-DT conjugate for regulation of the fertility tested in 5 female baboons (Papic anubis) showed high antibody titres against rec-bmZPI and remained infertile for 5 to 6 cycles, though one animal became pregnant when titres were less than 2000 antibody units. Reversibility experiments reveal that out of 5 animals, three became pregnant when titres were allowed to fall below 1000 antibody units. Along with these, two control female baboons became pregnant in the first and second mating cycles respectively.

Collaborations under consideration

Indo-China

Discussions were held with Chinese Officials on cooperative programmes in biotechnology. Seven proposals are pending discussion at the Joint S&T Committee meeting.

Indo-France

A Letter of Intent for cooperation in biotechnology between the National Centre for Scientific Research (CNRS) and Department of Biotechnology was signed on January 25,1998 between the Government of India and Government of France. Potential areas for cooperation included silkworm genome, bioinformatics related to genome research, human X-chromosome, mapping of genes for idiopathies generalised epilepsy, leishmaniasis and pharmocogenetics. As a follow up of this agreement, a DBT, CSIR, CNRS, joint workshop was organised at CCMB, Hyderabad on April 6-7, 1998 and specific pre-proposals in above areas were developed. Full proposals in respect of four specific projects in biotechnology are being developed for implementation. A Memorandum of Understanding for Cooperation in Biotechnology between the Department of Biotechnology, India and the National Centre for Scientific Research (CNRS), France was signed in Paris on June 10, 1998. Specific programmes have been identified for joint R&D. The agreement also has a scope to expand collaboration to other areas of mutual interest.

Indo-Israel

As a follow up of the Indo-Israel meeting of experts on Human Genome Research held at IISc. Bangalore in November, 1997, four projects have been developed on specific themes for consideration for cooperation.

Indo-Italy

Interactions were made for cooperation in biotechnology A new project submitted by NCCS, Pune is under consideration for implementation. At the Joint Committee Meeting on S&T, exchange visits have been agreed in the areas of Genetics including Human Genetics and Vaccines and Diagnostics.

Indo-Japan

As a follow up of the fifth meeting of the Indo-Japan Joint Committee on Science & Technology held at New Delhi in December 1997, a project titled "understanding biochemical and molecular control of differentiation" developed at JNU, New Delhi has been reviewed and the same is under consideration for implementation in the next Joint Committee Meeting.

Indo-Tunisia

Proposals are being developed in the area of vaccine and diagnostics development, plant transformations, biological pesticides, microbial production of bioactive compounds and bioinformatics.

Association of south east Asia nations

Specific projects have been developed in the areas of plant biotechnology with Indian counterpart scientists. Three projects are under consideration for implementation.

Collaboration among the SAARC countries

The 15th meeting of the SAARC Technical Committee on Science & Technology held in September-October, 1997 agreed to the concept proposal on "SAARC Biotechnology Council" and recommended consideration of the document by the Standing Committee and Council of Ministers. The document submitted to the Standing Committee is under consideration by the Member-States. The document will be considered by S&T Ministers of the Members States in March, 1999. Specific projects are being developed in the areas of vaccines and diagnostics, plant transformation, medicinal and aromatic plants. Concept paper for this has already been exchanged.

G-15 activities

National gene banks at CIMAP, TBGRI and NBPGR initiated under the aegis of G-15 GEBMAP have been further strengthened. The gene banks have made significant progress in terms of collection and conservation of species. The department participated in the G-15 exhibition held during the Eighth G-15 Submit at Cario during May, 1998. Exhibits on various aspects of medicinal and aromatic plants were displayed. The proceedings of the G-15 symposium on "State-of-the-art strategies and technologies for conservation of medicinal and aromatic plants" held at Kuala Lumpur during September, 1998 is being published by the FIRM, Malaysia. Egypt is bringing out the GEBMAP Newsletter. The department has participated in the exhibition during the G-15 summit at Jamaica in February, 1999.

Farmer centred agriculture resource management (FARM)—UNDP/FAO

The Biotech Node coordinated the activities related to biotechnology demonstration and information exchange, networking etc. in all eight member countries.

DBT has been coordinating the implementation of activities at the National level in India at the 3 sites selected—Coastal (Arcot, Tamil Nadu), Mountain (Almora, UP), Arid (Alwar, Rajasthan). All proven biotechnologies (IPM, Micropropagation, Biofertilizer, etc.), are being effectively demonstrated in association with local farmers. The demonstrations are being conducted in an integrated manner in association with State Departments, Ministry of Agriculture land Ministry of Environment & Forestry.

The Biotech Node successfully documented the Field Demonstration Case studies of four countries -China, India, Philippines and Vietnam. In addition Technology Bulletins on the proven technologies ready for transfer and-adoption by the farmers have been published.

For the Bioinformatics activities a referral centre has been set up in DBT. A regional directory and database on the FARM activities is being consolidated. A database on TCDC experts is also being complied. The referral centre has been connected through Internet. E-mail connectivity has been provided to all focal persons including India. This is now being extended to connect the Chairpersons of the Country Coordination Committee in all member countries. E-mail database on FARM addresses is available. A regional database on FARM resource persons is being compiled for the Internet. A Directory of Resource Persons was made available through the Home Page. A database of all FARM publications has been prepared and linked to the Home Page. A database of the proven technologies, of all the member countries has been collected for the internet. Training Programmes have been held at three levels—scientists, trainers, local farmers. Farmer field schools and Melas were organized. Information material in local languages was distributed for awareness generation and technology dissemination. Approximately eighty farmers were trained for application and successful demonstration of need based rural biotechnologies.

A Regional Training and Workshop on "Application of Biotechnologies to rainfed Farming Communities including Bioindexing emphasizing participatory approach at Community Level" was organized at the MS Swaminathan Research Foundation, Chennai. The main aim of the workshop was to synthesize the biovillage experience of 8 member countries of FARM and also building the capacity of site working group members to handle biotechnologies including bioindexing. The participants were exposed to the bioinformatics network and access to databases. The workshop was very successful and attended by over 40 participants from member countries.

The Biotech Node organized a "Participatory Assessment and Planning" (PAP) training for the three sites - Almora, UP: Alwar, Rajasthan and Sriperumbudur, Tamil Nadu. The main objective was to introduce the PAP approach to the FARM field sites in India. It was felt necessary that the FARM field sites adopt PAP as a key approach to establish a Farmer Centred Resource Management development process at the community level. It aimed at bringing the farmer to the centre of the decision making process and help prepare their own development plans. The training was attended by 20 participants from the 3 FARM sites-Almora, Uttar Pradesh; Alwar, Rajasthan and Sriperumbudur, Tamil Nadu.

Jute biotechnology

Under the UNDP supported project "Biotechnology for improvement of fibre Jute Crop" activities continued in the first phase. The main objectives of the programme are development of an efficient enzymatic retting protocol, tagging of genes of significance with molecular markers, development of transgenic jute genotypes with desirable genes and their field testing.

An enzymatic retting protocol as an alternative to the conventional retting procedure was standardized at laboratory level. Process, optimization for upscaling at field level is underway. The protocol is being optimized to enable retting of both green and dried ribbons, reduce retting time and upgrade fibre quality, genetic lines with desirable character such as short stature, good fibre development and less lignin content. Studies are underway for gene tagging. Molecular markers have been developed. Genomic library is also being constructed. Regeneration protocol has been standardized, Genetic transformation protocol for gene transfer is being developed. Genes for development growth patterns and also those influencing lignin biosynthetic pathway are being isolated.

A programme for Phase II activities is being formulated which concentrates on developing a cost effective pilot scale enzymatic retting protocol, categorization of Jute genotype, molecular dissection of the genome and generation of novel genotypes and testing of genotypes in different agroclimatic regions.

9

Autonomous Institutions

National institute of immunology, New Delhi

The National institute of Immunology is contributing to generate competence in modern biology; nurture novel and appropriate biomedical technologies of special relevance to the nation. Meetings of the SAC, RAP, Governing Body and Society were held as per schedule. Major areas of research are immunology, infectious diseases, molecular design, reproduction and development.

Basic immunology

Factors involved in differential priming of T cells are being investigated, using Salmonella typhimurium (Stm) model. It has been shown that the live microbe induces a Th1 type of response while dead ones induced Th2 type response. The persistence of live Stm was not critical to the quality of the response. Pentoxylline and dibutyryl cyclic AMP are being investigated for their ability to enhance commitment to memory cells. Amongst the effector markers investigated, CD25 showed a qualitative change in the T cells primed with pentoxylline over those that did not receive pentoxylline.

An attempt to target antigens to antigen presenting cells via the scavenger receptor is being made to understand its consequences in terms of tolerance or antigenicity. Maleyl antigens induce sustained levels of peptide-MHC complexes leading to altered immunogenicity. T cell hybridoma lines were generated and rat antisera raised against them were found to be stimulatory.

Antigens have been tested for their ability to induce oral tolerance to Leishmania, Salmonella and E.coli. It appears that the frequency of exposure contributes to hyporesponsiveness in a dose-dependent manner. Intraperitoneal administration of soluble antigen was also found to induce hypo responsiveness.

Immunomodulatory products from plants were investigated for both immuno potentiating as well as imunosuppressive properties. NII-60 an isoquinoline isolated from Berberis aristata was shown to possess T cell inhibitory property as assayed by mixed lymphocyte reactions. Preliminary results are indicative of its efficacy in endotoxin induced septic shock. Studies have also indicated that this compound inhibits the hydrolysis of phosphatidyl inositol. A flavinoid from Azadorachta indica was seen to inhibit phospholipase A2, a player in inflammatory reaction and in the establishment of infection by certain parasites. Another glycoprotein from T.cordifolia was able to induce nitric oxide production by macrophages. These compounds may have the potential in combating certain infections or tumours.

Immunology & infectious diseases

Japanese encephalitis virus is being studied in order to determine the genetics of virulence. A less virulent Indian isolate of JEV as compared to the virulent prototype JaOAR has been isolated and partially sequenced. The 3' region of the non-coding regions of the structural gene between them was found to be dissimilar. The NS1 (nonstructurals) gene has been cloned under the SV40/ CMV promoter and is being optimized as a putative DNA vaccine.

A hammer-head ribozyme that could cleave the truncated 178 bp long HIV-1 envelope gene in vitro has been developed. Studies on the CCR5 coreceptor suspected to aid viral entry and progression of the disease have been carried out. One Indian was identified with a heterozygous mutant allele for the CCR5 coreceptor.

The role of adhesion molecules in metastasis of colon adenocarcinoma cell lines are being investigated. The anti-cancer peptide combination MuJ-7 developed earlier was seen to have antiangiogenic property. Several analogues have been synthesized and their cytotoxicity evaluated. Glioblastomas and neuroblastomas are also being subjected to peptide combinations as a possible therapeutic intervention.

The Mycobacterium w - based leprosy vaccine has progressed through immunotherapeutic and immunoprophylactic trials at Delhi and Kanpur dehat respectively. No relapse of the disease has been observed in the cases followed up for 1-7 years. Cellular immunity was upgraded in the vaccines. In the immuno-prophylactic phase of the clinical trials, 23,950 of the 29,420 household contacts identified were administered the vaccine/ placebo in double-blind trials. Two follow up surveys have been completed and the data is being analysed. Clearance of the Drug Controller for the manufacture of trial batches of the vaccine has been obtained. Cadila laboratories has taken up commercial production of this vaccine.

Multidrug resistance in tuberculosis is another area that is being explored with genetic probes. RFLP analysis have been translated into molecular epidemiology. PCR primers specific to RNA polymerase b-subunit have been designed to reveal mutations that lead to resistance against rifampicin. Most mutations have been found to be point mutations.

Molecular design

Glycosil inositol phospholipids (GIPLs) are crucial to survival and infectivity of Leishmania. By understanding the synthetic pathway, it is possible to delineate points of intervention in the parasite's life cycle either chemically or immunologically. For this, isolation and characterisation of GIPLs is being carried out. The precursors for GIPLs were biosynthesized and incorporated into promastigote cultures. GIPLs & lipophosphoglycan have been isolated and chemically characterized. The presence of a link in either the lipid and GIPIs / LPG pathway is evident. This could be exploited for meaningful intervention.

For a site-specific drug delivery system, investigations were made on the prospects of targeting antisense molecules into vesicular stomatitis virus (VSV) infected cells using the scavenger receptor on the cells of the macrophage lineage. Poly G was used as an effective ligand to ferry antisense molecules into J774E cell line that were later infected with VSV. Drug targeting strategy was also employed to overcome multidrug resistance in human cancer cells.

Ribonucleases - restrictocin, human pancreatic ribonuclease (HPR) and eosinophil cationic protein (ECP) were under investigation for deciphering the mechanism of their action based on structure - function relationships. Tumour explants in nude mice treated to restrictocin-anti-TFR(scFv) could initiate necrosis of these tumours. By engineering a proteolytic site between the ligand and the toxin to free the toxin at the target site, efficiency of restrictocin immunotoxins was enhanced. Another immunotoxin made by coupling antihuman transferin receptor antibody to HPR was shown to be effective against a human T cell leukaemia cell line in a dose-dependent manner. It is believed that its cytotoxicity could be enhanced by enabling proper folding which could also prevent its interaction with cellular ribonuclease inhibitors of the target cell.

In the baculoviral expression system, the late gene transcription element was analysed. The hr1 sequence was mapped to its enhancer and ori functions. The motif of the host factor that binds to hr1 has been characterized. It was observed that hr1 was capable of enhancing reporter gene expression from non-baculoviral promoters in mammalian cells. The baculoviral anti-apoptotic gene p35 has also been studied. Oxidative stress-induced apoptosis could be neutralized by transfection with p35 gene inserts in Sf9 cell lines. Full length DNA of p35 has been cloned :o biochemically characterize the product.

In the cloning and expression of human growth hormone, the earlier strategy involving a histidine tag has been abandoned in favour of one without the tag. The yield has been found to be the same by the new method. The role of different signal sequences in the transport of cytosolic proteins into the periplasm in V.cholerae and E.coli were analysed using human fructose 1,6 bisphosphatase, a cytosolic protein.

Reproduction and development

A birth control vaccine for women based on hCG is being optimized. In order to achieve greater coverage, the immunogenicity of the vaccine formulation is being enhanced by the inclusion of T helper epitopes. Peptides derived from measles virus F protein, from influenza haemagglutinin and HIV reverse transcriptase have been investigated. Higher responses were generated by the peptide conjugates. Bonnet monkeys have been immunized with a selected cocktail vaccine preparation from these peptide conjugates, to assess their effectivity The problem of carder-mediated suppression encountered with the vaccine is also being mimicked in mice by sensitization with the carrier prior to immunization with the immunogen-carrier conjugate.

The zona pellucida of oocyte has been investigated as a potential antifertility vaccine candidate. Synthetic immunogens to B cell epitopes of zona pellucida (ZP) have been made and their immunogenicity evaluated. Bonnet ZP1 and ZP2 have been cloned and expressed. These recombinant proteins were used for immunization of primates, Animals immunized with recombinant ZP1 produced high titres and remained infertile. Antibodies generated by rZP2 immunization of rabbits recognized both native as well as recombinant bonnet ZP2. Human zona was also characterized using polyclonal antibodies generated against recombinant bonnet ZP1, ZP2 and ZP3. Dog zona pellucida 3 has been produced in a reactor and yielded 30mg/L of culture as against 4mg/L in a shake flask. This will be useful to control stray dog population.

A research programme aimed at producing transgenic animals has been initiated using, two reporter transgenes namely, green fluorescent protein (GFP) and neomycin resistance (Neor). Of the 64 pups born, five were positive for the transgene as confirmed by Southern blotting, PCR, sequencing, RT-PCR and germ-line transmission to F1 progeny. Similarly, the jellyfish green fluorescent protein gene was also introduced into mouse embryos. Some of the microinjected embryos were also cultured in vitro into blastocysts. These are being examined for transgene expression. A transgenic mouse model for hepatitis B is also underway. Transgene constructs involving the X gene of hepatitis B virus have been made. Four of the 165 pups born have the transgene insert.

Ovine growth hormone was cloned and expressed with a view to create a perennial source of this product at an affordable price. Expression in E.coli earlier yielded just 2.3 mg/ L. By adopting high cell density fed batch system of fermentation, a yield 3.2gm of the hormone was obtained. This is the highest yield ever reported for hormones.

Other activities

The doctoral programme of the Institute continued to receive the best talent from across the country. Research collaborations with laboratories overseas and within the country continued. A few collaborative research proposals from overseas laboratories were received.

The Institute continued as a WHO Collaborating Centre for Research and Training in Immunology, on FAO's Asian Network on Biotechnology as Applied to Animal Reproduction and Health, UNESCO's Centre for Molecular and Cellular Biology, as a Centre of Excellence of the Third World Academy of Sciences and as a node of the Hybridoma Databank.

Sixty research papers were published in peer reviewed International Journals. Out of 9 patent applications filed: India (4) Overseas (5). two patents secured allowance in USA and Europe. Dr. James D. Watson, Nobel Laureate visited the laboratories and also delivered a special lecture.

National Centre for Cell Science (NCCS), Pune

The National Centre for Cell Science (NCCS), Pune was established as a national repository of animal cell culture, manpower development programmes in animal tissue culture and to extend infrastructure facilities to researchers and institutions in biomedical sciences and conduct the state-of-the-art research and development in the area of modern biology. The Governing Council, Society and SAC met during the year. SAC has been reconstituted with Prof. G. Padmanaban as its chairman. Many young scientists have been recruited.

Cell repository

Over the past few years, the cell repository has increased the collection to 1127 cultures derived from 25 different species, including hybridomas. During the current year, 252 cell cultures, comprising of 112 different cell lines were supplied to 72 research institutes across the country.

Human resource development

NCCS continued the activities for training programmes in animal tissue culture and related areas such as hybridoma, molecular biology, etc. A summer training programme was organized for the post-graduate students of the University of Pune and Devi Ahilya University, Indore.

Research projects

The institute has developed and transferred two technologies to recipient hospitals/ centres for clinical use. These technologies are: a) large scale expansion of human skin in culture for the treatment of burns, vitiligo and nonhealing ulcers: b) cryopreservation of cord blood and haematopoetic stem cells. The technology for human skin culture has been transferred to the Armed Forces Medical College, Pune, K.E.M. Hospital and Sion Hospital, Mumbai. As a follow up of the technology transfer, NCCS conducted special training programmes for the laboratory personnel from the Armed Forces Medical College. In vitro rapid expansion of human skin from small biopsy provides large sheets of live skin for covering wounds. The technology developed is based on use of a new feeder layer and growth media, which promote faster growth rates of the keratinocytes.

In cancer patients undergoing radical chemo and radio-therapy, the stem cells are destroyed.. Low temperature storage of stem cells make self and nonself cells available for the generation of all normal blood cells in these patients. The development of cryobiological methods for the safe preservation and storage of bone marrow provides a method for the widespread clinical application of autologous haemopoetic stem cells. Cryopreservation of the cord blood was accomplished by the scientists from Cancer Research Institute, Mumbai while cryopreservation of bone marrow was standardized at NCCS. Use of anti-oxidants and trehalose in the freezing mixtures supported better recovery of the cryopreserved cells which in turn yield celi populations of various haematopoietic lineages as characterized by Colony Forming Units (CFU) assays.

Regulation of melanin skin pigmentation was evaluated for two aspects ie.: dendtritogenesis and phosphorylation in melanogenesis. B16 melanoma model is being used for assessing the role of melanogenic enzymes during remelanization. These cells expressed a high molecular weight form of tyrosinase. Studies on the identification of melanoma oncogenes were continued using Cloudman Melanoma clone M3 as an experimental cell system. Efforts were made to characterize the gene in detail using mRNA expression studies and Fluorescent Activated Cells Sorter (FACS) analysis of the transfected cells. Attempts are underway to sequence this gene to understand its role in the signal transduction cascade.

As observed earlier, the bone marrow mononuclear cells releases TGF beta 1 in response to erythropoietin. TGF beta 1 in turn was found to confer an adhesive phenotype on the stromal cells leading to both homotypic as well as heterotypic interactions. The heterotypic interaction of CD34+ stem cells with stromal cells was found to result in amplification of stem cells. The signal transduction pathways involved in the stem cell amplification as well as the amplified population of the stem cells are being evaluated. These studies revealed that the stromal regulation of stem cell proliferation appears to be dependent on the activation of phophokinase C (PKC) and rise in intracellular Ca+2 mediated via PC-PLC pathway.

Fetal liver infusion (FLI) therapy has been attempted in certain major disorders like immunodeficiency syndrome, aplastic anemia, leukemia and genetic or metabolic disorders. Human subjects have shown extremely variable responses to transplantation, even with single clinical categories. Studies have been initiated with a view to understand the mechanism of autologous recovery of adult hematopoiesis in response to FLI. These studies will pave the way to establish quality control criteria for the infusion material and to improve the success rate of FLI therapy. The results obtained so far indicate that the fetal liver cells bring about stimulantion of haematopoiesis by secretion of TGF beta 1.

The co-stimulatory molecules and the antibodies against them, their receptor on the target cells and the antibodies against the receptors can be of immense importance in understanding the immunobiology of various pathogenic infections like malaria, tuberculosis, leishmaniasis, leprosy, especially selective regulation of immune system. These molecules are therefore being studied in detail The B7.1 and M150 are potent costimulatory molecules ex pressed on B cells and macrophages. M150 has also been shown to act as a costimulatory molecule in the activation of CD8+ T cells.

A growth factor from pancreatic islets (3 has been isolated and partly characterisation. It is a kDa protein and N-terminal sequence of 35 amino acids has been carried out. Comparison with the existing database suggests it to be a new protein molecule.

Basic studies in cell biology, neurobiology and parasitology have been continued. The neuroblastoma cell lines, such as Neruo-2a, are useful models to study cell differentiation. The changes in adhesion to collagen-I have been studied after inducing differentiation in these cells. The differentiated cells exhibited increased binding to collagen as compared to undifferentiated cells. Cytochemical analysis of the cells induced to migrate by serum or growth factors suggested down regulation of epithelial markers such as keratin, epithelial specific antigen, and redistribution of desmosomal proteins, reduced expression of Beta-1 integrin and absence of laminin, absence of fibronectin. Concurrently, there is up regulation of mesenchymal markers such as vimentin, fibroblast surface protein, and reorganization of tracks of focal contacts detected by vinculin and talin. The migrating cells exhibit extended G1 phase of the cell cycle, resulting in delayed recruitment of these cells into S phase. All these changes were found to be temporary and reversible.

Establishment of in vitro extra eryothrocytic strains of Plasmodium falciparum appear to have been achieved. Monoclonal antibodies raised against the intracellular parasites also react with these extracellular forms. PCR studies are underway to confirm the species of the parasites. Since there is no interference of RBCs in culture, these extra erythrocytic strains will prove very valuable for experimental studies on biology and immunology of the malarial parasite, action of and resistance to antimalarial drugs such as chloroquine.

A patent has been granted in India for improved nutrient composition useful for effective maintenance of hybridoma cell line. Two technologies have been transferred. There were 30 publications in reputed journals.

Centre for DNA Fingerprinting and Diagnostics (CDFD),

Hyderabad

This Centre established as an autonomous institution, provides DNA fingerprinting services in medico-legal cases. The centre also investigates the molecular basis of a number of diseases. The total number of forensic cases received at CDFD during the year were 150. CDFD received 89 cases involving paternity, 9 cases of rape, 46 cases of murder and 2 cases of hospital swapping of infants. The remaining 4 cases included one each for, DNA fingerprinting to establish identity of seized animal skins, DNA typing of chilli seeds to establish the familial relationship for the purpose of kidney transplantation and sex determination. Out of 89 paternity cases received at CDFD, 60 were forwarded through Courts and 29 were from private parties. Of the paternity cases forwarded to CDFD, 29.2% were from Kerala and 24.7% from Andhra Pradesh. Paternity cases constituted 59.33% of the total cases. During this period, 2 cases of familial relationship from foreign countries (Bangladesh and New Zealand) were sent to CDFD for an opinion. CDFD reports in these cases were useful for immigration purposes. In nine rape cases, DNA fingerprinting was used, out of which 4 cases were from Andhra Pradesh followed by 2 cases from Maharashtra.

There was a significant rise in the number of murder cases forwarded to CDFD in comparison, to previous year. In all, 46 cases of - murder were received. Andhra Pradesh Police utilized the DNA fingerprinting services in 12 murder cases, Which amounted to 26% of the total murder cases. The Kathmandu Forensic Science Laboratories, Nepal, forwarded one case of murder. The State of Delhi forwarded 8 cases of murder to CDFD for opinion.

There were two cases of child swapping in hospitals, one from Andhra Pradesh and the other from Kerala. A total number of 578 forensic exhibits were handled by CDFD.

A concerted effort towards the provision of molecular diagnosis for various common genetic disorders like Fragile-X Syndrome, Beta Thalassemia, Sickle Cell Anemia, Duchenne and Becker Muscular Dystrophy, Huntington's Disease and other triplet repeat associated diseases were initiated and CDFD started providing diagnostic services for the same.

CDFD is currently operating from the Centre for Cellular and Molecular Biology, Hyderabad as an interim facility. Building plans have been firmed up and construction activities are to be initiated. Hands on training courses have been organised by the Centre which have been attended by scientists including forensic scientists both from India and abroad. The Centre has recruited scientific, technical and administrative manpower. The Governing Council met on 18th August, 1998 and the Society met on December 10th, 1998 to approve the Annual Report and audited accounts. Eleven publications/ presentations were made during the year.

National Brain Research Centre (NBRC), New Delhi

The Department announced the establishment of a National Brain Research Centre with the main objective of consolidating the efforts made in the area of neurosciences and basic brain research. An interactive session on "Vision for Neurosciences in the Next Millennium was held during the year in which neuroscientists from all over the country participated. An Action Plan for the research activity during the next decade was drawn out with emphasis on the following:

1. Networking of centres/institutes doing neurosciences research;

2. Identification Of a few centres as collaborative centres and others as satellite centres;
3. Generation and dissemination of data bases; improved communication amongst different groups;
4. Evolving comprehensive neuroscience courses;
5. Creating Neuroscience Post-doctoral positions;
6. Establishing multidisciplinary-interactive groups between biologists, physicists, mathematicians, computational scientists and clinicians;
7. Provide centralised facilities for
   - Sophisticated and high value equipments;
   - Transgenic Animals;
   - MEG, Laser microscopy;
8. Organize
   - Multidisciplinary symposia
   - Hands-on training workshops;
9. Initiate activities in the field of
   - Cognitive Neuroscience
   - " Theoretical Neuroscience"
   - " Neurophysics"

Areas have also been identified for future research. The focus would be on:

(i) Neuroimmunology: Neuropeptides and cytokines and their role in growth and regulation of nervous system; control of cognitive function; psychoneuroimmunology including yoga, meditation etc.

(ii) Neurovirology: Immunodiagnostics; viruses and

psychiatric disturbances; use of viruses in genetic engineering and vector development.

(iii) CNS Infections: Molecular epidemiology; immunodiagnostics; antigen mimicry between host and parasite; chronic infections and their role in neurodegenerative diseases; glial functions, their repair and neuro-glial inter action.

(iv) Neuro-genetics: Use of clinical material, (neurological, psychiatric/behavioural) for predictive, diagnostic and preventive purposes; collaboration between clinicians and basic scientists.

(v) Neurochemistry: Study of receptors, expression and characterisation of specific genes; development of diagnostic markers; oxidative stress/repair mechanisms; protein kinases; ion - channels and neurotoxicology.

(vi) Neurophysics: Molecular spectroscopy; computers, neural network, modeling, newer optical and ESR technologies their application; biomolecular structure and function dynamics and biomemory.

(vii) Neuropharmacology: Effects of drugs on brain; drug development through high level screening of biodiversity; use of indigenous medicines.

Networking, co-ordination and support for training, workshops and symposia have been initiated during the year. These are being implemented through NIMHANS, Bangalore. The centre is likely to shift soon to its premises near Gurgaon.

National centre for plant genome research, New Delhi

The National Centre for Plant Genome Research (NCPGR) started functioning in the JNU Campus. The Governing Body met and took various pending decisions. A one day brain storming session was organized to discuss the scope of the plant genome research, the priorities and work plan.

The major research projects in progress at the centre are as follows:

Organization and expression of two novel genes namely AmAl (seed protein) and OXDC (Oxalate decarboxylase)

(a) Organization and expression of AmAl: In an attempt to improve the nutritional quality, the coding sequence of AmAl was stably introduced into potato plants using a simple and reproducible regeneration protocol. The protein was expressed in transgenic tubers under the control of CamV 35S and GBSS promoters. A significant increase in most essential amino acids except serine was observed. On an average, the amount of essential amino acids in tubers was increased by 2-7 fold. AmAl coding region has been cloned under the control of nmtl promoter in pREP1 vector. The clone was named as pRAC.S.pombe strain harbouring pRAC overexpressed AmAl protein which was 6-7% of the total soluble protein. To study the plant gene splicing in S.pombe, the AmAl genomic DNA was cloned in pREPI. The clone was named as Prag, where the coding region along with the single intron has been cloned under nmt1 promoter. S.pombe strain harboring this construct under induction did not produce the AmAl full-length protein, instead it showed a smaller molecular weight band which cross reacted with the AmAl antibody.

(b) Organization and expression of OXDC: In an attempt to remove the nutritional stress factor namely oxalic acid from some commonly use d vegetables, the coding region of OXDC gene was cloned under CamV 35S and pE8.2 promoters. The constructs under the control of CamV 35S promoter were transferred to tomato as it has high content of oxalic acid. Transgenic tomato showed stable expression of the foreign protein and also accumulated very little oxalic acid in comparison to wild type plants. The wilting test suggested that the enzyme was active in vivo. The transgenic plants were found to be resistant to infestation by Sclerotinia sclerotiorum. Molecular and physiological analysis of the transgenics harbouring construct where the OXDC coding region is under the control of pE8.2 is now in progress. Further, in order to study the structure of OXDC gene, the full length genomic clone was sequenced and analysed. Sequence analysis revealed the presence of eukaryotic transcription factors like SPI, AP1, CAAT and TATA binding elements. The presence of oxalic acid / HCL responsive factor was demonstrated. The factor can only bind to a 490 bp fragment of the promoter. South-western analysis revealed that the factor has MW 280 kDa under non-denaturating condition. In vivo promoter analysis in Saccharomyces with different deletions of promoter DNA construct showed the basal level of expression.

Expression pattern of AtPAL1 and AtPAL2 gene in transgenic tobacco

Since PAL catalyses a crucial step in the pathway leading to synthesis of antimicrobial phytoalexins and signal molecule salicylic acid, it was conjectured that up-regulation of this enzyme may enhance the synthesis of these compounds. Such plants with higher levels of phytoalexins and salicylic acid may have enhanced disease resistance potential. Attempts have been made to up-regulate PAL by introducing a complete Arabidopsis PAL1 gene into tobacco plants. The 4.8-kb EcoR I fragment containing complete AtPAL1 gene was sub-cloned into a binary vector Ppzp111. The gene construct was transferred to tobacco plants by Agrobacterium - mediated transformation method. The transformants were selected on kanamycin plate. They were transferred from shoot inducing media to rooting media to small pots in a growth chamber and finally to field.

On the basis of growth and development, the transgenic plants carrying complete AtPAL1 gene could be grouped into three categories: (i) plants with extremely stunted growth (ii) plants showing retardation in growth and having morphological abnormalities; and (iii) plants with apparently normal growth.

The plants are in T1 generation and are still to be analysed with respect to levels of PAL.

Differential Expression pattern of Atpal1 and Atpal2 in transgenic tobacco plants: The upstream region of AtPAL2 was isolated and cloned in the binary vector pBl 101 upstream to the GUS coding sequence. The gene consruct was transferred to tobacco plants using the Agrobacterium mediated transformation method and transgenic tobacco plants carrying PAL2 promoter-GUS constructs. The expression pattern of these constructs was compared with the plants carrying PAL1 promoter-GUS construct. Transgenic seedlings show that both AtPAL1 and AtPAL2 promoters are developmentally regulated. During germination and early stages of growth, the level of expression of AtPAL1 GUS is low. However, 10 days after germination, the pattern of expression undergoes a drastic shift and finally confining to vascular tissue. In the case of AtPAL2 gus, early stages of seedling growth, showed GUS expression and at later stages, the GUS activity was localized in the apical vascular tissue. Both AtPAL1 and AtPAL2 promoters show tissue specific and organ specific expression. Atpal1 promoter is inducible in response to wounding, whereas the AtPAL2 promoter does not show a similar response.

Biochemical and molecular basis of differentiation and genetic improvement of brassica and cicer arietinum

(a) Transformation and regeneration studies: Pursuing the earlier attempts to get transgenic Cicer, modified, protocols using different selection markers and particle bombardment techniques along with standard Agrobacterium mediated transformations were tried. Problems based on improved efficiency of transformation and better selection systems were solved by using co-transformation method with desensitized AK and Psm2 (Gus-Basta construct). New Cambia vectors were also used for their versatility as reported in literature. For all these experiments, tobacco controls were used.

On screening with Kanamycin and Basta, some plants we re successfully recovered. Southern hybridization with desensitized AK probe also yielded some positive results. These transformants are now being reared for genetic analysis.

(b) Biochemical and molecular basis of differentiation: Importance of amino acids, polyamines and ethylene in induction of differentiation and their interactions had earlier been reported. Comparative studies of free amino acids and polyamines (free, conjugated and bound forms) in embryogenic, regenerating and proliferating cultures of Vigna mungo had also been conducted. Their morphogenic capabilities had also been assessed by giving exogenous treatments.

Work on synchronization of carrot suspension cultures, which aims to understand the molecular mechanism of plant cell cycle, also progressed. Efficiency of various cell cycle blockers in getting synchronization and the best results were found by using an amino acid analog-mimosine.

Role of phosphorylation/dephosphorylation in stress signalling in Brassica juncea

Involvement of phosphorylation and dephosphorylation in stress signalling in Brassica juncea seedlings are being studied. The seedlings were grown at 25°C or 4°C (to give low temperature stress) and were treated with the inhibitors of kinases. The control seedlings showed phosphorylation of a 55 kDa polypeptide. The phosphorylation was enhanced in the presence of PMA, a PKC activator while it was blocked by the PKC inhibitors. A calcium/calmodulin inhibitor W-7 had no effect. These observations suggest that phosphorylation of the 55 kDa polypeptide is PKC dependent. The same polypeptide was dephosphorylated under low temperature stress. The dephosphorylation started 10 min after treatment and the polypeptide was completely dephosphorylated by 30 min. Findings suggest that the phosphatase may be PKC dependent. Attempts to purify PKC type kinase from B.juncea are in progress.